# POVERTY AND POLICY
# IN AMERICAN HISTORY

# STUDIES IN SOCIAL DISCONTINUITY

*Under the Consulting Editorship of:*

CHARLES TILLY
*University of Michigan*

EDWARD SHORTER
*University of Toronto*

*In preparation*

*Manuel Gottlieb.* A Theory of Economic Systems

*Published*

*Michael B. Katz.* Poverty and Policy in American History

*Arthur L. Stinchcombe.* Economic Sociology

*Jill S. Quadagno.* Aging in Early Industrial Society: Work, Family, and Social Policy in Nineteenth-Century England

*J. Dennis Willigan and Katherine A. Lynch.* Sources and Methods of Historical Demography

*Dietrich Gerhard.* Old Europe: A Study of Continuity, 1000-1800

*Charles Tilly.* As Sociology Meets History

*Maris A. Vinovskis.* Fertility in Massachusetts from the Revolution to the Civil War

*Juan G. Espinosa and Andrew S. Zimbalist,* Economic Democracy: Workers' Participation in Chilean Industry 1970-1973: Updated Student Edition

*Alejandro Portes and John Walton.* Labor, Class, and the International System

*James H. Mittelman.* Underdevelopment and the Transition to Socialism: Mozambique and Tanzania

*John R. Gillis.* Youth and History: Tradition and Change in European Age Relations, 1770—Present: Expanded Student Edition

*Samuel Kline Cohn, Jr.* The Laboring Classes in Renaissance Florence

*Richard C. Trexler.* Public Life in Renaissance Florence

*Paul Oquist.* Violence, Conflict, and Politics in Colombia

*Fred Weinstein.* The Dynamics of Nazism: Leadership, Ideology, and the Holocaust

*John R. Hanson II.* Trade in Transition: Exports from the Third World, 1840—1900

*Evelyne Huber Stephens.* The Politics of Workers' Participation: The Peruvian Approach in Comparative Perspective

*Albert Bergesen* (Ed.). Studies of the Modern World-System

*Lucile H. Brockway.* Science and Colonial Expansion: The Role of the British Royal Botanic Gardens

*James Lang.* Portuguese Brazil: The King's Plantation

The list of titles in this series continues on the last page of this volume

# POVERTY AND POLICY
# IN AMERICAN HISTORY

Michael B. Katz

University of Pennsylvania
Philadelphia, Pennsylvania

ACADEMIC PRESS
*A Subsidiary of Harcourt Brace Jovanovich, Publishers*
New York   London
Paris   San Diego   San Francisco   São Paulo   Sydney   Tokyo   Toronto

The cover illustration is from the poster of the Philadelphia Exhibition of the Society for Organizing Charity, 1916, courtesy of the Historical Society of Pennsylvania.

ACADEMIC PRESS, INC.
111 Fifth Avenue, New York, New York 10003

*United Kingdom Edition published by*
ACADEMIC PRESS, INC. (LONDON) LTD.
24/28 Oval Road, London NW1   7DX

Library of Congress Cataloging in Publication Data

Katz, Michael B.
    Poverty and policy in American history.

    (Studies in social discontinuity)
    Includes index.
    1. Public welfare--United States--History. 2. Poor--
United States--History. 3. Poor--Government policy--
United States--History. 4. Almshouses--United States--
History. 5. Tramps--United States--History. 6. Depend-
ency (Psychology)--History. I. Title. II. Series.
HV91.K35  1983      361.6'0973      83-3700
ISBN 0-12-401760-6
ISBN 0-12-401762-2 (pbk.)

PRINTED IN THE UNITED STATES OF AMERICA

83 84 85 86   9 8 7 6 5 4 3 2 1

For Dan Calhoun

# CONTENTS

Preface      ix

Acknowledgments      xi

Introduction      1

CHAPTER 1

FAMILIES AND WELFARE:
A PHILADELPHIA CASE      17

The Sullivan Family      18
Themes in the History of the Sullivan Family      41

CHAPTER 2

POORHOUSES, PAUPERS,
AND TRAMPS      55

PART I
From Family Refuge to Old Age Home: The Demographic
History of the Erie County, New York,
Poorhouse from 1829 to 1886      57

Aggregate Trends in Poorhouse Composition      61
Conclusion      86

PART II
Early Social Science and the Causes of Pauperism        90

The Design of the Report                                94
The Sample                                              98
Institutional Demography: Age, Sex, Birthplace          100
Hoyt and the Causes of Pauperism                        103
The Act of 1875 and the Creation of Poorhouse Records   116
Poorhouse Demography                                    119
Conclusion                                              129

PART III
"The Morphology of Evil"                                134

The Problem of Social Categories                        134
The Demography of Dependence                            142
Conclusion                                              153

PART IV
New York's Tramps and the Problem
of Causal Attribution in the 1870s                      157

The Tramp Problem                                       157
The Characteristics of Tramps                           166
The Problem of Causal Attribution                       174

CHAPTER 3

AMERICAN HISTORIANS
AND DEPENDENCE                                          183

Historians and Philanthropy: *Urban Masses and Moral Order in
America* as the Culmination of a Historiographical Tradition   184
Historians and Institutions: David Rothman and Asylums  201
The History of Public Welfare: Roy Lubove on Social Insurance   218

Epilogue: The Significance of Welfare History           239

Appendix                                                243

Index                                                   281

# PREFACE

This book is about people who needed help in the nineteenth and early twentieth centuries. Some of them lived in poorhouses, mental hospitals, and other institutions. Others depended on public and private charity. With rich, fascinating, and hitherto unused sources, I have asked who these people were, why they needed help, and how accurately they were described by contemporaries.

Therefore, this book also is about policy. It is about the ways in which the perception of poverty and other forms of dependence affected the development of public programs and the conduct of voluntary reform. This is not, however, a history of welfare. Rather, it is a series of discrete probes into the past, a set of images which suggest what a new picture of welfare in America might be like.

Because this book wants partially to reorient the study of poverty and policy in American history, it also is about the the ways in which people have written about welfare. I argue that the historiography of dependence is too fragmented, too caught in conventional categories, insufficiently concerned with the actual experience of people, and too removed from the state and local contexts in which most decisions about welfare were made.

Finally, this is a book about the present. It shows that many popular ideas about welfare are myths. It points to the stale, repetitive, and self-serving character of ideas about poor people in American social thought. And it suggests that the welfare state may be a lot more fragile than many people think. There is an American style of welfare. It is old. It is no cause for pride or satisfaction. It is what this book, ultimately, is about.

# ACKNOWLEDGMENTS

This book is like the tip of an iceberg. The parts that do not show are the help I received from the many people who participated in the research on which it is based; the agency that funded the work; the colleagues, friends, and family who gave moral support; and the many scholars on whose work I have drawn for ideas, interpretations, and data. For all of the help and support I am deeply grateful. Without it this book would not have been written.

For programming assistance with the project out of which this book grew I am grateful to Linda Hughes and Laura Gaynard, and for secretarial assistance to Barbara Redman. Brenda Donahue of the State University of New York at Buffalo helped with research on that city and Charles Bland and Shonnie Finnegan, also of the State University of New York at Buffalo, assisted the work in various ways; Sally Sorenson worked on the background of superintendents of the poor; Paul Eisenhauer did very careful research for the project on the history of the Elmira Reformatory and other subjects in the New York State Archives in Albany, whose staff has been consistently helpful. The Family Service Association of Philadelphia kindly made its old case files available. Caroline Zinsser and Gail Glicksman helped in various ways with the preparation of the manuscript. Michael Frisch gave me characteristically insightful comments on a draft of Chapter 3. Charles Tilly read the entire manuscript and made exceptionally useful suggestions. Mark Stern collaborated on the project. Together we worked on the demography of the Erie Country Poorhouse, but his assistance includes, as well, supervising the technical work and programming. Susan Davis's exceptionally thorough and penetrating work on Brooklyn, Philadelphia, and Indianapolis has been a major source of my education in the historical politics of welfare. During the year 1980–1981 most of the sections of this book were criticized in the project group formed around this and another research project. Its members enjoyed a first-rate seminar with one another, and, if it need be said, they have been enormously helpful to me. The members of the project group were David Hogan, Mark Stern, Walter Licht, Susan Davis, Bruce Bellingham, Paul Eisenhauer, Gail Glicksman, and Mark Winther.

The research on which the book rests was supported by the Center for Studies of Metropolitan Problems of the National Institute of Mental Health (Grant No. RO1MH32520). I want to thank the Center's director, Elliot Liebow, whose recognition of the importance of history and whose courage have had a major impact upon scholarship in the last dozen or so years.

The final version of this book was written almost entirely at Clioquossia, in Oquossoc, Maine, where it is a pleasure even to work. I would like to thank my friends and neighbors there and, especially, my wife Edda and youngest daughter Sarah, who shared the summers when this book was written.

# INTRODUCTION

The early 1980s are like the 1870s. Then, as now, respectable citizens worried about rising crime and radicalism and complained about high taxes spent on useless public programs. They thought that social programs wasted their money on the idle and immoral. Hopes faded that institutions could rehabilitate, cure, or even educate as mental hospitals, penitentiaries, and reformatories became frankly custodial. Economy, efficiency, and the superiority of the private sector became guidelines for public policy. Local, state, and federal governments fostered the growth of giant corporations, supported attacks on the labor movement, and cut back on civil rights. They also cut welfare. Private philanthropy, they said, would fill any genuine gaps left by the reduction in the public sector.

Despite decades of social science research, popular images of people on welfare have not changed very much in the last century. Their problems, it is thought, are largely their own fault. How are we to account for the resilience of the individual interpretation of poverty? For the punitive and degrading character of the welfare system? For the continuation of a welfare system that nobody likes? American historical writing does not help answer these questions nearly well enough. Its fragmentation of the subject, its division between public and private spheres, its too easy acceptance of popular stereotypes, its neglect of local case studies, and its too frequent Whig bias all stand in the way of coherent interpretations of policy toward poor and dependent people in the American past. This book is offered as a step toward the reconstruction of a more accurate and useful version of poverty and policy in American history.

Welfare in America is shot through with ironies and contradictions that conventional histories do not explain very well. Consider, first, the fragility of progress. Not long ago it could be argued that the modern history of welfare had two great periods: before and after the New Deal. The New Deal marked the point at which the federal government assumed the leading role in welfare. Despite its imperfections, the New Deal introduced the policies that would eventually create a welfare state in America. For a time this seemed a plausible version of history because the New Deal did transform the administration of welfare and because welfare did in fact spread into new areas for about 4 decades. Only now, the counterattack on welfare shows how fragile those gains were. Progress, it appears, is by no means inevitable; the state can shed as well as assume responsibilities.

The fragility of welfare and its rhythms remain two themes that require more historical attention. Another is the meaning of reform. Welfare reform has swept through America fairly often. Indeed, one can identify welfare reform movements in the 1820s, 1850s, 1870s, and 1890s, to take only nineteenth-century examples. These movements shared at least two characteristics. One is that they failed to reduce the social problems that they set out to solve. The other is that they defined reform as reducing public expenditure on welfare. In fact, welfare reform always has been partially a synonym for saving money.

The mean-spirited nature of reform requires emphasis. Charity and welfare reform are laced with noble rhetoric. Opponents of public welfare have argued that the American spirit of voluntarism would relieve all the truly needy, and sponsors of new institutions, such as mental hospitals or reformatories, have held out extravagant expectations. But voluntarism has not proved an adequate social policy, and institutions never have reached their rehabilitative goals. Part of the reason is that they never have been properly funded. Voluntary agencies have constantly complained that the public has been unwilling to support their efforts adequately, and legislatures never have appropriated the funds necessary to give major social institutions (or other social policies) the chance to work as projected.

Both the reasons why reforms have failed and the reasons why Americans have been so unwilling to fund welfare adequately require more exploration. Part of the answer, surely, rests in the dominant view of dependence in American culture, for if the spirit in which the relief of dependence has been undertaken has been mean, the perception of dependent people has been vicious. Two points about these long-standing popular perceptions of dependent people are especially important. The first is the definition of poverty as a moral condition. In this view poverty is not simply the lack of money; it is the lack of the capacity to earn money. In a society where self-sufficiency is available to all people of ordinary talent and reasonable energy, poverty reflects personal weakness. It is an individual rather than a social condition. At the same time—and this is the second point—there is not much real distinction between the various categories of dependence: poverty, crime, and ignorance, to take three major types, shade into one another as the various categories of dependence are collapsed into a metaclass that is, despite an occasional burst of sentimentality or the annual appeal to help the neediest, despised.

Popular media, social policy, and political debate often seem willfully blind to the actual circumstances and characteristics of dependent people. Indeed, contemporary social science, which has undermined so many of the standard ideas about people on welfare, has made a very small dent in popular thought. Although comparisons usually show how the demography of dependence contradicts its stereotypes, with surprising vitality roughly similar images have dominated discussions for the last 175 years.

In general, dependent people have a passive image within both popular stereotypes and even much academic thought. They are by definition people for whom and to whom things are done, recipients of charity and inmates of institutions who lack dignity, autonomy, and self-respect. Yet another long-standing current criticizes dependent people for opposite reasons. The clever street urchin, the wily tramp, and the manipulative welfare cheat point to the limits of the passive stereotype. The poor have always managed to survive. They have found ways to exploit the interstices of the system and to manipulate institutions to their own purposes. On occasion, they even have forced concessions from authorities. Indeed, Frances Fox Piven and Richard Cloward would argue, only by their own activity have the poor won anything at all. Yet, the activity of the poor on their own behalf has not received very much historical attention, and the strategies by which the poor have survived await systematic historical treatment.

What accounts for these resilient and inaccurate ideas about dependent people? The very question, some critics would argue, is naive. People are prisoners of their moral and cognitive systems, trapped within paradigms of social structure and individual behavior, unable to escape prevailing value systems and religious beliefs. To expect them to transcend their own milieu and socialization is arrogant and ahistorical. One historian, in fact, has argued that the mode of causal attribution dominating American society until the 1890s made it literally impossible for observers to see the complex and deeply rooted sources of poverty. In a later chapter I will show why this view is wrong on empirical grounds. Here I want to offer a brief word in defense of history as moral criticism.

There are at least two consequences of straining all moral judgments out of history. One is the loss of all critical capacity. If we cannot criticize people in the past, how can we do so in the present? If all behavior merely reflects the incapacitating weight of socialization and the confinement of cognitive prisons, how can we move beyond a radically relative approach to moral life? Are there no historical actions that we are prepared to disapprove? A second consequence of rejecting moral criticism in history is a constriction of vision, a closing down of alternative futures. Historical actors trapped within their own mental and moral limits have had little choice. Indeed, given their constricted vision and the pressure of circumstances, most have had few alternatives. Their action—hence, history itself—becomes inevitable. We are all, by implication, travelers on a very narrow road, plodding unhappily in the same direction unless, almost magically, the paradigms that blind us from seeing other routes fall suddenly away. Nonetheless, in every era some men and women have traveled without blinders, pointing out sane and reasonable alternatives. The issue, then, is not the failure of human imagination but the reasons why intelligent people have chosen some possibilities rather than others.

I have rejected the idea that historians cannot be moral critics, and I have treated the discrepancy between the image and facts of dependence as a serious problem whose resolution goes straight to the core of American social history: the translation of social class relations into social policy.

However, this book is not a history of welfare. Rather, it consists of a series of probes that point to some new directions in welfare history. *Welfare* here is a broad term that refers to the provision of relief and rehabilitation for dependent people. It encompasses both private and public action and activity both inside and outside of institutions. Even though this book does not tell the story of welfare in a systematic way, it is important to sketch some of the major features of welfare history in America in order to establish the context of the individual probes.[1]

---

[1]For a general history of welfare, which includes an excellent bibliography, see James Leiby, *A History of Social Welfare and Social Work in the United States* (New York: Columbia University Press, 1978); on the role of business in making welfare innovations, see Edward Berkowitz and Kim McQuaid, *Creating the Welfare State: The Political Economy of Twentieth-Century Reform* (New York: Praeger, 1980); also of major importance on twentieth-century

The first point about welfare is its profoundly local nature during most of American history. Influenced by British precedents, colonial American towns and parishes assumed responsibility for their own poor. Assistance usually was given in a casual and unsystematic way, and needy strangers were warned out of town. Some of the larger cities built workhouses that took in not only the poor but the sick as well. In the early nineteenth century growing relief expenses and new strands in transatlantic ideas about the relief of poverty stimulated several states to try to systematize their poor laws. They hoped to reduce outdoor relief (the term for public welfare) by tightening eligibility laws and, especially, by requiring the destitute to enter poorhouses, which they expected would discourage them from applying for relief.

State governments entered the area of welfare in the 1820s mainly by requiring counties to establish poorhouses. Although their construction was ordered by state law, the poorhouses built in a number of states were controlled by local governments, either town or county. In this way early nineteenth-century legislation modified but did not erode the local basis of welfare. The establishment of poorhouses did not eliminate the problem of outdoor relief, as their sponsors had predicted. Most people who needed assistance continued to get aid outside of institutions through a variety of public mechanisms: small amounts of money, food, or fuel. Sometimes these were distributed by specially elected boards, sometimes by super-intendents of poorhouses, and sometimes by other public officials. Thus, the administration of relief within individual states remained complex, if not chaotic, despite periodic attempts to systematize poor laws.

Most histories of welfare pay more attention to voluntary than to public relief efforts in the nineteenth and early twentieth centuries. Indeed, voluntary activities have taken a wide variety of forms, including casual, ad hoc relief given by churches; the aid given to immigrants by ethnic societies; and more widespread, systematic philanthropy. Especially noteworthy are the often heroic efforts of the Catholic church, which have not received nearly the credit they deserve in American social history.

---

welfare is James T. Patterson, *America's Struggle against Poverty, 1900–1980* (Cambridge, Mass.: Harvard University Press, 1981); on the development of social work as a profession, the best study is Roy Lubove, *The Professional Altruist: The Emergence of Social Work as a Career 1880–1930* (Cambridge, Mass.: Harvard University Press, 1965); an excellent overview of the voluntary reform tradition is Paul Boyer, *Urban Masses and Moral Order in America, 1820–1920* (Cambridge, Mass.: Harvard University Press, 1978); a more radical view of welfare, its functions, and its history is Frances Fox Piven and Richard Cloward, *Regulating the Poor: The Functions of Public Welfare* (New York: Random House, 1971), and, by the same authors, *Poor People's Movements: Why They Succeed and How They Fail* (New York: Pantheon, 1977).

Despite the poverty of its largely immigrant congregation, in the nine-teenth century the Catholic church created an impressive array of hospitals, orphanages, schools, and organizations that gave outdoor relief. Other voluntary organizations mixed relief with moral uplift. In the antebellum period evangelical Protestant women began missionary work among the poor in large cities. Between the 1820s and the 1840s their emphasis gradually shifted from distributing religious tracts to providing relief, and their work with individual families was the precedent for the "friendly visiting" that formed the core of the "scientific charity" move-ment of the 1870s, represented by the establishment of Charity Organiza-tion Societies in most cities after 1878.

The Charity Organization Societies led an attempt to differentiate the worthy from the unworthy poor, systematize charity, and restore the relations between social classes through the agency of friendly visitors who would advise poor families on how to escape dependency. At the same time, the Charity Organization Societies spearheaded an attempt to end all public outdoor relief. In this they were partly successful for a time because several of the country's largest cities abolished outdoor relief, and between the late 1870s and the mid-1890s, many others reduced the amount they gave. Despite its emphasis on the force of personality, the importance of individual contact, and the drawbacks of "machine charity," voluntarism became bureaucratized in the early decades of the twentieth century through the creation of Social Service Exchanges, Community Chests, and, eventually, the United Way, whose quasi-official status blurred the boundaries between public and private that late nineteenth-century voluntarism had unsuccessfully tried to draw precisely and permanently.

The advocates of voluntarism have been the most articulate writers about relief, and historians have paid more attention to their efforts than to public relief. However, it is important to stress that after the initial period of settlement, and outside of the South, public relief always has been more widespread than private. Public relief is an American tradition with roots firmly planted in the colonial period. During the nineteenth and early twentieth centuries, even prior to the New Deal, far more people received public than received private assistance, and most money for relief came from local taxes.

Despite the continued local base of welfare, state governments played an increasingly important role throughout the nineteenth century, assuming welfare responsibilities in stages. First was the attempt to reform poor laws early in the nineteenth century; second was the great wave of institutional creation that also started after 1820. As I will discuss in more detail in

Chapter 3, a new faith in the capacity of institutions to solve social problems was reflected in the creation of specialized institutions for the poor, mentally ill, juvenile delinquents, adult criminals, blind, deaf and dumb, and idiots and even in the form of public schools for the ignorant. These institutions originated through varied and complex mixtures of public and private initiatives that, nonetheless, in virtually all cases reflected a heightened role for state governments in the promotion of social welfare.

By the 1860s relief networks in the more densely populated states had become complex. States attempted to regulate poor laws, ran some institutions, and provided whole or partial funding for many others. They did all of this with relatively little supervision or coordination. As a result, they knew little about how their policies actually worked, and they had almost no effective mechanisms of control. In order to improve the coordination of their relief activities, state legislatures established boards of state charities under various titles. The first was created in Massachusetts in the early 1860s, and others soon followed. These boards gathered statistics, visited institutions, and collected other forms of evidence, which they used to make recommendations to state legislatures. With little power, and often resented by the institutions and voluntary agencies they supervised, state boards could accomplish relatively little by themselves and often had a rocky history. The New York board, for instance, repeatedly fought for its survival during the nineteenth century. However, these state boards were the precursors of the state departments of public welfare established in the early decades of the twentieth century.

State departments of public welfare—indeed, the transmutation of the term *relief* into *public welfare*—reflected two important processes. One was the attempt to distinguish public from private and to define a clear public sphere of action. This process never was wholly successful. Although much welfare has remained nominally voluntary, many agencies and institutions have received most of their funds from some level of government in the form of either flat grants, as for hospitals in Pennsylvania between 1870 and 1910, or per capita grants, as in New York. Still, the growth of public activity and the attempt to define a permanent role for the public in welfare are clear.

The second process reflected in the creation of state departments of public welfare is professionalization. Throughout the nineteenth and early twentieth centuries welfare activities crystallized into distinct, specialized occupations. First came the creation of a series of special occupations related to the new institutions founded in the antebellum period. There were, after all, no professional superintendents of mental hospitals, reform

schools, or public school systems in the early nineteenth century. The first
administrators of public institutions all came from other professions and
learned their work on the job. As they acquired experience and made
contact with their counterparts throughout the country, they developed
national journals and associations and, eventually, training programs,
standards of admission, and the other characteristics of a profession. In the
case of poorhouses a direct line can be traced in New York from the first
Convention of County Superintendents of the Poor in 1870 to its
transformation into the New York Association of Public Welfare Officials
in 1913.

Professionalism affected the conduct of relief work as well. Throughout
the nineteenth century charity workers and friendly visitors had no special
training, and the first serious social-work education began in the early
twentieth century. Within social work a shift from a focus on relief to
therapeutic case work and a decreased emphasis on social reform
accompanied professionalization. The major exception to the emphasis on
therapy was the work of the settlement houses founded in poor
neighborhoods in the late nineteenth century, for more than any other
group settlement workers combined work among the poor with a
commitment to social reform.

Even before the New Deal the federal government paid some attention
to problems associated with relief, although for the most part its efforts
were limited to publicizing issues through conferences and reports. The
most notable examples are the White House Conference on Children in
1909, which was influential in persuading a number of states to establish
mothers' pensions, and the Children's Bureau, created in 1912 and headed
by Julia Lathrop, a former settlement house worker who had been active in
social reform in Illinois. Probably the most interesting federal innovation
of the early twentieth century was the Shepperd–Towner Act (1921–
1929), which funded the establishment of community health centers for
women and children.

In the early twentieth century state and city governments also inno-
vated. The most notable state accomplishments were mothers' pensions
and the first workmen's compensation legislation. Although both programs actually assisted very few people and gave minimal amounts of
relief, they set important precedents. Within cities, a movement for the
creation of municipal departments of public welfare started in Kansas City
in 1913 and spread throughout the country in the next several years. Cities
also experimented hesitantly with various ways of relieving unemployment.

In some ways more welfare innovations came from private industry than
from any other source in the late nineteenth and early twentieth centuries.

These innovations were part of what has been called welfare capitalism and reflected the efforts of large industries to alter their labor management policies. Welfare capitalism was an attempt to integrate an often hostile, foreign, unstable labor force into the social order by winning the commitment of workers to individual firms and to American capitalism. It involved a number of strategies: establishing model towns such as Pullman, Illinois; raising real wages; promoting home ownership; and introducing pensions and other benefits. As limited in scope and coverage as these policies were, they were bolder than almost any government scheme and provided models that governments used when they hesitantly began to expand welfare in the 1920s.

Throughout the nineteenth and twentieth centuries social and political commentators wrote incessantly about rising expenses for poor relief, increasing crime, the dangers of ignorance, and the plight of neglected or hungry children. Although, by and large, they did not diagnose problems or describe dependent people very accurately, the depth and persistence of their concern testify that dependence was a major problem in nineteenth- and twentieth-century America. The reason why is not hard to understand. Even a cursory review highlights the way in which the process of American social development created and sustained dependence as a major social problem. Indeed, periodic dependence was a predictable, structural feature of working-class life.[2]

---

[2]There is no satisfactory overview of the social history of capitalism in America. The book that started the revival of interest in the history of social and population mobility is Stephan Thernstrom, *Poverty and Progress: Social Mobility in a Nineteenth-Century City* (Cambridge, Mass.: Harvard University Press, 1964). Especially important, too, is Herbert G. Gutman, *Work, Culture, and Society in Industrializing America* (New York: Knopf, 1976). An excellent discussion of the intellectual response to wage labor is Daniel T. Rodgers, *The Work Ethic in Industrial America, 1850–1920* (Chicago: University of Chicago Press, 1978). For an important examination of the early transition to industrialism, see Anthony F. C. Wallace, *Rockdale: The Growth of an American Village in the Early Industrial Revolution* (New York: Knopf, 1978). Samples of some of the newer approaches to nineteenth-century social history are in Theodore Hershberg, ed., *Philadelphia: Work, Space, Family, and Group Experience in the 19th Century* (New York: Oxford, 1981). An important discussion of changing demographic patterns, including age-structures, is Peter Uhlenberg, "Changing Configurations of the Life Course," in *Transitions: The Family and the Life Course in Historical Perspective*, ed. Tamara K. Hareven (New York: Academic Press, 1978), pp. 65–98. The problems of youth, particularly in the late nineteenth century, are discussed in Joseph K. Kett, *Rites of Passage: Adolescence in America 1790 to the Present* (New York: Basic Books, 1977), and in Paul Osterman, *Getting Started: The Youth Labor Market* (Cambridge, Mass.: MIT Press, 1978), esp. chap. 4. An essay of extraordinary importance on the early history of capitalism and the distinction between capitalism and industrialism is Raphael Samuel, "The Workshop of the World: Steam Power and Hand Technology in Mid-Victorian Britain," *History Workshop Journal* 3 (Spring 1977): 6–72. On the social structure of mid-nineteenth-century cities, see also Michael B. Katz, *The*

The emergence of capitalism in the late eighteenth and early nineteenth centuries changed social relations. The defining feature of capitalism was the spread of wage labor. No one has precise figures for the proportion of wageworkers at different points in American history. As an example, though, one historian points to an increase in the proportion of laborers—the people who were most unambiguously wageworkers—in New York City's work force from 5.5% to 27.4% between 1796 and 1855. Other research shows clearly that by the mid-nineteenth century most artisans in North American cities were wageworkers.[3] One feature of capitalism with special importance for welfare was an increase in population mobility, for the creation of a mobile class of wage laborers often broke the ties between individuals and communities. As it became increasingly difficult to define the community to which any individual belonged, the concept of settlement—on which relief had been based—became anachronistic. At the same time, landless poor people on the move in search of work often needed relief for short periods when they lacked jobs.

Because people moved so often, they had fewer kin who could help them in difficult times or during crises. With the low wages that most people earned, they found it almost impossible to save for their old age, and unless they had children nearby who were willing and able to care for them, elderly working-class people were often left destitute, dependent on public relief or the poorhouse.

The problem was exacerbated by the separation of home and work, which was the major shift in household organization during the transition to a wage-labor and market economy. As households ceased to be centers of work and residence, they became smaller, more specialized, less able to incorporate needy kin. Few urban working-class families had enough physical space in their houses to take in their needy relatives, and, at a time when food took well over half of their income, they often could not afford to feed anyone else.

The shift in social relations fostered by the spread of wage labor did not depend on—indeed it preceded—mechanization. But mechanization itself also had an important impact on dependence as the growth of industrial opportunities pulled people off the land and into towns and cities, where they worked irregularly for low wages. When mechanization involved the

*People of Hamilton, Canada West: Family and Class in a Mid-Nineteenth Century City* (Cambridge, Mass.: Harvard University Press, 1975), and Michael B. Katz, Michael J. Doucet, and Mark J. Stern, *The Social Organization of Early Industrial Capitalism* (Cambridge, Mass.: Harvard University Press, 1982).

[3]Carl F. Kaestle, *The Evolution of an Urban School System: New York City, 1750–1850* (Cambridge, Mass.: Harvard University Press, 1973), p. 102; Katz, Doucet, and Stern, *Social Organization*, chap. 1.

rapid deskilling of crafts, as in the case of shoemaking after about 1850, it created special hardships for adult workers who, if not thrown out of work, had to accept lower wages.

Irregular work was the outstanding characteristic of wage labor in the nineteenth century. Indeed, even more than low wages, the lack of steady work plagued nineteenth-century workers. Irregular work reflected, first, capitalism's dependence on a mobile class of wage laborers ready to move where needed, a reserve army willing to work long hours at low wages. It was exaggerated, however, by labor market practices. By hiring unskilled workers on a daily basis from among a pool waiting at the factory gates, nineteenth- and early twentieth-century industrialists contributed to an extraordinary rate of labor turnover (100% per year was quite a usual figure in American manufacturing firms). They also contributed to labor turnover and irregular work for individuals by laying off workers during periods of business slack, which arose from market conditions or the periodic depressions that defined the business cycle. Finally, work was irregular because many jobs, such as those in construction, were seasonal. As a result, most workers probably did not work steadily throughout the year, and few had the savings necessary to sustain themselves and their families during anything but very short periods without an income.

Until the introduction of cheap mass transportation late in the century, everyone had to live near his or her work. This meant that changing jobs often meant moving one's home. In this way the irregularity of work and the geographic relation between home and workplace combined to promote transience and periodic dependence among many workers. Indeed, the need for some form of relief probably was a common element in the lives of most workers rather than the experience of a shiftless and incompetent minority.

Women had especially serious problems. Until late in the nineteenth century there were almost no pensions; few men left much in the way of savings when they died; and life insurance spread slowly, especially among the working class. Because the poorest men worked hardest at the least healthy jobs, they were often sick and died relatively young, and women, then as now, usually outlived their husbands. Thus even though divorce was uncommon, very large proportions of women with children lived by themselves. With no Social Security and with little paid work available to them, the plight of widows was especially pathetic.

Women's problems were exacerbated by changes in their economic role. Domestic manufacture (making articles for home consumption, under contract, or for sale) dwindled in the early years of the nineteenth century as factory production replaced the putting-out system and as more and more household goods were purchased rather than produced. In rural areas women had tended gardens and cared for family dairies. Often they could manage a farm by themselves or with the help of a hired laborer or child. By contrast, and contrary to popular stereotypes (which are based on the minority of young women who worked in mills), there was very little industrial work open to any women in towns and cities before the late nineteenth century and almost none to married women even throughout the early twentieth century. If a widow was lucky, she would have a child old enough to support her, and many widows often earned a little cash by taking in boarders or washing. Until the twentieth century most domestic jobs required servants to live in, and so even housekeeping was closed to widows or married women with children.

Immigration heightened problems related to dependence. Between 1830 and 1930, 30 million immigrants came to the United States. The first great wave, the Irish, fled the potato famine and desperate poverty. Although they probably were not the most destitute people in Ireland, they arrived with few industrial skills and with few resources. They quickly made up the majority of unskilled laborers and domestic servants in towns and cities, and, not surprisingly, their need for assistance was great. Indeed, in most categories of dependence they were represented far out of proportion to their share of the population.

Massive immigration fueled the development of American industry and increased the pace of urbanization. Lacking adequate housing facilities, sewers, water supplies, or other services, American cities became breeding grounds of disease and sites of frequent epidemics. The suffering of the poor within nineteenth- and early twentieth-century cities has been documented too often to need elaboration. What is important to stress is, first, the implication of that suffering for dependence. A mixture of sickness and poverty defined life in the great zones of poverty that disfigured American cities. Second is the inadequacy of relief. Neither public relief nor private charity could effectively alleviate poverty in these years. Third is the connection of relief with politics. Every account of the attempt to reform relief in nineteenth-century cities stressed the interplay of relief with corruption. Supplying poorhouses, distributing relief, and building institutions all offered great opportunities for graft. Politicians, so reformers said, manipulated the poor to stay in power and used relief money to line their own pockets. Without doubt, relief was corrupt. However, it is the meaning of corruption and machine politics that historians have begun to question. In the absence of municipal services, machine politicians provided the assistance without which many poor people in cities might not have survived, and the image of a friend of the poor, so assiduously cultivated by city bosses, may not have been entirely cynical.

Some of the improvements in the lives of the poor in the late nineteenth and early twentieth centuries were ironical in their outcome. The decline in the infant death rate after about 1880 certainly was unambiguous, but the extension of the adult life span was not. Throughout the late nineteenth and early twentieth centuries the age structure of the population gradually shifted, and the proportion of elderly people rose. This increase preceded the spread of pensions and the introduction of Social Security. At the same time, because marital fertility was decreasing, there was no corresponding increase in the proportion of children able to care for their parents. Thus, just as their lives began to lengthen, elderly people had fewer children to whom they could turn and few, if any, additional resources of their own.

Young people, as well as the elderly, faced special problems. There were, in fact, two great crises of youth in the nineteenth century. One happened in the 1830s and 1840s. As young people crowded into cities in these years, they found few jobs open to them. Lengthy, formal apprenticeships had mostly disappeared, and few employers needed the labor of adolescents. At the same time, few educational institutions served young people during their teenage years. Thus it is not surprising that social observers complained over and over again of idle youth hanging about street corners, engaging in petty crime, and annoying passersby. This first youth crisis was solved in two ways: the introduction of more schools for adolescents; and, starting around 1860 or 1870, industrial work. In its early years large-scale industrialization in the metal industries, shoemaking, and other trades opened up a great number of jobs for young people from the age of 14 or 15 upward. These jobs proved enormously attractive to both young working-class men and women; young men left school and young women left domestic service to work in the new factories. By the end of the nineteenth century, however, technological progress had begun to shrink the need for unskilled and semiskilled labor, and the new immigration from southern and eastern Europe made it possible to replace teenagers with adult workers. As a consequence, young people found it increasingly difficult to get work, and the jobs available to them often led nowhere. This second crisis of youth, which was widely discussed in the late nineteenth and early twentieth centuries, fueled the creation of a number of social innovations, including settlement work, youth groups, playgrounds, vocational education, and vocational guidance. Here the significance is in the way in which the impact of industrial development on the youth labor market created periodic crises of youth and helped shape a definition of youth as a special, useless, and dependent population.

The conditions that made dependence a structural feature of working-class life during the nineteenth and early twentieth centuries and the characteristics of welfare during these same years are the backdrop for the rest of this book. The book grows out of a research project whose official title was "Institutions and the Casualties of Industrial Society." I originally intended to focus on the demography of institutions. Recent historical writing on institutions stresses the public goals of administrators and reformers, official views of inmates and their families, and detailed accounts of internal developments. As valuable as these studies are, the actual identity and features of inmate populations have remained relatively unstudied, and it became clear from my own work and the research of historians working in other areas that popular and official descriptions rarely matched actual behavior. I wanted to know who the inmates were, how inmates of various types of institutions differed from one another, and how their characteristics changed over time. As the research progressed, the same empirical questions remained important, but my emphasis shifted. My earlier formulation of the questions, I saw, was limited by the way in which historians had carved up the field of dependence. What struck me as most important was the question of dependence itself. What were the features of dependent populations? How did they contrast with popular and official images? What were the links between the reasons for dependence, perceptions, and social policy?

The turning points in the reseach occurred when I began to read the debates about outdoor relief in the 1870s and the proceedings of the annual conventions of the county superintendents of the poor in New York State. These made me see that outdoor relief is one of those nasty little questions that have been brushed aside in American historical writing and that the whole question of relief policy is vastly more complex than I had realized. As a result, I commissioned some case studies of relief policy at the local level. These have only strengthened my impression that the history of dependence in American needs to be rewritten from the bottom up, that is, through a series of local case histories set in a comparative framework and through an analysis of the lives and experiences of the poor themselves. This is the task that this book tries to begin.

Chapter 1 uses case records to describe the life and death of a poor family in early twentieth-century Philadelpha. It attempts to show many of the themes in the lives of the poor through the close analysis of one extended example. By focusing on a single family and its experience, the case shows the interaction of a family with the agencies of welfare, the features of welfare itself, and something about the way in which poor families managed to survive, and it especially highlights the role of sickness in the life of the poor.

Chapter 2 moves back in time and consists of four case studies drawn from the project's empirical research. The first case study takes a neglected institution, the poorhouse, and shows that it has a history. It shows how internal population shifts reflected changes in function and how the very poor sometimes used the poorhouse in ways for which it had not been designed. The second case reports on a remarkable survey of the causes of pauperism undertaken by the New York Board of State Charities in the mid-1870s. It examines the report's conclusions as an example of early social science, assesses their internal validity, and reanalyses a portion of the data. The analysis shows how the reported findings, which were extremely influential, distorted the data and how those distortions were built into the way in which statistics on poorhouse inmates were collected throughout the rest of the century. The analysis also points to some of the underlying features of pauperism in the nineteenth century. The third case study continues the theme of the relation between the perception of dependence and its actual patterns by analyzing a sample of the seven special schedules of the 1880 U.S. census, which enumerated the "defective, dependent, and delinquent" population. It takes as its special problem the creation of social categories—in this case, a metaclass of defective people who, upon analysis, appear to have been quite different from one another. The final case deals with tramps. It uses a register of tramps from various places in New York State during the mid-1870s to assess the relation between popular images of tramps and what appeared to be their actual characteristics. Again, as in the other studies, the variation is quite wide. Using the findings of the analysis, the case study ends by taking up the question of causal attribution in history, that is, by asking whether it is in fact legitimate to criticize nineteenth-century social administrators and commentators for misrepresenting the objects of their attention. And it offers a few speculations about why particular misrepresentations were so serviceable.

The third chapter of the book is historiographical. Using the results of the project's research and other recent work on related topics, it looks at American historical writing about dependence as a field and offers a sympathetic critique. I have tried to make it a provocative and synthetic discussion that will interest at least some historians in taking new directions in the study of dependence. Indeed, the intent of this book is not to offer a definitive account of welfare as much as to open up the field in some fresh and useful ways.

I began the research on which this book rests before the current attempt to roll back the welfare state. Since then, American politics has made the underlying questions about dependence especially timely, even urgent. As in so many areas, social policy rests more on myths about the past than on history. Those myths about the past coupled with myths about the poor will increase the amount of insecurity, misery, and turmoil in this country. I hope this book will be helpful to those people in search of a more accurate, and equally usable, past.

# CHAPTER 1

## FAMILIES AND WELFARE: A PHILADELPHIA CASE

In neither the past nor the present can family life among the poor be disentangled from the practice of welfare. For centuries poor families have depended for their survival on charity, relief, or, as it is now called, welfare, while welfare agents—from the benevolent ladies and friendly visitors of the nineteenth century to the social workers of the twentieth—have set out to alleviate family destitution and prevent family disintegration. Nonetheless, historians have paid surprisingly little attention to the intersection of families and welfare. Despite several histories of welfare policy, there is no account of the way in which welfare practice actually affected families in the nineteenth and early twentieth centuries. Likewise, although historians of the family have written about family organization, the characteristics of the life-course, and the general relations between the family and the state, they have revealed relatively little about the internal dynamics of poor families and about the actual day-to-day interaction between families and social institutions.

To be fair, the texture of family life among the poor and the impact of welfare practice on individual families are topics about which it is difficult to know very much. However, one source of evidence remains largely untapped: case histories of welfare agencies. From at least the late nineteenth century onward, agencies that relieved the poor kept records of their activities. Sometimes these records are sketchy, little more than notations of aid given, but sometimes they are remarkably full. For example, the Charity Organization Societies, founded in most cities in the late nineteenth century, were especially compulsive. Their agents visited clients in their homes, not only recording demographic and economic information about families but also describing living conditions, behavior, and conversation. Because the Charity Organization Societies believed that relatives should help one another, they tried to contact as many kin as possible. Because they were concerned with discriminating between the worthy and unworthy poor, they also talked with employers, landlords, and sometimes neighbors. Unfortunately, most case records have been destroyed, but where they do exist, their careful accounts of their contacts make up detailed case studies of the lives of the very poor, often over several years. They make possible the reconstruction of the lives of the poor and of the intersection between families and welfare with a richness of detail that is available nowhere else.[1]

About 50 case histories of the Society for Organizing Charity in Philadelphia (founded in 1878) exist for the early twentieth century. None of the nineteenth-century cases have been preserved. What follows is a reconstruction from these documents of the history of one family and its interaction with the agencies of welfare in the early twentieth century. The first part of the reconstruction is a narrative history of the life and death of the family; the second is a thematic analysis of its meaning.[2] (Please note: In the interest of privacy the names of all family members and their friends, neighbors, and employers have been changed.)

## THE SULLIVAN FAMILY

On February 15, 1909, the Society for Organizing Charity (SOC) in Philadelphia received a postcard with the following message written in pencil:

Dear Madam
    Will you please call and see Mrs. Willem Sullivan 2726 Oakdail st I have

---

[1]On the history of the charity organization movement, see Frank Dekker Watson, *The Charity Organization Movement in the United States* (New York: Macmillan, 1902). On the origins of the movement in Philadelphia, see Julia B. Rauch, "Unfriendly Visitors: The Emergence of Scientific Philanthropy in Philadelphia, 1878–1880" (Ph.D. diss., University of Pennsylvania, 1974).

[2]The case histories that have been saved are in the files of the Family Service Association of Philadelphia.

two very sick children and my husband has no work and I am sick my self so
I would like you to oblige me please for god sake not for me

Mary Sullivan, the author, was 34 years old. Like her American-born 35-year-old husband, William, she had lived most of her life around Philadelphia. She and her husband had several relatives nearby: On Oakdale Street were Mr. Sullivan's brother and mother and Mrs. Sullivan's sister. Elsewhere in the city were another of Mrs. Sullivan's sisters, her aunt, a cousin, and, floating from place to place in the same area, her father. Nearby, too, was Mr. Sullivan's married cousin.

Mr. Sullivan, a teamster, was out of work. He and Mary had four children: William, 7 years old; John, age 6; Mary, 3, and Francis, 2. Mary was 1 month pregnant. All six of them lived in three rooms, for which they paid $6.50 per month.

The day after Mary's postcard arrived at the office of the SOC an agent visited the Sullivans. She found Mary and "all the children living in the kitchen, as this was the only room she could afford to heat." Mary was a "tall, slender woman, very light complected, light brown hair." The older children had just returned from the Municipal Hospital, where they had been sent with measels and chicken pox. Since their return home, they all had become ill again with measels. Mrs. Sullivan had no coal or groceries and no income whatsoever. Her husband, usually employed as a teamster by George Mohr, had not worked lately because of the weather. His mother lived in the front of the house, using two rooms and paying half the rent. However, she would have nothing to do with her son's family. According to Mary Sullivan, Mrs. Sullivan, Sr., had a "pension and is very well able to get along and could help her if she would. This she declines to do." The SOC agent sent 68 cents worth of groceries and promised to return the next day.

When the agent visited again a week later, Mrs. Sullivan reported that Dr. Ludon had sent her daughter Mary to the Municipal Hospital because she had chicken pox. Her husband, she said, was still looking for work but unable to find any. If the weather held, she thought, he soon would be reemployed by Mr. Mohr. On this visit the agent gave Mrs. Sullivan 50 cents for coal.

Three days later the agent telephoned Dr. Ludon. Dr. Ludon told her that the child Mary had died the night before in the Municipal Hospital. If the rest of the children did not improve, the doctor stressed, he would send them to the hospital, too. He thought that Mrs. Sullivan was "careless" and did not "know how to care for the children." Realizing, perhaps, that the Sullivans' situation would not improve soon, the agent sent them one-quarter ton of coal.

Mrs. Sullivan, however, blamed the doctor for her daughter's death. For "several days the children were in the hot kitchen on pillows and chairs, the door was constantly opening on them, and the kitchen was full of steam from washing. The doctor insisted that the children be taken upstairs, not knowing that she had no stove there." Mrs. Sullivan was convinced that the "change to the cold room gave Mary a chill which proved fatal."

The SOC agent visited the Sullivans on the same day she learned of their daughter's death, arriving as the family was returning from the cemetery. The house smelled strongly of formaldehyde. Mrs. Sullivan reported that the two young children were doing well; the doctor did not need to send them to the hospital. Father Gough had given her a lot in Holy Cross Cemetery and paid the funeral expenses. He would have given her an order for groceries, too, but the "Conference has been over burdened with relief work." Nonetheless, the neighbors had been "very kind," and she was "grateful to me for the coal and two orders of groceries we had sent." Mrs. Sullivan thought it useless to ask her sister, living on the same street, for help. However, she did not ask for any more relief and requested only some sheets and pillowcases for which she would be "very grateful."

Despite Mrs. Sullivan's advice, the SOC agent visited her sister. As Mrs. Sullivan had predicted, her sister claimed it would be "utterly impossible" for her to assist the Sullivans. Even more, she asserted that "Mame Sullivan was a great deal better off than she is. The child's illness and death cost her nothing; the funeral expenses were paid for, she got a lot in the cemetery, and will receive $17 insurance on the life of the child. Besides all this, groceries and all other kinds of help have poured in abundantly." Mrs. Sullivan's sister was sorry about the death of the child but thought her sister "exceedingly well provided for" and able to "get along." To some extent Mrs. Sullivan's sister was right. Her husband had managed a little work the previous week, earning $2, but his employer, on learning of his bereavement, had given him $6.

Shortly after the death of young Mary, the SOC received an unsolicited letter from one of the Sullivans' neighbors:

Dear Miss Clark in referance to Sullivans 2726 I main to tell you a little about them did she have the nerve to take you to her bed room to let you see the toilet set indeed a credit to a woman married 9 or 10 years Miss Clark she is a person you could cart in and she would cart out next day by going out a little I found out plenty the tavern gets even and to the few Stamps she receives in the stores she sells them every time she can he is sitting home today till the charities are all out he is a loafer from the word go the man he worked for last summer would not give him [illegible] but you drink to mutch for me that is what he told Mrs. Sullivan when she asked him to take him back they are all a pack of whiskey drinkers even to his old mother she always drank and the woman you went to see down 2710 Oakdale they are a disgrace to the square there is home mission St. Columbia 28 ward and all the neighbors helping them and the answer she gave me yesterday I asked if you were around yes I was disepointed I thought she would give me a dollar or two She got insurance but she could never get enough she is one of them crying beggars if you don't know her 8 weeks her children were in the hospital she worked 3 and 4 days a week and he worked and did you see anything for it A woman told me the other day not to have a thing to do with her think people will never be better he is sitting in the tavern on 27th st all the time and she is no better always crying for help drop them of give the relief to some poor people that is worthy and in want and be thankful. Miss Clark your own sences can tell you a respectal person not take you to such a room as that you know there should be something at the back if young people like them should have a little more respect for themselves than let any one see a poor widow could be that bad of that would to [illegible] out to feed her children then her pride would get a head of her and could not let the public see but that there is no pride there but grasp all you can get if I could see you I would tell you more but this is an eye opener must close hoping to meet you some time respectfully Mrs. Walsh to Miss Clark keep this to yourself.

Miss Clark did keep the letter to herself, apparently ignoring its advice, for a few days later, on February 24, an agent visited George Mohr, Mr. Sullivan's employer. Mohr confirmed that Sullivan worked for him, describing him as a "very good man" who drank but "no more than the ordinary teamster and never lost any time because of it." Next, Miss Clark looked for another of Mrs. Sullivan's sisters, who was not at home.

A few days later Miss Clark learned that the Sullivans had been reported to the Society for the Prevention of Cruelty to Children (SPCC) and that another child had contracted diptheria. Concerned by the report, she visited the Sullivans again on March 6, only to find the report true. The oldest boy, ill for several days, had been sent by the doctor to the Philadelphia Hospital. Mrs. Sullivan had telephoned the hospital a couple of times and learned that her son, who had a tracheotomy, was "very feeble, and it was uncertain whether he would recover." On the bright side, the children with measels and chicken pox were recovering fairly well. Mr. Sullivan, unfortunately, had had little work that week, earning only a few dollars. At present, Mrs. Sullivan said, they were not in need, but if her husband did not find work soon, they would "require some help." Also, her mother-in-law had moved out of their house.

Four days later an SOC agent checked to see if the Church was still helping the Sullivans, and she also visited the doctor to discuss the SPCC's allegations against them. The doctor "had seen no evidence of cruelty or actual neglect." Indeed, when she visited them the same day, the agent found the "family in the kitchen, which was warm and tidy." The child in the hospital remained in very serious condition, not expected to live. The Sullivans owed $13 in back rent. They recently had paid $2.50 but still were $10.50 in arrears. They had not asked Father Gough for more help because he had done so much when their child had died. The family had received coal on credit. Meanwhile, Mrs. Sullivan thought that an aunt who lived with her sister had some money and might help if the SOC asked. The agent sent a grocery order for $1.05 and also ordered a quart of milk for the children daily for 2 weeks.

Two days later the agent visited Mrs. Sullivan's sister, who claimed that she had done all she could to help the Sullivan family. She blamed all her sister's troubles on her husband, who, she asserted, was a "worthless drunkard." The so-called rich aunt living in the same house was about 70 years old and supported herself by sewing. She had no spare money. The agent also visited the cousin. Like the sister, she was not willing to help Mrs. Sullivan "as long as her husband" was at home. Mr. Sullivan, the cousin claimed, "could get plenty of work if he would only stay sober." She blamed the family's troubles on his drinking.

Shortly afterward, on March 23, Miss Clark received another postcard from Mrs. Sullivan:

> will you please call and see Mrs. Sullivan 2126 0 I have my boy home from the hospital and am very much in need of food for him oblige me.

The agent learned that when Mrs. Sullivan had telephoned the hospital to find out about her son's condition, she was told that the boy was well enough to come home. She asked the hospital to keep him a little longer because she "was not prepared with proper food for him." But the hospital refused and sent the child home in a carriage the next day. His lower legs were paralyzed and he was pale and thin. The agent found him sitting "in a big chair on pillows. The two younger children look much better—chicken pox crusts still visible on John. All comfortably dressed and fairly clean— the kitchen very tidy. Turnips and potatoes cooking on the stove." Mr. Sullivan was working now. He had earned $5 the previous week from his old employer and used $4 for rent. If the weather stayed good for teaming, he could earn $10 during the current week, with which he had promised to pay $5 in rent. The Sullivans had onions to cook, but their flour was gone.

They ate meat only on Sundays. The agent promised 3 pints of milk (one for each child) daily for the next few weeks and sent a bag of flour and yeast cake worth 42 cents. The children, she commented, "really need the milk."

When the agent visited again on April 3 Mrs. Sullivan reported, happily, that her husband had steady work and would earn $10 during the week, of which $4 would go to the landlord for the February rent. She also wanted to know if the SOC could send a little coal because it cost so much to buy it by the bucket. The boy who had diptheria still felt the "effects of it." The doctor "thought he should have nourishing food, but she has not been able to afford it." Mr. Sullivan was supposed to be paid that day, and if he was, she would try to buy some eggs. She asked that the SOC continue to send the milk a little longer and give her another grocery order in a few days. The agent offered to ask her supervisor about the request.

For a month and a half the Sullivans managed without the help of the SOC. Then, on May 17, Mrs. Sullivan came to the District Office. Her husband, she said, had been working about 5 days a week, earning $1.75 a day, but he had not given her all of his money. "They needed so much for the children and were so in debt she has not been able to pay rent." The constable had "levied" her a few days before, and, to make matters worse, her husband's brother, who lived on the same street, had committed suicide a few days before. His widow kept Mr. Sullivan "from work to help her find a house and rent it for her." She wanted her brother-in-law and his family to move in with her, but because she was "a rough drinking woman, as are all belonging" to Mr. Sullivan, Mrs. Sullivan refused to go. Instead, she wanted the SOC agent to persuade her husband to borrow from his sister-in-law so that the family could take a house alone or, failing that, to send her and the children to a home.

When the SOC agent visited the Sullivans at their home the same day, Mr. Sullivan had not returned yet. Mrs. Sullivan thought she would not be evicted before morning, and, possibly, "by that time her husband would return." He had left with $20, and she thought he might have gone to the country to rent a place because he always had been anxious to live in New Jersey. She promised to let the SOC know of any further developments "but thought she would be allright." Just to be safe, the agent gave her a note admitting her to an SOC lodge in case she was evicted suddenly.

Sadly, Mrs. Sullivan had to use the note. Within a few days she and her children no longer lived in their own home. Upset at finding his wife and children in a SOC lodge, Mr. Sullivan, "partially under the influence of liquor," appeared at a local SOC office "asking for his wife." The agent on duty who thought it would be better if he did not see her "in his present condition," did "not like the responsibility of the interview" and sent Mr. Sullivan to the District Office. There he again asked for his wife and children, claiming that he would be paid $4 the next day and would rent a room for his family or would give his wife the money. His sister-in-law had been arrested and "taken away by the SPCC the day before to be placed three months in the House of Correction and the children were given over to the SPCC." He admitted that he had taken the $20 and made "a fool of himself." He did not think he had used it all for drink and believed part of the money had been stolen from him when he was drunk. "He would not take the pledge for the SOC agent but he told her he was goint to try to cut out the drink and try to provide a good home for his wife and family." The SPCC had a warrant for his arrest but told him that he could have 2 weeks' trial. He promised to go to work the next day.

After telephoning Mrs. Sullivan at the lodge where she had gone with her children, the SOC agent suggested that all of the Sullivans' furniture be put in storage. Mr. Sullivan had begun to sober up and promised to work steadily. The SOC agent arranged to draw his $4 pay, and he promised to give her money to hold for the family during the next 2 weeks. As soon as he was "ahead enough," he would rent a place other than furnished rooms. Mrs. Sullivan, meanwhile, would give her husband another "try," and the SPCC would hold its warrant for 2 weeks.

Mr. Sullivan, reported the agent, was "good hearted but easy and liable to go off on a drunk at any time. When he takes the pledge he will keep straight for a month at a time, however." So there was at least a faint hope that the reunited family could manage on its own. Because Mrs. Sullivan was pregnant and "rather helpless," it seemed, on balance, "best for her to try" her husband one more time.

The lodge at which Mrs. Sullivan and the children were staying was eager for them to leave. Especially because the baby was "very cross," it was "a great deal of trouble" to house them. The SOC told the lodge that the family would leave as soon as Mr. Sullivan drew his pay. However, he worked only a short week. He boarded in the same house as his single brother and had to pay $4 for his room and meals. Although this expense reduced the amount he could save, Mrs. Sullivan expected to have enough money to leave the lodge by the end of the week. Indeed, she was "very anxious to get out of the Lodge" and during the first week asked only for groceries, which the SOC said her parish should provide.

Within a few days Mr. Sullivan had "steady work" as a night watchman with his old employer. He expected to earn $10.50 for his week's work.

With this amount he could "hardly do better than furnished rooms." As Mrs. Sullivan and her children left the lodge to join him, the SOC agent noted that they would be closely supervised and that she would have the "children committed at the first outbreak."

On August 9, only little more than a month after she had left the lodge, Mrs. Sullivan again wrote to the SOC:

> Mrs. Wood I am in great need both myself and children have no food in the house my husband was taking sick and had to go to hospital and my health is in no condition to make a living so hope you would be kind enough to call 2442 Marston St.

The next day the agent visited Mrs. Sullivan, who had left Oakdale Street "because they could not stand living with those people any longer, they were so common and used such foul language." Instead, counting on her husband's income, they had taken a house with her aunt, who was to pay half the rent. They paid the rent until August 3, when her husband became sick and had to leave work. Now he was hospitalized. Her aunt, Mrs. Kelly, had bought food, but she was "only a poor woman" and could do no more to help the family. Mrs. Sullivan, who expected to give birth in October, had no other relatives who could help. She wanted to go to a hospital but did not know what to do with her children. Desperate, she asked for help until her husband could return to work. "She had to send the little boy down to ask for a loaf of bread this morning and is afraid if she does that very often the Cruelty will get after her. Someone gave her a bag of coffee and that is about all they have in the house." The agent promised to "see what we could do."

The SOC agent telephoned the SPCC, which wanted to "move on the case," even though the SOC was "very doubtful of getting evidence." However, the SOC agreed to the SPCC request that it stay out of the case for the time being.

Mr. Sullivan, who had been discharged from the hospital, did not pay any rent between August and December, and the family was evicted. Moreover, during those months he did not live wholly at home. His landlord reported him as "lying drunk" and offered to appear as a witness against him in court. On December 22 Miss McConnell of the SPCC swore out a warrant for Sullivan's arrest. Although her family offered help, Mrs. Sullivan decided to return with her children to the Wayfarer Lodge because she was afraid of her husband. On December 29 the SPCC argued its case against the family before Judge Magill, who ordered Sullivan to pay $5 a week but decided that "as Mrs. Sullivan seemed to be perfectly respectable, and fond of her children, he did not think it just to take the children away from her." Thus, the case returned to the SOC.

By the middle of January Mrs. Sullivan, who had given birth to another son in October, still had not received any money and decided it would be "better for her to place William and John in St. John's home and take a service place." She had heard that her husband was staying with his mother and was "quite determined" never to return to him. Obviously "anxious," Mrs. Sullivan sought the agent's "advice about her future plans."

When Mrs. Sullivan's sister visited the lodge in January she agreed that it would be best for the children to be put in an orphanage and for her sister to take a service job. She, too, had no money and could not help the family. One reason why it was so important to move Mrs. Sullivan far away from her husband was that she "always has been very easily managed and she gives into her husband when he talks to her. Mrs. Sullivan means to be a good mother to the children and has done the best she could with the little money Mr. Sullivan has given her, but it is quite useless to start her up in a room or house as her husband would surely come back and bother her."

Throughout January the SOC tried to collect some money from Mr. Sullivan, who, it later learned, had sent the money to the wrong address. At the end of the month Mr. Sullivan went to the lodge to look for his wife but was not allowed in. Waiting until the Millers, the superintendents of the lodge, were at church, Sullivan returned and called to his wife, who came out on the pavement to talk with him. When the Millers returned and saw the couple talking on the street, they "sent Mr. Sullivan away."

Although Mr. Sullivan, who by now had paid his support money, wanted to return to his wife, the SOC did not approve. Pressing his case, Sullivan, a "rather tall, well built" man with "reddish brown hair and moustache, blue eyes, fresh complexion, dressed quite well," appeared at the SOC office. He had not been drinking that morning but, nonetheless, "seemed to be recovering from the effects of a spree." His "very disagreeable manner" did not help his claim. Sullivan demanded a written order to the lodge permitting him to see his wife. He had a "proposition" for her that he would make to no one else, and "if it were not for those who come between them, he and his wife would get along very well." The agent told Sullivan that when he had paid his wife regularly for some time, stayed in work, and kept away from drink, that the SOC "may consider having her go back to him." At this reply Mr. Sullivan became "very nasty," saying he would refuse to pay any more for support. Angry, he left the

**Plate 1.** From the exhibition of the Philadelphia Society for Organizing Charity (1916). Note the interconnection of public and private agencies and the symbol of the telephone. (Courtesy of the Historical Society of Pennsylvania.)

SOC office and returned to the lodge, where he "threatened to do terrible things" if not allowed to see his wife and children.

Two days later the agent talked with Mrs. Sullivan, who did not want any more contact with her husband and asserted that the only reason she had gone out to speak to him on Sunday was "because she was afraid he would make a fuss and she knew that the Millers were not in to manage him." She promised "never to do such a thing again, not to answer his letters or to have anything to do with him." She showed the agent a letter from a cousin, who reported that Mr. Sullivan had come to claim some of the family's furniture, which the cousin refused to give him. Her husband's purpose, said Mrs. Sullivan, had been to make her return to him so that he would no longer have to pay support to City Hall and "would get some benefit of the $5 he already had given her." She was afraid that he might try to take "the little boys, as he threatened to do, claiming to be very fond of the children."

On the same day Mrs. Miller called to report that she had had to get a doctor from the Children's Homeopathic Hospital to see one of the boys who had been very sick. Fortunately, the boy had only a slight sore throat and bad cold. To aid his recovery, the SOC asked Mrs. Miller to give him milk.

Within a few days the SOC agent visited Mr. Hickey, the agent for Catholic Children, to get an application form for William's and John's admission to St. John's Home. The application was supposed to be signed by the parish priest best acquainted with the family. Meanwhile, Mr. Sullivan sent $2.50 as a partial support payment. As she tried to work out a more long-term solution to the Sullivans' problems, the SOC agent visited the Children's Bureau and talked with an official there who promised to see if the bureau could take the case over entirely. The following day Miss True from the bureau called to say that the bureau would be glad to place Mrs. Sullivan and her youngest child at service but thought Mr. Hickey should place the older boys.

Thus, on the next day the SOC agent visited Mrs. Sullivan at Lodge Number 2 to have her sign the application for John's and William's admission to St. John's. Mrs. Sullivan thought that her sister might take Francis for a while if the SOC requested it. This was an important possibility because Mrs. Miller, the superintendent of the lodge, reported that Francis was "more trouble than the baby and the two older boys. He whines continually, though there seems to be nothing wrong with him. The cook complained because she has to sleep in the room next to the Sullivans."

The SOC wrote to Mrs. Sullivan's sister and arranged for Mrs. Sullivan to go to the Children's Bureau for an interview. But 2 days later, on

February 7, Mrs. Miller called to report that John had developed a sore throat and a problem with his nose. She sent him to the Northern Dispensary to see a physician, who transferred him to the nose and throat specialist. The appointment with the specialist was set for the same afternoon, and the SOC agent agreed to meet Mrs. Sullivan and John at the dispensary. The specialist found that although John's tonsils were hardly swollen, his adenoids should be removed. The operation was set for the next day. This time the SOC agent, Mrs. Sullivan, and John went to the Roosevelt Hospital, where the doctor "removed the adenoids after placing the boy under ether." The task was difficult because John was "very unmanageable and gave the doctor and agent a good deal of trouble. His mother has apparently no control over him at all." The agent arranged to take him back for a checkup the next afternoon. Then she took John and his mother back to the lodge, where the boy was "quite sick" from the operation. The agent bought him Phenol Sodique for 15 cents.

On the next day the agent met John and his mother at the dispensary. The doctor's assistant examined John's nose with "difficulty as he cried and struggled a good deal." Everything appeared to be healing properly. Again, the agent bought some medicine and arranged for Mrs. Sullivan to have "access to the bathroom so that she could treat John's nose as instructed." On the same day Mrs. Sullivan had also taken Francis to the doctor, who have her some medicine for him as the child seems to be nervous and poorly nourished." The agent arranged with Mrs. Miller to give milk to the three children.

With the medical emergency past, the agent visited St. Columbus Church to ask Father Gough to sign the application for the orphanage, but he was out. On the same day Mrs. Sullivan's sister visited the lodge and offered to take Francis for a time, but when she tried to take him home with her, "he cried so much she could not manage it." The agent instructed Mrs. Miller to tell Mrs. Sullivan to take her child to her sister's herself "as he would be much better off than at the Lodge, and it would be much better for the other children, as he makes so much noise at nights and keeps them all awake."

Finally, on February 14, Father Gough signed John's and William's application to St. John's Home. The agent then took the signed application to the Catholic agent, Mr. Hickey, who promised to "hurry" the case. In the meantime Mrs. Sullivan had taken Francis to her sister, but he was so "fretful and peevish" that her sister returned him and instead took the baby, Charles.

The arrangement lasted only a week. Mrs. Sullivan's sister called the lodge to say that the baby had to be removed immediately. To the agent the situation seemed "queer" because Mrs. Sullivan reported on Saturday that her sister "was much pleased with Charles, as was also her husband, and they would like to adopt it permanently." Because the streetcar drivers were striking, it was very difficult to reach Mrs. Sullivan's sister's home, and Mrs. Miller at the lodge did not know what to do.

The agent telephoned the SOC office nearest Mrs. Sullivan's sister and asked someone there to investigate right away. The local agent reported that Mrs. Sullivan's sister would not keep the baby another night and insisted that the mother come for it. The baby seemed to be "doing very well on the bottle," but because he had been used to being fed at night by his mother, he screamed all night and kept the family awake. They could stand it no longer, not even 1 more day. Mrs. Sullivan, the lodge reported, had started to "walk over to Kensington for it."

By the end of the week when the agent visited the lodge she found Mrs. Sullivan "very worried about matters in general" and "much disappointed that her sister would not keep the baby." She also had not heard from her husband. Wanting to pursue the payment due to Mrs. Sullivan, the agent telephoned the SPCC. Miss Sharp, the agent there, promised to send him a notice right away and, as well, said that Mrs. Sullivan should "come to City Hall on March 9 at 1 p.m. for an attachment against him." She was to go to room 580 but "must not ask for Miss Sharp."

The day Mrs. Sullivan was to appear at City Hall Mrs. Miller telephoned the SOC. Mrs. Sullivan, she reported, had received a letter from her husband a day or two before that she had "forgot to speak to her about and that he stated he had been in the Episcopal Hospital for some time very ill and wanted his wife to come and see him." The agent checked with the hospital, which confirmed that Mr. Sullivan had been admitted there suffering from some serious heart trouble "which is practically incurable." He was discharged about March 1 and was supposed to have gone home. Informed of Mr. Sullivan's condition, Miss Sharp said she had already sent him a notice that he was in arrears with his support payments, but she would not have him arrested until something more was learned about his condition and his ability to work.

About a week later one of the Sullivan children again took sick. This time it was the oldest boy. According to the doctor, the illness was not serious, only a fever and bad cold. Perhaps worn down by illness and poverty, Mrs. Sullivan told Mrs. Miller that she was "willing to turn the children over to the SPCC if they will take them as she is unable to manage the boys." Under pressure from the SOC, Mr. Hickey promised to place the boys in St. John's on April 10 after an examination by Dr. Eagen. On that morning the SOC agent went to the lodge to take the boys to Dr. Eagen, who examined them and gave them a certificate of health. With the permit from Mr. Hickey in hand, she then took the boys to St. John's

Home, where the mother superior "received them." She called Mrs. Sullivan at the orphanage to tell her that the boys were safely at the lodge and that she could visit them once a month.

Only a week later the lodge reported that it was quarantined with the measels and that the two remaining Sullivan children might contract the disease because another child from a different family who had been sleeping in the same room with them had just been taken to the Philadelphia Hospital. The next 6 or 7 days would reveal whether the Sullivan children also had contracted the measels. Fortunately, reported the lodge nearly a month later, the Sullivan children had not caught the disease. However, Mrs. Sullivan had heard that her husband was very ill in the Women's Homeopathic Hospital and was "anxious to see him" right away. Again checking the information, the agent discovered that Mr. Sullivan, suffering from cardiac asthma, was "in a serious condition, but not dangerously ill," and Mrs. Sullivan was given permission to visit him.

On the same day the agent telephoned Miss Brophy at St. Vincent's, another Catholic children's home, and asked her to admit Francis so that the SOC could place Mrs. Sullivan and the baby in a job. Miss Brophy called 2 days later to say that arrangements could be made to admit Francis in 5 days, on May 10. She had visited the lodge to see the family and wanted to take Mrs. Sullivan and the baby into "her home to try her for a week or so to see how she does her work, it may be that permanent arrangements can be made to keep her at a small salary." The only problem was that Miss Brophy lived with her brother, a doctor, and her sister, a schoolteacher. Thus, the house was empty part of every day, and she wanted to know if Mrs. Sullivan could be trusted. The agent told Miss Brophy "that we have made no special inquiries as to Mrs. Sullivan's honesty, but she had always been well spoken of."

The day before Francis was to go to St. Vincent's, Lodge No. 2 reported that the Sullivan baby had the measels and that Dr. Brody had sent for the ambulance to take it to the Philadelphia Hospital. Because Francis had been sleeping very close to the baby it was quite likely that he would contract the measels, and because Mrs. Sullivan was nursing the baby, the whole family had to be sent to the hospital. After the family left, the lodge notified the Bureau of Health and asked them to fumigate. Notified of the new events Miss Brophy said that she would be willing to honor her commitment once the family was well. However, Francis had to be entirely recovered before he could enter St. Vincent's, and this meant a delay of at least several weeks.

Within 2 days the hospital telephoned Mrs. Miller at the lodge to say that the Sullivans were ready to be discharged. Mrs. Miller called the SOC agent, who incredulous, telephoned Mr. Bohler, the house agent for the Department of Public Health and Charity of the Bureau of Charities. How, she asked, could the family have recovered from measels in 2 days? Mr. Bohler answered that the child already was convalescing when admitted. The agent protested that the whole family should be kept under observation for a week or two. Mr. Bohler agreed to keep them only until the next morning, "under protest," Several telephone calls followed. Finally, the assistant secretary of the SOC reached Dr. Cairns of the Bureau of Health and Charities and explained the case. Dr. Cairns agreed that it would be risky to discharge the family. By the next morning Mr. Bohler had agreed to keep them for 2 more weeks. Meanwhile, Mr. Sullivan had been discharged from the hospital and gone home (probably to his mother's).

On May 30 the SOC agent went to the Philadelphia Hospital to meet the Sullivans, who were leaving. Francis looked very well, but "the baby does not seem in very good condition." However, the nurse said that "the child is all right." When the family returned to the lodge, the agent called Miss Brophy, who said that St. Vincent's would wait a week or two to make sure that all danger of infection had passed.

The lodge called the SOC 10 days later to report that the Sullivan baby was very sick. Dr. Brody, who examined it, wanted to send the baby to the hospital, but Mrs. Sullivan "would not let it go." The agent, after conferring with Dr. Brody, told Mrs. Miller that "she had better persuade Mrs. Sullivan to take the child to the hospital." By evening Mrs. Miller had prevailed, and Mrs. Sullivan and the baby left for the hospital in an ambulance. The ambulance doctor felt "hopeless" about the baby, who apparently had pneumonia.

While Mrs. Sullivan waited to learn her baby's fate, the SOC agent visited Mr. Sullivan's mother in order to learn her son's address. Mrs. Sullivan, Sr., told the agent that her son had died a few days before at the Medico Chi Hospital, where he had been a patient for 10 days. "They were very good to him at the hospital, and she was with him until he died. He did not ask for his wife. They tried to find her but did not know the exact address of the Lodge or even the name of it, so they could not let Mrs. Sullivan know." Mr. Sullivan had left no insurance, and his mother had to "get credit at the undertaker's to have him buried." She did not "speak bitterly about Mrs. Sullivan but says, 'She is a very bad manager and does not know how to take care of the children.'" It was "absolutely impossible" for Mrs. Sullivan, Sr., to do anything to help her late son's family.

The SOC agent then went to the Philadelphia Hospital to tell Mrs. Sullivan of her husband's death. Although Mrs. Sullivan felt "rather badly," she said, "she is thankful that she will not be bothered by him any longer." During her visit the agent saw the baby, Charles, who seemed "to be in a dying condition." The next day he died.

Obviously distraught by the simultaneous deaths of her husband and child, Mrs. Sullivan asked for a discharge from the hospital, failing to tell Mr. Bohler that her child had died. She disappeared for a day or so, returning late on a Saturday night saying, "she had no place to go and must wait in the hospital for the [SOC] agent." Mr. Bohler took her in and kept her until morning, when he gave her carfare to the lodge.

Arrangements then had to be made for the baby's funeral. The SOC agent contacted a Protestant undertaker in West Philadelphia who agreed to bury the baby in Arlington Cemetery and provide a carriage for Mrs. Sullivan, all for $8. However, Father Gough arranged for his undertaker to bury the baby. The Church could not provide a carriage or arrange for Mrs. Sullivan to see the baby before he was buried, but it would inter Charles in the same lot with Mary in Holy Cross Cemetery. Mrs. Sullivan preferred the latter plan because Arlington was not "consecrated ground." The Church's undertaker offered to bring Mrs. Sullivan to view the baby's body at the hospital, and the agent agreed to accompany her. But Mrs. Sullivan "decided she would rather not go." The undertaker then gave her a dollar "out of his own pocket." Mrs. Sullivan, observed the agent, "seems very much worn out after all her trouble." She said "that they were not very nice to them at the hospital on Saturday." She blamed the hospital "because there was a great delay in caring for the baby on the night they were taken there in the ambulance. The ambulance stopped at the police station and took in two men, so that by the time they reached the hospital it was about 11 o'clock and in all this time the baby had received no attention."

Mrs. Sullivan had no reprieve. The next day Francis developed sore eyes. The doctor examining him thought it was pinkeye and worried that it might develop into whooping cough. However, a specialist, the brother of one of the SOC agents, visited Francis and diagnosed his condition as the aftermath of the measels. He advised the SOC to take Francis to the hospital every day until the condition improved. By early July the lodge reported that his eyes were "quite well again." Equally encouraging, Mrs. Sullivan had heard of a job to which she could go with Francis.

The job was offered by a friend of a Mrs. Hall, who had a delicatessen store on York Street between 27th and 28th streets. Mrs. Hall was in the mountains but would be home in 10 days and was willing to take Mrs. Sullivan and Francis and to pay $3 in wages. Mrs. Sullivan was anxious to try the place, and the SOC agent saw no harm in the arrangements. However, Mrs. Sullivan needed clothes badly, as did Francis, a condition she felt all the more sharply because she had learned that her late husband's family "had a drunked spree on the proceeds of the collection taken up to bury" him.

Within 2 weeks the promised job fell through. Mrs. Hall had changed her mind about taking Mrs. Sullivan with Francis. Now, Mrs. Sullivan began to press for a place through the Children's Bureau. While the bureau looked for a place for her, the Northern Lodge, where Mrs. Sullivan and Francis now were staying, reported to the SOC that a Mr. Schmidheiser of 27th and Susquehanna streets had come to the lodge and given her $5 to "help her along." More than a little suspicious, the SOC investigated. Questioned about Mr. Schmidheiser, Mrs. Sullivan said that she had known his family when they lived in the same neighborhood. His mother was an old lady who was "quite interested in the children." She lived at 27th and Susquehanna streets next to a bottle store. Her son Fred worked at the feed store at 22d and York. They "felt sorry for Mrs. Sullivan on account of the death of her husband and Charles . . . .Mrs. Schmidheiser sent her son with the $5 for her." While questioning her about her recent gift, the agent gave Mrs. Sullivan "some old clothes." Mrs. Sullivan repeated that she wanted to go to work.

By the third week in July the Children's Bureau had found a place for the Sullivans. Mr. E. F. Hunt of Mullica Hill, New Jersey, "came to the Lodge himself with an automobile, talked with Mrs. Sullivan, helped her to get her belongings tied up and took her away with him. He promised to let us know if she was not satisfactory."

From her new home in the country with the Hunts—described by the agent as "very nice people" who made Mrs. Sullivan work hard but were "very kind to her"—Mrs. Sullivan sent the first of a steady stream of letters back to the SOC on July 21, 1910:

Dear Miss Cashwell

I thought I would write to let you know that I have got a place in the contry and I think I will like it very much we have 6 or 7 men to meals all darkies and I have to tell Francis not to call them niggers as he would and I know they would not like that I will go out to see my boys the firt sunday of the month I have to get up at 4 o'clock in the morning and Francis is up a soon as he misses me out of the bed he is taking at sleep now and I am in my room with him writing to you and taking in the contry pickture of the corn fields will you . . . write to me soon and I would like to let Mrs. Schimather know where I am also . . . but I do not know her number any letters that come for me to Mrs. Millers tell her to send them as that man told me he would write I think that is all I have to tell you hoping you will look after me untill I get my family to getter again.

Yours truly
Mrs. Sullivan a worried mother

Three weeks later, on August 11, she wrote to Mrs. Miller, superintendent of the lodge where she had stayed:

> Mrs Miller
>     Pardon me for writing to you but I tink of the trouble you had with me and as I can not pay in any other way at preasant I think I could write to let you know that I have not for got you and Mr. Miller I hope you are well as I am getting along good with my boy I had a little trouble with him at first he would get up at 4 in the morning and I thought the lady would not keep me for she did not like him crying so much but I have him so good that he is no trouble to me or her but my troble is not over as I received a letter from Miss Wood telling me my father would like me to help him what do you think of that before I get started on myself so I do not know what to do if I have some place I could take him to mind Francis and go out to work I think I could make more money as I have it [illegible] for $2.50 a week. The lady is so busy some days that we have no time to eat coming and she says that sattday work is worth one dollar and she had to pay that much by the day when she was without a girl so you can know that it is hard—how is Miss M. Cashell I wrote a letter to her but I have not got no ancer—that is all at present yours truly Mrs. Sullivan.

By September 20, over a month later, Mrs. Sullivan still had not received a reply from Miss Cashell, so she wrote again, asking why her letter had not been answered. "I am fine," wrote Mrs. Sullivan, "and my boy is big and fat as butter." However, she was worried because her older boys at the orphanage had been unwell; her father was still asking for money; and she had no clothes. The Hunts held out the prospect of a house that she could rent in the spring, and that, she felt, would enable her to take both her boys and her father. What, she asked the SOC agent, should she do? Could she have some money for furniture? "I am only," she concluded, "asking God to let me live for my tree little ones that is left to me to take care of that is all I ask if I had the money to go to the contry sails you can get bed and washtand for 25 cents so you know it would not take much."

On September 27 the Northeast Office assistant called the SOC District Office where Mrs. Sullivan had received aid. Mr. Murphy, Mrs. Sullivan's father, had appealed to the district for assistance, and agents there had written to Mrs. Sullivan. When about a week earlier Mrs. Sullivan had come to Philadelphia to see her sister, she had also visited the SOC Northeast Office. Mrs. Sullivan explained that another office had been dealing with her and had placed her through the Children's Bureau. The agent on duty advised her not to worry about her father. She also advised her not to take the boys out of the orphanage at present and not to take in her father. Mr. Murphy, still seeking aid from his daughter, refused shelter at the lodge and "disappeared from view." On the same day another SOC agent wrote to Mrs. Sullivan and also advised her not to help her father and to leave the boys in the home at present.

In the middle of October Mrs. Sullivan and Francis, in town for the day, visited the SOC. The agent, who reported them "both looking very well," discussed with Mrs. Sullivan the possibility of renting the house offered by the Hunts in the spring. "It may be," ruminated the agent, that Mrs. Sullivan could "get enough work to support herself and three children by that time . . . . There is a good country school within a half a mile of the farm and of course higher schools in Swedesboro." Mrs. Sullivan still was "bothered" by her father who had written requesting $5. Mrs. Sullivan's sister felt she "ought to help him," but the SOC advised her "not to send her father any money, but refer him to the SOC if he is in need of assistance." The agent also promised to visit Mullica Hill when the busy season on the farm was over and to find "any old clothes" for Francis and Mrs. Sullivan. The older boys, still in the home, seemed "to be getting along very well."

Mrs. Sullivan wrote again 2 weeks later to Miss Cashell, thanking her for a letter and repeating that she could not help her father. "You may know that I have nothing to put on my back and Francis has no coat to put on when the winter comes." She asked if she should approach the Children's Aid Society (CAS) about clothes.

> I am trying to get $50 put away untill spring and the lady will rent me the house as she would like me to wash for her. I have it very hard now as we have 16 in the house to work for but as soon as the sweet potoes is gone then them men will go. I was thinking that I could get all the eating such as potoes and tomaoes and beans as the lady told me she would help me out that way and she thinks that I ought to try and get my boys home . . . . Francis is looking good the lady was up in the city and she got me a bottle of Kunkels worm syrup as I thought he was troubled with them it is $1 a bottle but I think it will do him good. did you go up to see that man that gave me the $5 as you did not tell me in the letter also let me know if Mrs. M. got the letter . . . . I heard she is a grand mother what do you think of that So write soon.

Only 2 days later she wrote again, asking Miss Cashell to visit her, pointing out that the farm was not so busy because the men had gone home. She also wanted information about her father, and she continued to press her concern about clothes, especially a coat for Francis.

On November 4 Miss Cashell answered her letters. She would visit when she could. She was looking for clothes. She had not heard from Mrs.

Sullivan's father, but Mrs. Sullivan was not to worry about him. In her usual prompt way, Mrs. Sullivan answered the next day, reporting that her sister had sent her a letter about her father. She had $35 now and would receive $3 per week if she would do the ironing. She had heard that her aunt had rented a house and was keeping roomers, but her aunt had said not to tell her because she was sure to ask for help, so "I wrote her how she liked keeping roomers and I have not got an ancer yet so I guess she is mad at me." Now that the heavy work was done she was picking beans for 1 cent a quart and felt she could take her father in for the winter.

This time Miss Cashell answered promptly, again discouraging Mrs. Sullivan from taking in her father. A couple of days later, again on a day off, Mrs. Sullivan and Francis appeared at the SOC office showing a letter from her father, "in which he makes a pitiful appeal for money, and also suggests that she might have him down in Mullica Hill." Mrs. Sullivan also had received a letter from a cousin asking for a loan of $5. The agent advised her to "write to her father that she could not help him and also to tell the cousin that she needed the money for her own children."

Mrs. Sullivan's father, Mr. Murphy, had been staying in Riverton with a relative but was unhappy there because he was "asked to do odd jobs about the house." This the agent found unacceptable. "We told" Mrs. Sullivan "that we thought Mr. Murphy should be glad to have a home and willing to do whatever" was asked.

Two days later a former neighbor answered one of Mrs. Sullivan's letters. Mrs. Sullivan had asked him if he knew that her husband had died. He replied that he knew "Will" was dead. Indeed, he said,

> a few of us got a collection of $50 together and payed the undertaker and had him Buried I am sorry to state though he was not taken in church as we could not afford to pay for same as we done all we could to Pay the Burial. I have been repayed in this about the same as in other cases with hard knocks is it then No Wonder that a man gets disgusted with labor of helping other's along when they are down.

Her former neighbor's discouragement obviously upset Mrs. Sullivan, and she wrote him herself. She also wrote Miss Cashell, enclosing the letter. "I received one that I would like you to ancer so that they will not be disgusted helping others as I wrote and thank him very much for all he has has done for me and I think if you would do the same he would think more like keeping on with his good works." She had not, she added, heard more from her father and cousin. Nearly a month later Miss Cashell replied that she would write to the neighbor.

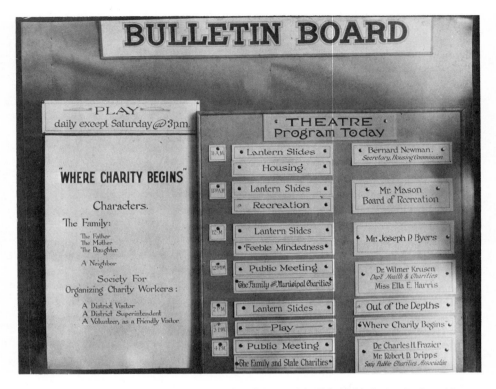

*Plate 2.* Bulletin board showing activities at the Exhibition of the Philadelphia Society for Organizing Charity (1916). Note the variety of concerns represented on the program. (Courtesy of the Historical Society of Pennsylvania.)

Characteristically, Mrs. Sullivan's good fortune did not last. On December 21 she wrote to Miss Cashell that she had had "some trouble." She had gone to the city to see her boys. Because of the cold weather, she had told the Hunts she would not return that night. Thus, no one was prepared to meet her. However, she had decided not to go to her sister's because she would be expected to bring Christmas presents. Instead, she decided to come home after all. She did not remember the Hunts' telephone number and tried one she thought correct, but it was wrong. So she had to go from the station to Mr. Hunt's father's, where she called for a ride home.

The lady was mad . . . .well the next day she was finding fault with Francis and said that Mr. Hunt was sorry that he did not get someone without a child and he wasted so much and I do not no what all so I could not stand it any longer so I told her that was going up in the city and see what I could do for I was crying and she got me so upset . . . but her husband ask her if she wanted me to go or what was the trouble and she did not tell him what she had said to me but told him that I wanted to go up to the city and he told her to go to Mrs. Gwynne [Children's Aid Society] at Arch St and get her to write me and see if I would not make up my mind to stay so she said I wrote and so I wrote and tell her all about it said will tell you what the ancer will be as soon as I get one Mrs. Hunt read her letter to me that she sent and it was very nice but all the trouble was put on me and you know that every story has two sides so I will tell you when I see you.

Miss Cashell answered almost immediately, urging her to stay with Mrs. Hunt and counseling patience. She also said that she had a box of toys for Francis at her office. Miss Gwynn at the CAS also wrote promptly, advising her to stay at least until spring. Work, she observed, was hard to get in the city. There was virtually "no day work." At the same time she reminded Mrs. Sullivan that she was entitled to 1 full day off per month without any loss of wages.

Two days after Christmas Mrs. Sullivan answered Miss Cashell. She wanted to get the toys for Francis because "he has nothing to play with and he gets lonesome but I do not like to take a day of as you see she will not pay me." Nonetheless, she had had a good Christmas at Mrs. Hunt's sister's house, where 26 people gathered for dinner. "Mrs. Hunt's sister," she observed, "is very nice she has no children her name is Hunt to she is looking for a girl so if you know of some I tink that it would be a very nice place." As for her own problems, "I do not think Mrs. Hunt ever thought that I would think of leaving her as things are going very nice." Thus, she said she would stay at least for the winter and asked that the toys for Francis be sent.

Early in January Mrs. Cashell answered, again urging her to stay at her place and telling her that she would hold the box of toys until Mrs. Sullivan could come to town. Mrs. Sullivan answered almost at once because she had received another letter about her father. Her sister had put her father out. Her Aunt Nora had taken him in, but she did not think he would be "allowed to stay long" because Nora's husband would object. Nora wanted $3 for rent because "my old lazzie father" had not paid her "one sent she said and he got her room black with his oil stove so that is the latest he has nothing to do but read the paper and paint so she would not put up with that." At the same time Mrs. Sullivan reported another argument with her employer. This time the object was wages. Mrs. Sullivan knew that she had earned $80, but "after all has been taken out that I got I only have $20.95." Her "books" and those of her employer differed dramatically, and she asked help in resolving the discrepancy. Miss Cashell promised to talk with the CAS about settling the wage dispute and, at the same time, advised her not to send money to her father.

The dispute with Mrs. Hunt continued throughout the month. Mrs. Sullivan intended to have a "papper made" showing all that was owed her. In the same letter, Mrs. Sullivan asked Miss Cashell if she ever had written to Mr. Avery, the neighbor whose discouragement about good works had so troubled her. Ruminating more generally, she asked Miss Cashell, "how is the world getting along have you any more poor mothers with a family like me to get starting out if you have I am sorry for them I hope I will soon get my boys home with me as I would be very happy working for them." Most seriously, almost as an afterthought, she reported that she would soon need a new place because the man and woman who had worked for the Hunts before her were returning in March.

In February illness again dominated Mrs. Sullivan's life. This time Francis was "very sick." She took him to the doctor in Philadelphia and spent "all sunday night" at her sister's with Francis, who was "afraid that I am going to leave him there as the doctor said he was alright and I had no trouble with him since I come home. He is happy with his box of toys. I thank you very much." Again, she reminded Miss Cashell that her time at the Hunts would end in early March. What she wanted, she said, was a house rather than a room, and she urgently needed advice about how to get one. She expected to receive about $30 and would "like to spend it wise as you know I had to work hard for it." Mrs. Gwynn at the CAS, she added, "thought that living alone would not be safe for me."

With Mrs. Sullivan about to lose her place, uncertain about where to live, anxious to get her boys back, worried about her father, the narrative ends. There are no more reports, no more letters, only a record of subsequent addresses. At the end of March she moved to Conshohocken, where she lived at the same address for 4 months before moving in July to another address in the same town. There she remained for a year and 3 months, until November 18, 1912, when she moved to the Shady Hill Poultry Farm, Willow Grove, Pennsylvania, a home that lasted 4 months. In February 1913 she drifted back to Philadelphia, living on Memphis Street for a year and 4 months until she moved to East Elkhart Street in Dresherton, Pennsylvania, an address also good for but 4 months, after which Mrs. Sullivan was listed only as in care of the CAS.

## THEMES IN THE HISTORY OF
## THE SULLIVAN FAMILY

### Contact with Agencies and Officials

The Sullivan family came into contact with an amazing variety of agencies and officials in the roughly 1½ years during which the records of the SOC narrate its history. First were the charitable agencies: the Society for Organizing Charity, the Society for the Prevention of Cruelty to Children, the Children's Aid Society, the Children's Bureau, St. John's Home, St. Vincent's Home, the Bureau of Health, the Bureau of Charities, and the local Catholic church. Encounters with the law came through the constables who evicted them, the city officials prepared to enforce support orders against Mr. Sullivan and to arrest him, and Judge Magill, who refused to break up the family. Then there were the hospitals: the Municipal Hospital, Philadelphia Hospital, Children's Homeopathic Hospital, Northern Dispensary, Episcopal Hospital, Women's Homeopathic Hospital, and Medico Chi Hospital. Finally, the Sullivans dealt with several doctors: Dr. Ludon, Dr. Brady, the eye specialist, the ear, nose, and throat specialist, and the doctors who treated Mr. Sullivan.

Agencies kept in touch with one another, cooperated, and, as a result, formed a loose network that provided a variety of types of assistance: cash, counseling, child care, housing, job placement, medical care, legal assistance, and burial. At the center was the SOC, whose agents managed the case, attempting with varying degrees of success to coordinate the efforts of the other sources of aid. For instance, when it became clear that the family could not remain together, the SPCC orchestrated an effort that involved the CAS, the Catholic church, and the Children's Bureau in an attempt to find homes for the Sullivans.

Tensions inevitably arose, as when the SOC reluctantly agreed to stay out of the case while the SPCC attempted to break up the family. Indeed, territorial issues between agencies must have been sensitive, because the SOC did not object when the SPCC brought the family to court, even though the SOC agents thought the evidence against the Sullivans insufficient. Another time the SOC was furious with the city official who tried to return the Sullivans to the lodge after only 2 days of hospitalization for measels. Using its authority, the SOC managed to reach his superior, who reversed the decision. Some tension as well, seems, to have marked relations between the SPCC and the city, as illustrated by the SPCC agent's instructions to Mrs. Sullivan not to mention her name when she went to City Hall for an attachment against her husband. Sometimes the tension between agencies resulted simply from the pressures on them. For instance, the Catholic agent who placed children seemed to the SOC to take an inordinately long time arranging for the admission of the two oldest Sullivan boys to St. John's, although the agent, Mr. Hickey, pointed out that the orphanage was overcrowded.

It is not useful to describe the network of agencies among which the Sullivans moved either as public or private. The SOC was private. Some of the hospitals were public. The city ran its own Bureau of Charities. But the SPCC, a private group, could initiate court proceedings intended to break up families. The SOC agents worked with both private and public agencies. The Children's Bureau coordinated child care services for a variety of agencies both public and private. Certainly, strains existed between sectors, and finances came from different sources. But public and private agencies combined to form a loosely coordinated network for the alleviation of dependence.

### The Nature of Assistance

Assistance was inadequate; of that there can be no doubt. The few groceries given to the Sullivans kept them just above starvation. Inadequate medical care may have killed two of their children. In no instance was material relief sufficient to move the family out of poverty; nor was it intended to be. Material relief, clearly, was seen as temporary, an expedient to tide the family through difficult, short-term crises occasioned by periodic unemployment or sickness. The structure of charity was not intended for the long-term relief of destitution. Rather, when the family clearly became unable to support itself, the policy was to break it up, to send some children to an orphanage and the mother out to service. As harsh as the policy was, in the short term it apparently improved the mental and physical health of the family. The older children at St. John's were well; Mrs. Sullivan was almost cheerful; Francis was "fat as butter."

SOC agents were unsentimental. They had relatively little to offer and probably would not have given much larger amounts of assistance if they could. But they were neither moralistic nor uncaring. They refused to accept negative descriptions of the Sullivans without checking, and they scarcely criticized the family in their reports. And they worked hard and promptly. The day after the SOC received a postcard from Mrs. Sullivan, an agent visited her home. The agents personally called on every nearby relative to check for possible help; agents accompanied the Sullivans on many trips to hospitals and doctors; they were their advocates before the hospital officials who wanted to send them home prematurely and the Catholic agent who needed prodding to get the boys admitted to St. John's. They coordinated the assistance from other agencies, answered letters, and always were available to advise Mrs. Sullivan when she appeared at their offices. In general their advice was sensible, especially when they counseled her not to assist her father and other relatives who suddenly appeared as soon as she had earned a few dollars.

The ideology of charity organization provides only a marginal guide to understanding the administration of charity. Clearly, daily confrontation with the problems of the very poor shaped attitudes and responses. Whatever the larger role of charity in reinforcing social inequality and low wages, SOC agents probably thought very little about such general issues as they spent their days trying to alleviate the endless crises in the lives of their clients. Just how experience reinforced or modified the way they thought about their role or their clients remains unknown. But it is a topic that can only be understood through an analysis of their actions and on-the-job responses, not deduced from official ideology. (It is quite likely that early twentieth-century SOC agents began their work with a considerably more complex view of poverty than did their predecessors in the 1870s and 1880s. In his history of charity organization, for instance, Frank Watson points out that within the SOC movement moralism began to give way to environmentalism during the early twentieth century.)[3]

## Characteristics of the Poor and the Problem of Perception

What were the Sullivans like? The answer is complex because so many different responses were given. Dr. Ludom called Mrs. Sullivan careless and a poor manager. Her mother-in-law agreed. The neighbor who wrote the poison-pen letter implied the same thing, adding that she was vain, lazy, and a drunk. Both the SOC agents and her sister felt that Mrs. Sullivan was weak and easily persuaded by her husband.

However, whenever the SOC agent visited the Sullivan home she found it clean and tidy. The St. Vincent's Society agent was so impressed by Mrs. Sullivan that she wanted to take her into her home as a resident domestic. When Judge Magill was asked by the SPCC (known by the poor as "the Cruelty") to break up the family, he refused because Mrs. Sullivan appeared to be respectable and to care for her children.

---

[3]Watson, *Charity Organization*, pp. 526–527.

Mrs. Sullivan's behavior showed both the positive and negative qualities attributed to her by observers. At times she was not strong; she did seem easily influenced by her husband; and she not only accepted most of the advice offered by the SOC without resistance but also became increasingly dependent on its agents.

Still, the story is far more complex. She survived an 18-month period during which two of her children and her husband died and her family was broken up. She herself remained unbroken, able—even eager—to work hard, save money, and plan for the reunification of her family. Clearly she wanted her boys back. Despite her family's general reluctance to help her, she felt obliged to help her father, who had ignored her during her greatest difficulties. She even remained able to play a little joke on her aunt, as in her letter about the boarder. Her language was at moments almost poetic, as in her sudden aside about the view from her window, her metaphor ("fat as butter") about Francis, or her question to the SOC agent about the state of the world. She learned which agencies could help her, turning to them in times of need, requesting help only when desperate, making specific requests, and admitting when she did not need help for a time. Spent by her experience with the death of her child, she resisted the hospitalization of her baby. When she learned, almost at the same moment, of the deaths of her husband and baby, she broke down briefly— for the only time during this period of disaster in her life—but recovered and within a day or so was coping with another child's illness. Indeed, her devotion to her children was striking. It was only when she could see no alternative, when she understood that it was in their best interests, that she agreed to separate from them. But she viewed the separation as temporary. Despite everything that happened to her, when an old neighbor wrote that all he received for trying to help others was hard knocks, Mrs. Sullivan immediately wrote to him and tried to persuade the SOC agent to reply as well. Mrs. Sullivan, in short, was a remarkable woman: intelligent, compassionate, fiercely loyal to her children, and, in some ways, strong and resilient.

Mr. Sullivan remains a more ambiguous figure. There can be no doubt that he drank a great deal. Every account confirms this. The question is whether drink caused his problems. Here the evidence does not support Mrs. Sullivan's relatives, who roundly condemned him. His employer called him a good worker, no heavier a drinker than the ordinary teamster and never drunk to the point that he could not work well. Is it possible that he drank progressively more as he became unable to find work and his health failed?

Again, he behaved inconsistently toward his family. At first he appears to have turned over almost all of his wages to his wife; later he ceased to support her and even lived at home irregularly. Yet his pathetic attempt to force the SOC to allow him to see his wife, his protestations of affection for his children, his claim that the SOC and other agencies had come between him and wife cannot be dismissed out of hand. The last several months of his life, after all, were a progressive assault on his sense of self-worth, his dignity, even his manhood. Through no fault of his own he was out of work and unable to support his family (which survived only through his wife's requests for charity), he was sick, one of his children died, his brother committed suicide, and courts ordered him to support his family at the very time that women charity workers persuaded his wife to leave him and—perhaps the final insult—refused even to let him see her. Is it any wonder that Mr. Sullivan—sick, poor, humiliated, and bitter—turned to drink and, in the final hours of life, did not ask to see his wife?

## Residential Mobility

Transience, so much a part of recent writing about American social history, is also a part of the Sullivan's story. It is unclear how long they had lived on Oakdale Street, but they moved as a family to another street within a few months of their first contact with the SOC. in the course of the year and a half during which the SOC records follow their history, Mrs. Sullivan and her children also lived at two or three different lodges; the older boys ended up in an orphanage; the baby for a short time lived with Mrs. Sullivan's sister; and, of course, Mrs. Sullivan and Francis moved to the farm in New Jersey. After the period covered in the narrative case record, Mrs. Sullivan moved about every 4 months during the next year or two. Mr. Sullivan lived not only with his wife and children but also with his mother, with his brother in a boarding house, and, very likely, in one or two other places as well.

All of these movements were of a relatively short distance. Until the boys went to the orphanage, the moves all took place within a relatively small section of Philadelphia. Relatives, too, lived for the most part nearby. In this way the Sullivans and their kin seem more like the casual poor trapped in East London, described by Gareth Stedman Jones, than the wandering or transient poor of North American social history.[4] It is significant that when Mrs. Sullivan finally left Philadelphia—and again the move was of a relatively short distance—it was to take a job. Indeed, once she entered the wage labor market, her history resembled that of the poor who appeared to pass through North American towns and cities in such

[4]Gareth Stedman Jones, *Outcast London* (London: Oxford, 1971).

great numbers during the nineteenth and early twentieth centuries. In this way the Sullivans' history points to opposing forces at work on the urban poor. One set of forces consisted of local kin ties, connections with charities, and relations with employers. These acted to keep people from moving very far, even though they changed residence often for a variety of reasons: eviction, changes in family circumstances, inability to get along with the neighbors. At the same time, the difficulty of finding work and the limitations of the local labor market encouraged men and women to move beyond the bounds of their neighborhoods, especially when a job possibility beckoned. Just how these forces interacted depended on a variety of factors: a family's health and energy level, relations with kin, the state of local labor markets, and the kinds of jobs available to men and women. Mr. Sullivan, a teamster, did not need to live where he worked, and the possibility of work when the weather improved made it worthwhile for him to stay in the neighborhood. Mrs. Sullivan, by contrast, could work only as a domestic, which meant living with her employer.

## Sickness

The Sullivans' history is a tale of sickness. The story opens with the children newly home from the hospital, where they were treated for measels and chicken pox. Soon they become ill again, and the youngest dies. The others fall in and out of ill health. Another almost dies in the hospital but manages to recover. Just as the older boys are about to go to St. John's, Francis to St. Vincent's, and the baby and Mrs. Sullivan into service, the whole family is rushed to the hospital, allegedly again with the measels. Afterward the baby dies. Meanwhile, Mr. Sullivan moves in and out of hospitals at least three times during the final months of his life. Even on the farm illness haunts Mrs. Sullivan. She worries that the boys in the orphanage are sick; sometimes she is not well; and, despite his generally more robust health, Francis gets sick during the winter.

If one could make a time budget for Mrs. Sullivan, it would show an extraordinary amount of her life spent in hospitals, taking children to doctors, or caring for a sick child. In fact, when she was living with all of her children, at least one of them was sick practically all of the time. Were they an especially unhealthy family? I suspect the answer is no. It was difficult for them ever to recover fully. They lacked adequate fuel with which to warm their home. They always lived on the edge of starvation. They could not afford the diet recommended by doctors. They did not have enough warm clothing. They slept together in the same bed.

To these factors, which undoubtedly were common among the very poor, must be added the quality of medical care. By no means was it all bad.

Certainly the doctor who sent the young child to an unheated room probably did kill it; the nurse who said the sick baby was "all right" made a bad mistake; the ambulance that took hours to reach the hospital probably eliminated any chance of the baby's recovery. Yet the specialists gave competent advice, and Mr. Sullivan received medical and nursing care that his mother referred to as kind. One of the Sullivan children even recovered from a serious illness in the hospital. Indeed, the degree to which medical care took place in a hospital and the at least mixed ability of physicians to cure some diseases probably separates the history of the very poor in the twentieth century from their history even 20 or 30 years earlier.

### The Role of the Catholic Church

Not only secular agencies but also the Catholic church were deeply involved in relief work. Both Father Gough's comment that he could not provide groceries for the Sullivans because his funds had been exhausted and the overcrowding at St. John's reflect the Church's burden. At certain times, though, the Church—whatever its load—helped, as when Father Gough paid for an undertaker and gave the Sullivans a lot for their children in a Catholic cemetery, relieving Mrs. Sullivan, who did not want her baby buried in unconsecrated ground. Mrs. Sullivan did not think that the Church's help had been inadequate. She was, in fact, very grateful for its help when her first child died and was reluctant to go to Father Gough for more aid. In the end the Catholic church was a major source of support for the Sullivan family because, through its St. John's home, it took care of the older boys.

### Kin

Kin play a key role in the Sullivans' history. First, the SOC clearly assumed that people with enough money or a large enough house should help their less fortunate kin. Therefore, agents tried hard to identify and contact all of each client's kin. Indeed, a large part of the agent's time was consumed with tracking down the Sullivans' relatives. In Mrs. Sullivan's case, with her mother apparently dead, the closest bonds were between sisters. No one in the family seemed very close to her father. Mr. Sullivan, by contrast, seemed closest to his brothers and to his mother. Mrs. Sullivan's family had no use for her husband and his kin, and Mr. Sullilvan's mother did not even speak to her daughter-in-law. Very likely, within working-class families intense bonds united mothers and their children throughout their lives, whereas for adults ties were strongest between siblings of the same sex. At the same time, tension and hostility often characterized the relations between in-laws.

If the Sullivans were typical, kin relations among the very poor were not always warm, close, and supportive. Mr. Sullivan's mother lived in one-half of the house occupied by her son's family, and although, according to Mary Sullivan, she had a pension, she refused to help or even to deal with them in any way. One of Mrs. Sullivan's sisters tried to minimize the Sullivan family's needs. All of the others refused to help by giving money. Two based their refusal on Mr. Sullivan's alleged drunkenness, but their protestations sounded at least partly self-serving. Only after Mr. Sullivan died did one of Mrs. Sullivan's sisters offer to help by taking in one of the children. But she was unwilling to put up with the inconvenience of a young, undoubtedly frightened baby who had been abruptly weaned.

Yet kin expected help from one another. When Mr. Sullivan's brother committed suicide, he took time off from work to help the brother's widow find a place to live. When he himself was sick, out of work, and his wife in a lodge, he went to live with his mother. As soon as Mrs. Sullivan's kin learned or suspected that she had saved a little money, they began to ask for help. It was not hard to turn down a cousin's request, but her father proved a more difficult problem. Her sisters had taken in their father for short periods, but the old man did not want to help with work around the house, he paid no rent, the smoke from his pipe was a nuisance, and her sisters' husbands objected. In some ways it did seem as though it was Mrs. Sullivan's turn, or at least it could be made to seem that way. Clearly, though, when she had been in trouble, her father had ignored her, and her sisters had been unwilling to help. Now she needed every cent if she was to save enough to reestablish a home for her boys. She knew all this, but kin obligations were strong, and she felt guilty.

The Sullivans' story both supports and modifies Michael Anderson's argument that kin relations among the poor were primarily instrumental.[5] Certainly, there often seemed little sentiment in the relations between Mrs. Sullivan and her relatives. With nothing to gain, they were reluctant to help one another. Yet, on the other hand, they clearly shared a sense of obligation, a feeling of responsibility based solely on kinship unmediated by the possibility of a reciprocal exchange of services. The SOC exploited this sense of obligation, as it tried to persuade kin to help one another. Although the Sullivans' relatives were sometimes moved by appeals for help, mostly they were preoccuped with a daily struggle for survival that drained kin relations of much of their sentimentality. In the end, poor

---

[5]Michael Anderson, *Family Structure in Nineteenth Century Lancashire* (Cambridge, Eng.: Cambridge Univ. Press, 1971).

*Plate 3.* Scene from the play, "Where Charity Begins," produced by the Philadelphia Society for Organizing Charity in Philadelphia at its Exhibition (1916). (Courtesy of the Historical Society of Pennsylvania.)

families oscillated between assuming kin responsibilities, such as taking in a sister's baby or a father, and then rejecting them, literally casting their relatives out of their households. This erratic pattern of acceptance and rejection—perhaps overlaid with nagging feelings of guilt—probably characterized kin relations among the very poor.

## Neighbors

Neighbors seemed more reliable and willing to help one another than did kin. When the first Sullivan child died, neighbors sent groceries and other supplies. A kind neighbor sent $5 to the lodge when she heard of Mrs. Sullivan's troubles. Neighbors took up a collection to bury Will Sullivan. When kin networks failed, neighborhood ones proved stronger. The Sullivans and their neighbors thought of the streets in which they lived as distinct neighborhoods; people knew one another's habits, troubles, and resources. They lived within tiny villages rather than within the city. Although the city was large and impersonal, neighborhoods mediated the anomic character of urban life.

Petty feuds as well as friendships marked urban life among the poor. Indeed, relations between neighbors should not be romanticized because an undercurrent of envy ran through life among the very poor. It was hinted at when Mrs. Sullivan's sister pointed out to the SOC agent just how well off her sister was, exactly how much insurance had been carried on the life of the child, how much help had been provided by church and neighbors. But it was clearest in the unsolicited, semiliterate poison-pen letter sent to the SOC agent by a neighbor, envious of the aid and attention received by the Sullivans. Surely these two comments do not establish a trend definitively, but they do raise the possibility that the texture of daily life aroused not only mutual sympathy but also close scrutiny and suspicion. One reaction to privation and poverty was the careful assessment of each neighbor's and relative's income and possessions and resentment of another's good fortune.

The poison-pen letter, too, points to the way in which the concept of poverty prevalent among the SOC and most of the middle classes permeated even the reactions of the poor. In the end, the writer based her case on a distinction between the worthy and the unworthy poor. The Sullivans did not deserve aid, she said, because they were unworthy, morally unfit, and destitute because of weaknesses in their own characters.

### Employers

Not much can be said about the relation of Mr. Sullivan to his employer, except that Mr. Mohr accepted his drinking, supported his character to the SOC agent, and give him $6 when his child died. Mohr did not provide steady work throughout the year, but, then, he probably could not. It may have been Sullivan's need, though, that prompted Mohr to hire him as a night watchman, a job probably steadier than that of a teamster because it was less affected by the weather. Had Sullivan not taken sick, the job as night watchman might have enabled him to pull his family out of destitution.

The relations between Mrs. Sullivan and the Hunts are documented in more detail. Mrs. Sullivan worked as a servant, and she worked very hard, rising at 4 o'clock in the morning. Her main job was cooking for the men on the farm. Although hard, the work rhythm was seasonal. When the harvest was over, the pace slowed considerably. Mrs. Sullivan was expected to work 7 days a week. Indeed, her agreement called for only 1 paid day off per month, and her employer tried to deny her even that.

The relation between Mrs. Sullivan and the Hunts deteriorated over time. At first, despite the hard work, Mrs. Sullivan was pleased, probably willing to overlook exploitation because she had a comfortable room and plenty of food for herself and Francis. Mrs. Hunt, moreover, took at least some interest in Mrs. Sullivan and advised her on personal questions, for instance, to take her boys out of the orphanage as soon as possible. And, although it is hard to tell exactly, she seems to have worked hard alongside Mrs. Sullivan. Indeed, the Hunts appear to have been small, moderately prosperous potato farmers who needed help to run the family farm.

Yet Mrs. Hunt was inconsistent. When Mrs. Sullivan changed her plans and called for a ride home, Mrs. Hunt became furious. She reduced Mrs. Sullivan to tears, and then, if Mrs. Sullivan is to be believed, lied to her husband and to the CAS agent to whom she wrote. At about the same time, she began to give Mrs. Sullivan less than her full wages and, as well, to make it difficult for her to take off even the 1 day per month to which she was entitled. Just why Mrs. Hunt's attitude appeared to change is not clear. What is transparent, though, is how defenseless it left Mrs. Sullivan. If Mrs. Hunt chose not to pay her full wages, she could complain and write to the SOC, but she had no way to compel full payment. When Mrs. Hunt told her that the couple who previously had run the farm was returning, she had no choice but to go. Based on this case, it appears that the relation between employer and employee in domestic service was marked by dependence tinged with exploitation. That it seemed preferable to the life Mrs. Sullivan had been living is a commentary on the wretchedness of her existence, not on the desirability of her place.

## Authority

The Sullivan case shows the force of authority in the lives of the very poor. Most dramatic was the death of the Sullivans' first child. When the doctor ordered the child moved to a room that he did not realize was unheated, Mrs. Sullivan obeyed, even though she knew it was wrong. Her deference to authority simply was too strong. Her protest against the subsequent hospitalization of her baby was short-lived; she capitulated quickly when the lodge matron, under orders from the SOC, put on some pressure. Mrs. Sullivan clearly believed that the authority of the SOC was legitimate and powerful. She wanted the agent to ask her relatives for money because she believed that the force of the SOC might change their minds. She felt that a letter from the SOC to her neighbor who was discouraged about good works would be more effective than one from her.

Overall, Mrs. Sullivan's experience with authority was mixed. The SOC agents tried to be helpful, but bad medical attention killed one and possibly two children. Hospitals had treated her husband kindly, but her treatment had been callous. One hospital had been unwilling to hold her child long enough for her to get food in the house; it had tried to send her family home prematurely; it had treated her unkindly on the night when her youngest child had died. The SPCC had tried to break up her family, but Judge Magill preserved it.

If her experience left her ambivalent about medical authority, it did not produce mixed feelings about the SOC. Indeed, the main theme in her relations with the SOC was her increasing dependence on its agents, not simply for help but for advice. Within a relatively short time she was permitting the SOC and SPCC to make decisions about whether her family should remain together. When she violated lodge policy by coming out on the street to talk with her husband, she apologized and promised not to do so again. She asked permission from the SOC agent to visit her husband in the hospital. Most notably, when she moved to the farm, she wrote repeatedly to the SOC agent seeking advice on every issue that she confronted, and she became anxious and uncertain when she did not receive prompt replies.

Not all clients became passive and dependent, as Mr. Sullivan's behavior underscores. He obviously resented the intrusion of the SOC and SPCC into the life of his family, blaming them for its breakup. His belligerent and threatening behavior was exactly the opposite of his wife's. Neither deferential nor grateful, Mr. Sullivan appeared "disagreeable" to the SOC agent. Indeed, one price of continued SOC support clearly was gratitude. One reason why Mrs. Sullivan was an appealing client was her obvious appreciation of the help given her. Indeed, agents made a point of noting that she was grateful. The emphasis on gratitude reinforces the argument made by Gareth Stedman Jones in *Outcast London*.[6] The purpose of charity organization was not simply the reduction of pauperism and the more efficient relief of destitution. It was, at least equally, to inject the key features of gifts—sacrifice, status, and obligation—back into poor relief. Charity organization was a way of reuniting classes in a deferential and dependent relationship.

---

[6]Jones, *Outcast London*, pp. 241–261.

## Children and Spouses

Mrs. Sullivan also was influenced by her husband. All parties admitted that he could persuade her, against her better judgment, to live with him. But the bond between them eroded as Mr. Sullivan's lack of support and erratic behavior became intolerable. Lest Mr. Sullivan appear simply uncaring and irresponsible, it is important to stress that his behavior worsened as his personal situation deteriorated. With Mr. Sullivan unable to find work, increasingly sick, and insulted by charity workers, his commitment to his family weakened and his relation with his wife began to dissolve. Although Mrs. Sullivan retained at least some residual affection for her husband, by the time he died her main emotion was relief that he would not be able to "bother" her any more. In this context *bother* is an ambiguous term. Did she mean persuade her to live with him? Annoy her? Or did she mean sexual relations, especially the birth of more children, as well?

Mr. Sullivan probably was telling the truth when he said he was fond of his children, but there can be no doubt of Mrs. Sullivan's commitment to them. Even Judge Magill remarked on it. Indeed, her whole goal in life became to find a way of supporting her children by herself. Yet, despite her commitment, she was not always an effective parent. Her older boys were "unmanageable." Her inability to control them was one reason she was willing to send them to an orphanage. The boys' unmanageable behavior may well have reflected the strains in their family life as much as Mrs. Sullivan's parental weakness. Indeed, the scars of his family life showed especially clearly on Francis, obviously a very insecure child. His fear of separation from his mother made it impossible to send him to live with aunt for a while; on the farm he at first cried loudly at 4 A.M. when his mother left their bed to cook breakfast; and he had a terrible fear of being left with the doctor. The latter, certainly, was grounded in experience, since his youngest sister and brother recently had died.

The Sullivans' history contradicts the critics who described poor parents as uncaring and ineffective. To the contrary, the Sullivans' story is filled with affection, dedication, and even competence. The surface evidence to the contrary—malnutrition, sickness, begging, behavior problems—it did not reflect negligence. Rather, it was the pathetic product of lives distorted by unemployment, sickness, and destitution.

## Other Themes

One other theme was the family's constant need for clothes. Mrs. Sullivan complained that she and Francis had practically nothing to wear;

later she worried a great deal because Francis did not have a winter coat. She repeatedly asked the SOC for clothes. When agents gave her some, they always specified that they were "old," and they seemed remarkably slow to honor her requests. Surely, used clothing was not so hard to acquire. Or was it? Was there some reason why the SOC was reluctant to find clothing for its clients, or was clothing especially hard to locate? The answer is unclear.

Another theme is alcohol. Until Mr. Sullivan's death, alcohol played a steady role in the family's history. It was blamed for their condition when, of course, unsteady work and sickness were the real culprits. But it is clear that drink played an important part in Mr. Sullivan's life both on and off the job. However, just what that role was and what its effects were are far from clear. Indeed, the relation of alcohol to working-class life remains a key topic for social history.

Finally, and implicit in much of what already has been said, is insecurity. The Sullivans were never secure. Neither Mr. nor Mrs. Sullivan could count on steady work. Mr. Sullivan's income depended on the weather; Mrs. Sullivan's job depended on the changing whims of an employer against whose arbitrary actions she had no protection. Therefore, the family lived continuously with the threat of eviction and hunger. Even when Mr. Sullivan appeared to find more steady work, his sickness repeatedly undercut the family's tenuous stability. Indeed, illness made planning of any sort precarious, as when arrangements for Mrs. Sullivan and the boys had to be canceled suddenly on account of sickness. It was the insecurity rooted in sickness and unemployment, not character defects, that gave to the life of the poor its volatile and impulsive facade, that made impossible the prudent, calculating behavior with which middle-class philanthropists hoped to arm them against the disintegrating effects of poverty.

This was 18 months in the life and death of the Sullivan family. How representative was it of life among the very poor? Only further case studies will tell for sure. But none of the forces that impinged upon the Sullivans and none of the agencies that touched them were exceptional. Nor can their troubles be traced to the recency of their arrival in either the United States or Philadelphia or to their race. The Sullivans were native white Americans, long-term residents of Philadelphia. Their destitution was neither accidental nor epiphenomenal. It was rooted, rather, in the structures of work and inequality in early twentieth-century America.

# CHAPTER 2

# POORHOUSES, PAUPERS,
# AND TRAMPS

The Sullivans were only one of the thousands of families who needed help in early twentieth-century Philadelphia. Their story, nonetheless, points to many of the central themes in the lives of the very poor. Even more, it shows why dependence was a structural, predictable aspect of working-class life rather than an exception—why, that is, almost any working-class family might at some point need relief. There is nothing in the record to suggest that the Sullivans were especially shiftless, weak, incompetent, or immoral. Rather, the forces potentially disrupting all working-class families—irregular work, sickness, and inadequate welfare—combined to hit them with a lethal blow. It is exactly these qualities, the Sullivans' fundamental decency and the lack of any truly exceptional element in their experience, that makes their story of such significance.

The Sullivans have also given us the chance to see the welfare system, such as it was, from the viewpoint of individuals. As experienced by the Sullivans, welfare in Philadelphia was not so much a discrete set of institutions and agencies, each with its own philosophy and budget, as a loosely connected network that a poor person had to learn to read with some skill. It was, after all, a matter of some judgment to know when to go to the local church, when to the Society for Organizing Charity, and how to keep one's children away from "the Cruelty." But the Sullivans are not the only individuals in their case history. The other major actors are the agents of the Society for Organizing Charity, and the Sullivans' story shows their vantage point, too. Interestingly, it resembled the Sullivans' in some ways: a day-to-day struggle to keep the family afloat, an attempt to tap into the welfare network in the most effective way. For charity agents, too, successful action meant knowing how to read the system.

Still, there are other important issues to investigate. The Sullivans' story takes place in the early twentieth century, when a welfare network of sorts already existed. How did it develop? Only part of welfare was aid to people in their homes. Most nineteenth-century welfare reformers wanted to put dependent people in institutions, and they built many of them. Who actually ended up in poorhouses, insane asylums, and penitentiaries? The new institutions all reflected assumptions that denied that dependence was a normal, structural aspect of working-class life. Instead, welfare reformers attempted to use institutions and social policy to place the poor and helpless outside the ordinary working class, to define them as a special class joined together by the individual weakness and inferiority of its members.

Thus, part of the story of welfare is tracking the history of institutions and social policies and their interaction with the lives of working-class people. This involves finding out who exactly the inmates of institutions were, whether they were there for the reasons reformers and administrators predicted, and what role various policies actually seemed to play in the lives of the poor. We already know enough to anticipate discrepancies between the interaction of institutions and inmates, on the one hand, and the ideology of dependence, on the other. The question is the nature of the distortion, its origins, and its significance.

To begin to unravel these complex matters we need to turn to data that complement the Sullivans' story, material that extends farther back in time, covers large populations, and makes possible the comparison of ideas with demographic patterns and institutional results. For this purpose, only broad demographic studies of selected populations will do. This is what is offered in the four case studies that follow. They begin with the most hated and despised of institutions, one probably dreaded by the Sullivans: namely, the poorhouse. However, even though the pages that follow translate the lives of the very poor into statistical patterns, the Sullivans must not be forgotten. Their history should always be a reminder of the day-to-day suffering and struggle that is abstracted in the demography of dependence.

# PART I

# From Family Refuge to Old Age Home: The Demographic History of the Erie County, New York, Poorhouse from 1829 to 1886

There is no written history of poorhouses. The recent rediscovery of the institutional past has focused primarily on reformatories, penitentiaries, mental hospitals, and schools. An energetic group of medical social historians is starting to rewrite the history of general hospitals. But little attention has been paid to poorhouses. Eric Monkkonen has compared prisoners and paupers in mid-nineteenth-century Ohio; David Rothman wrote about the origins of almshouses in *The Discovery of the Asylum*, although he did not mention them in his second volume on the Progressive era; a few as yet unpublished dissertations have dealt with poorhouses. This is about the total of the treatment of poorhouses in contemporary historiography.[1]

Yet, poorhouses were at least as ubiquitous and important as other institutions in nineteenth-century America. The debate on outdoor relief, so widely written about in England, had its counterpart in America, where, to take an example, it began in Philadelphia in the late eighteenth century and remained a controversial issue through the early twentieth century. Indeed, in its transfiguration into debates over public welfare, outdoor relief remains very much a live issue today. Within the debate the poorhouse

---

[1] Eric H. Monkkonen, *The Dangerous Class: Crime and Poverty in Columbus, Ohio, 1880–1885* (Cambridge, Mass.: Harvard University Press, 1975); David J. Rothman, *The Discovery of the Asylum: Social Order and Disorder in the New Republic* (Boston: Little, Brown, 1971); Priscilla Clement, "The Response to Need: Welfare and Poverty in Philadelphia, 1800 to 1850" (Ph. D. diss., University of Pennsylvania, 1977); Stephen Edward Wiberley, Jr., "Four Cities: Public Poor Relief in America, 1700–1775" (Ph.D. diss., Yale University, 1975); Charles E. Rosenberg, "From Almshouse to Hospital: The Shaping of the Philadelphia General Hospital," *Health and Society*, Vol. 60: no. 1 (1982) pp. 108–154. Especially useful on the development of relief in Buffalo have been two unpublished essays by Charles L. Bland, "Institutions of Charity in Jacksonian Erie County: 1829–1861" (History Department, SUNY Buffalo, June 1975) and "Public Relief in Erie County: 1861–1896" (History Department, SUNY Buffalo, July 1976).

played a critical role because it was seen as an alternative to outdoor relief. Poorhouses were created not only to alleviate distress but also to discourage pauperism. When relief was available solely within poor-houses, argued their proponents, only the most helpless and destitute would apply for assistance, and the ablebodied shirkers who sustained themselves through public generosity would find jobs rather than face the deprivation and degradation of the poorhouse. In this way, the poorhouses established in early nineteenth-century America were as much reform institutions as penitentiaries, reform schools, and mental hospitals. Only they were expected to accomplish their goals not by reforming the characters of their inmates as much as through their deterrent effect: the stimulus to work—and so, indirectly, to character improvement—that they would provide. Of course, poorhouses did not work in the way their sponsors intended any more than did other nineteenth-century institu-tions, and they served multiple, sometimes unanticipated functions. However, they did affect large numbers of people.[2]

In fact, it must be remembered that in terms of contact with the people, poorhouses were among the most important nineteenth-century residen-tial institutions, touching far more lives than did reformatories or mental hospitals. Consider some statistics from New York State in 1900. In that year the New York House of Refuge for Women had, on the average, 279 inmates, the House of Refuge for Men, 801. Private mental hospitals took in 585 patients; on October 1, 928 remained within them. The state mental hospitals admitted 4862 and, again on October 1, 22,088 remained. By contrast, during the same year 85,567 people were supported in city and county almshouses, and on October 1 the number remaining was 13,846. Thus, although more inmates remained in mental hospitals, many more people actually spent time in poorhouses. The difference in the number actually resident at any one time reflects the longer term custody of most mental patients. The institutions most like the poorhouse in terms of the relation between intake and average population were the city and county jails (not the penitentiaries) and the hospitals. On October 1, 1900, city and county jails held 8032 prisoners, although in the course of the year they at some point housed 110,453 people. The county penitentiaries, again on October 1, had 2186 inmates compared with the 11,756 whom they received during the year. By contrast, the state prisons held 3375 on October 1 but received only 1732 during the year. Hospitals also treated

---

[2]For a discussion of the functions of poorhouses and poor relief in general, see Frances Fox Piven and Richard A. Cloward, *Regulating the Poor: The Functions of Public Welfare* (New York: Random House, 1971).

many patients for short periods. During the year the state's hospitals treated 86,985 patients, of whom 6128 remained on October 1.[3]

Clearly, poorhouses were major institutions, second only to jails in the number of people received during the year. (The poorhouses, it must be emphasized, dealt with only a fraction of the people receiving relief; during the year 209,092 received outdoor aid from public sources.) Yet, little is known about either their role or their clients. The image of poorhouse inmates generally has reflected contemporary stereotypes of paupers. Those who found themselves in poorhouses, it as been assumed, have been the most helpless and degraded poor, unwilling and unable to survive by their own efforts. Demoralized and incompetent, they sank into the poorhouse, where they lived the rest of their lives dependent upon the generosity of the public. This, of course, is a serviceable image. It has worked to reinforce the stigma attached to poorhouses and to make them a source of dread among the working class, a stimulus to exertion and self-sufficiency. But recent historiography has made it abundantly clear that the image of poor and dependent populations rarely has coincided with their actual demography and that clients have used institutions and organizations for their own purposes, shaping them sometimes in ways quite at variance with the intentions of their sponsors. In actual practice, then, the roles of social institutions have been complex, not easily deduced from the statements of sponsors or administrators. There is no reason to suspect that poorhouses and their inmates will be any different. In fact, as I will show, the history of poorhouse populations reveals the same tension between image and demography and the same complexity of role as does the history of mental hospitals, school systems, or reform schools.[4]

One key question about poorhouses is, Who used them? What kinds of people entered and how long did they stay? Did the populations of poorhouses come from a degraded lumpen proletariat, or are they better

---

[3]These figures are derived from *Thirty-third Annual Report of the Board of State Charities of the State of New York* (Albany: James Lyon, 1901); *Sixth Annual Report of the State Commision of Prisons for the Year 1900* (Albany: James Lyon, 1901); and *New York State Commission in Lunacy Twelfth Annual Report, October 1, 1889, to September 30, 1900* (Albany: James Lyon, 1901).

[4]For example, see the discussion of the magistrate's courts in Michael B. Katz, Michael J. Doucet, and Mark J. Stern, *The Social Organization of Early Industrial Capitalism* (Cambridge, Mass.: Harvard University Press, 1982), pp. 228–240; the uses of Victorian culture by the working class as described by Robert Q. Gray, *The Labour Aristocracy in Victorian Edinborough* (London: Oxford University Press, 1976), pp. 136–143; and the comments on the uses of the juvenile court in Steven L. Schlossman, *Love and the American Delinquent: The Theory and Practice of "Progressive" Juvenile Justice, 1825–1920* (Chicago: University of Chicago Press, 1977), p. 148.

thought of as part of the working class? Were poorhouse inmates demoralized and helpless or casualties of social inequality and economic development? Did most people who entered poorhouses remain there for the rest of their lives? The answers to these questions will provide a first step in a reconsideration of the role of poorhouses in American social history.

Questions about the composition of poorhouses can be answered only through a reconstruction of their populations. This is what this part offers for one poorhouse, the Erie County, New York, almshouse, between its opening in 1829 and 1866. In 1824 a committee of the New York State legislature, known as the Yates Committee, had reported on the problem of outdoor relief and the administrative difficulties posed by New York's complex system of poor law administration. Its major recommendation was the establishment of poorhouses in each county of the state. Within several years most counties, including Erie, had complied with the report's recommendation. Subsequent legislation called for the administration of most county poorhouses by a superintendent of the poor elected annually. The superintendent also gave outdoor relief, and within most towns outdoor relief was given, as well, by elected overseers of the poor, popularly known by the older title of poormasters.[5] These statements about the administration of relief are only a general and rough outline of the poor law. General statements are difficult to make because legal arrangements for relief varied greatly from county to county, and, even more, local behavior did not always conform to state law.[6]

Only three pieces of legislation seriously affected poorhouses until the end of the 1880s. The first was the 1873 legislation concerning state paupers. Troubled by the influx of foreign paupers without legal settlement, the legislature designated certain poorhouses as recipients of state paupers. Paupers without a legal settlement in any town were to be sent to one of these and their expenses paid by the state rather than by the county. Erie County was one of these poorhouses. Second, an attempt to

---

[5]On poor relief in New York State, see, Martha Branscombe, *The Courts and the Poor Laws in New York State, 1784–1928* (Chicago: University of Chicago Press, 1943), and David M. Schneider, *The History of Public Welfare in New York State, 1609–1866* (Chicago: University of Chicago Press, 1938).

[6]The variation in local provision for poor relief can be seen by inspecting the annual figures on a county-by-county basis as reported in either the annual reports of the secretary of state on poor relief or in the annual reports of the Board of State Charities. The discussions of the superintendents and overseers of the poor, as reported in the proceedings of their annual conventions, which started in 1870, are also full of comments on local variations and on the complexity of the law.

remove the chronically insane from local poorhouses began in the early 1860s. Its first major achievement was the creation of the Willard Asylum, to which all of the chronically insane were supposed to be sent. The asylum, however, was not large enough, and some counties, including Erie, were allowed to operate facilities for the chronically insane on behalf of the state until the 1890s, when legislation required their removal to enlarged state facilities. In terms of its impact upon poorhouses, the most important legislation was the so-called Children's Law of 1875, which required the removal of all children between 2 and 16 from poorhouses and their transfer to orphanages or other institutions designed especially for children. Children under 2 were permitted to remain if their mothers were residents, a regulation introduced because of the substantial numbers of unmarried mothers in poorhouses. Although the act of 1875 fundamentally altered the demographic composition of poorhouses and fostered the growth of orphanages and related institutions, the attempt to remove children from poorhouses had started prior to its passage and in some counties, including Erie, already was well under way.[7]

## AGGREGATE TRENDS IN POORHOUSE COMPOSITION

Between its opening in 1829 and the end of 1879 approximately 46,400 people entered Erie County's poorhouse (see Table A.1). The fewest, 212, entered in 1830 and the most, 1727, in 1874 as a result of the depression that began in the previous year. During the same period the county's population grew from about 35,700 to 220,000. Thus, only a translation of number of entrants into rates shows the actual trends in poorhouse size.[8]

With a few notable exceptions, the rate of poorhouse entrance remained generally stable throughout the period (see Figure 2.1 and Table A.1). Beginning at about 8.5 per thousand of the county's population, it rarely

---

[7]On the act of 1875, see David M. Schneider and Albert Deutsch, *The History of Public Welfare in New York State, 1867–1940* (Chicago: University of Chicago Press, 1941), pp. 60–71.

[8]The source of this analysis is the registers of the Erie County Almshouse, which are still housed in the institution, now renamed the Erie County Home and Infirmary.

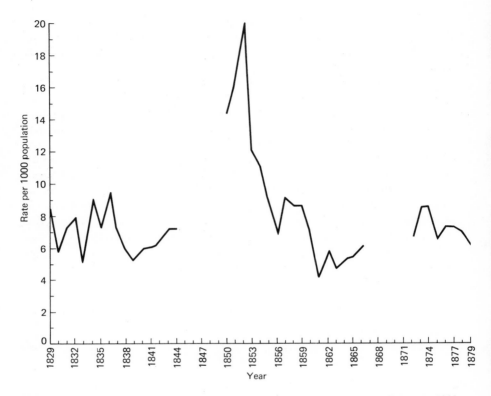

**Figure 2.1.** Entrants to Erie County, New York, Poorhouse, 1829–1879: Rate per 1000 population.

fell below 5 per thousand or rose over 10. During the early 1830s, the rate rose over 9 per thousand, peaked at 9.66 in 1836, and then returned to approximately 6 per thousand during the late 1830s and early 1840s. The most dramatic change occured in response to the immigration of the late 1840s and early 1850s. Although we lack data on the late 1840s, the annual entrance rate in the early 1850s was consistently above 10 per thousand, reaching 20.34 in 1854. From this peak the rate fell consistently to a mere 4.19 in 1861. During the Civil War the rate rose slightly but never exceeded 6 per thousand. Only an increase to 8.88 per thousand during the depression of the 1870s interrupted the rate's general stability. Slightly different figures compiled by the State Board of Charities confirm the general stability of the entrance rate. The "average" number of individuals supported in the poorhouse during each year generally fell between the

Civil War and the turn of the century. During the depression of the 1870s the rate rose to 4.14 per thousand and then declined, continuing to drop even during the depression years of the 1890s, when it reached 1.41 in 1894 and 1.71 in 1896.

The trends in poorhouse admission did not reflect a decline in poverty within the county, as figures showing the numbers receiving outdoor relief reveal (see Figure 2.2 and Table A.2). The rate, which far exceeded the rate of admissions to the poorhouse, remained generally stable between 1870 and 1875, when it more than doubled in 1 year from 20.7 to 50.4. After reaching a peak of 64.9 in 1876, the rate underwent a secular decline during the late 1870s and early 1880s, paralleling the rate for indoor relief. However, in contrast to the population of the poorhouse, the number of individuals on outdoor relief exploded during the 1890s, rising from 7.7 per thousand in 1892 to 29.6, 16.3, and 28.4 during the middle years of the decade. Thus, different factors affected the rates of indoor and outdoor relief. In a time-series analysis, year by itself accounted for only 1.2% of the variation in admission to the almshouses but 9.5% of the variation in the rate of outdoor relief.

In one important way the experience of the 1890s did not repeat that of the 1870s. During the earlier period the average amount of relief given to

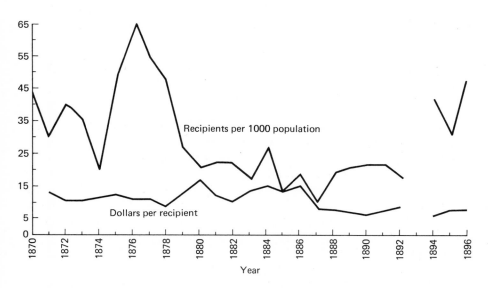

**Figure 2.2.** Recipients of outdoor relief per 1000 population and dollars per recipient: Erie County, New York, 1870–1896.

individuals had risen from a little over $10 to nearly $22 in 1874 (see Figure 2.2 and Table A.2). By contrast, the welfare "reform" movement of the next 2 decades succeeded in reducing the average amount of relief from around $10 in the late 1870s to $7 or $8 by the early 1890s. Indeed, as the number of individuals on relief rose during the 1890s, the average amount of relief declined to only $6.20 in 1894. This contrast between trends in indoor and outdoor relief shows that relief was not simply an automatic response to need. Rather, the politics of relief during this period make abundantly clear the interconnection of relief with a number of other factors: the electoral ambitions of politicians; movements for municipal reform; and the ability of the poor to manipulate welfare practices in their own interest. The expansion of outdoor relief during depressions and the stability in indoor relief, taken together, show that the former was more easily influenced by political and social factors. Patterns of seasonality in poorhouse entrance point to the same conclusion.[9]

Historians and economists have demonstrated the seasonality of need in the nineteenth century fairly well. Especially in a port city such as Buffalo, the closing of shipping and the lack of outdoor work during the winter caused a decline in casual labor, which led in turn to great hardship among the poorest members of the working class. Thus, one should expect poorhouse admissions to rise during the winter. Although this sometimes happened, the connection between seasons of the year and poorhouse admissions was surprisingly weak.[10]

Here the relation between entrance and seasonality is expressed by an index in which 100 means that one-twelfth of the inmates entered during a particular month (see Figure 2.3 and Table A.3). Index figures above 100 reveal months of heavy entrance, below 100, of light entrance. Individuals entered often in December and January. Yet, entrance was relatively low during the harsh months of January, February, and March. Indeed, the index for February, 77, was the lowest of any month.

During the half century from 1829 to 1879, significant changes occurred

---

[9]On welfare during depressions, see Leah H. Feder, *Unemployment Relief in Periods of Depression* (New York: Russell Sage Foundation, 1936).

[10]An excellent discussion of the effect of seasonality on labor is in Gareth Stedman Jones, *Outcast London* (London: Oxford University Press, 1971), pp. 33–51. Buffalo, of course, was a Great Lakes port and very much affected by the weather, especially in winter. On some of the problems in Buffalo in the late nineteenth century, see Brenda K. Shelton, *Reformers in Search of Yesterday: Buffalo in the 1890's* (Albany: SUNY Albany Press, 1976). For a general economic history of Buffalo, see Mark J. Stern, "The Demography of Capitalism" (Ph.D. diss., York University, 1979).

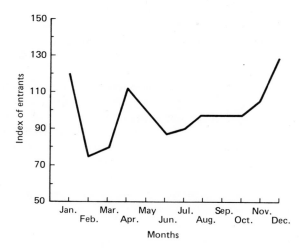

**Figure 2.3.** Index of entrants per month: Erie County, New York, Poorhouse, 1829–1871.

in the pattern of seasonality. In the 1830s and 1840s, people entered the poorhouse most often during the late summer and fall. During mid-century late fall and early winter were the periods of greatest entry. However, the most puzzling figures come from the depression of the 1870s. With one exception, between 1874 and 1879 the month of heaviest entrance was either April or May. Between 1872 and 1876 the index for these months was 158 and 125; between 1877 and 1879 it was 203 and 112. During these years, as will become evident later in this chapter, very large numbers of young men entered the poorhouse for short periods of time. It may be, then, that the spring entrants were young men out looking for work and out of money. As ablebodied strangers, they may have been considered ineligible for outdoor relief and forced into the poorhouse for short periods until they found work.

## Descriptions of the Erie County Poorhouse

I have found no descriptions of the Erie County Poorhouse during its early years. However, within about 25 years of its founding, it had become a foul and dangerous place. In the early 1850s the Erie County Medical Society attacked the poorhouse, pointing out its extraordinary rate of mortality. In 1848, 1 out of every 6 persons received in the poorhouse died; in 1849, 1 out of 8. And 6 years later, in 1854, the number had been reduced to 1 in 9.16. But this figure still was higher, even, than that for major hospitals. In New York Hospital during the same year the mortality rate was 1 in 11.125; in Charity Hospital, New Orleans, 1 in 11; in Pennsylvania Hospital, 1 in 11.87; and in the Quarantine Hospital, New York, during the "ship-fever of 1847" it was 1 in 16. "The whole policy of the Poorhouse," complained the editor of the *Buffalo Medical Journal*, "is niggardly and mean. Cheap provisions, cheap doctors, cheap nurses, cheap medicines, cheapness everywhere is the rule, forgetting that higher policy which finds true economy in a humane policy." The reason for the high mortality, according to one observer, "aside from insufficient ventilation and other causes incident to the construction of the building," was "the diet of the house—a diet which exceeds, in its accurate estimate of the starvation point, anything which Dickens ever described." Here is a description of the diet and of other aspects of care within the institution:

Breakfast—A piece of bread about 5 inches square by 3/4 of an inch thick, a little salt pork with coffee, made from barley, and sweetened with the cheapest of molasses. Dinner—Same as breakfast, minus the coffee. Supper—Bread and tea.
Once a week mutton soup.
As to quality, the nurse in charge of the children said that the bread was never sufficiently baked, and was frequently so sour as to curdle milk. On rolling it in the hand it worked up into dough very readily. No butter is given on the bread.
The pork was rusty, and slippery necks and shoulders. For a few days back they had had some mutton served out. The ration for the day was seen; about two ounces (bone and all) being given to each.
Vegetables—During three or four months of winter and spring none were given out. This was owing to the high price of potatoes, but no substitutes, such as beets, carrots or turnips were provided. Since the appearance of cholera, no vegetable of any kind. As a consequence of this beautiful management there has been one death from scurvy, (a disease hardly ever known except in ships on long voyages,) and four other cases are now in the house . . . .
The nursing is done by a sore-legged Irish pauper, who takes especial care of his fellow countrymen, at the expense of French or American paupers.
We intended to speak of the ventilation, but we are sick of the subject. Suffice it to say that the ground floor is on a level with the earth, paved with bricks, laid directly upon the clap; that all the dining, cook and wash rooms, are on this floor; and that the steam and stench of all the household offices find vent only through the joints of the floors above—none of the ceilings are lathed and plastered; and the foul odors of the basement ascend to the fourth story. There is not a hall in the building; and the ventilators connecting with the flues are perfect shams. Throughout the whole house there is a sickening, decaying odor. All these remarks apply to both buildings alike . . . .

Here are more than three hundred paupers kept in a foul, ill-ventilated building, on a diet which will just keep the wheels of life in motion.

For month after month the thing has gone on, producing its legitmate and murderous results. Lying-in women have died of fever, leaving their children, and the numerous foundlings brought to the house, to die of starvation together. Brought there as bright, healthy infants, these little offsprings of misfortune and crime have scarcely an average of four weeks of like in this great lazar house. Older children become idiotic, dwarfed, inanimate; and men and women die from a hundred diseases, written down upon the case-book with Latin names, but which might be better called starvation. [11]

Within a couple of years the physicians' campaign was successful. The old building, fortuitously, burned down, and a new one was completed in 1856. According to a select committee of the state senate that visited "Charitable Institutions supported by the State, and all city and county poor and work houses and jails," the new house, "kept in a clean and orderly condition," was a great improvement. The poorhouse was located about 6 miles north of Buffalo. It consisted of two buildings, one used for the poorhouse itself and one for the insane. The "main structure" was "sixty-five feet front, octagonal in shape, with wings extending 255 feet." Attached to the poorhouse was a 153-acre farm. The house had 34 rooms, or wards, "well warmed by stoves and partially ventilated." As many as 30 paupers occupied each ward. Men and women were partially separated during the day and completely at night. The staff consisted of six keepers, three men and three women, and the poorhouse supported an average of 300 paupers a week at cost of $1 each. A teacher was employed all year for the school, which averaged 45 children. Children were kept in the poorhouse until the age of 16, when they were bound out by the superintendent. A physician, paid $400 per year, visited the poorhouse twice a week, and a student physician lived there full time. Despite its improved facilities, there were "no arrangements for bathing." The insane asylum, built of limestone, was two stories high, 60 by 30 feet. It was described by the state senate committee as 'commodious, cleanly and well kept." The insane received "good care" and were "classified according to their different stages of insanity." The editor of the Erie County Medical Society's journal confirmed the improved conditions, which he attributed, with no modesty, to the efforts of the county's regular physicians:

It is necessary, to the proper understanding of this marked reduction in the mortality of the Erie County Poor-House, to state that, during the two years

---

[11] *Buffalo Medical Journal* 12 (1856): 184–186.

past, great reforms have been introduced into its construction and its entire
sanitary arrangment. To this, and to the succession of two healthy seasons, is
due, as we believe, the diminished mortality of the Poor-house. The history
of that reform constitutes one of the most interesting features in the history
of the Buffalo Medical Journal. [12]

However, by the late 1870s conditions had again deteriorated, although
not, it would appear, to their previous level. The "provision made for the
dependent classes, by this county," reported William P. Letchworth in
1878, "can not be said to be in keeping with the intelligence and liberal
spirit of its people." Letchworth complained, first, about the quality of
construction and ventilation. There was "no air space between the stone
and the plaster, the plaster being laid directly upon the solid masonry, thus
creating an unwholesome atmosphere within, nor was any plan for
ventilation considered in its construction." Nor was the site of the
poorhouse well chosen. The supply of water was not adequate. The "barns
and out buildings, except the horse stable, are not as good as the average
buildings of that class on farms in the country. To reach such of these
buildings as are located rearward, in wet weather, must be by walking
through the mud." [13]

Nor was Letchworth pleased with the administration of the poorhouse.
By failing to make ablebodied paupers work, the poorhouse keeper was
neglecting opportunities for both moral instruction and a reduction in the
public funds necessary to run the institution:

> During the late fall, winter and early spring, there is always a large force
> sufficiently strong to do out-door work, who are sitting idly in the men's
> sitting room, in total mental stupor . . . who should be continually employed,
> if for no other reason than for the benefit of the moral influence inculcated
> by systematic labor . . . . Upon a visit made during the winter months, a few
> years ago, it was estimated that there were about two hundred men in the
> poor house who might under a proper system do a fair day's work. [14]

The appearance of poorhouses, stressed Letchworth, varied with the
season. He contrasted the image of the "average poor house after its spring
house-cleaning" with its picture during the winter. In the spring the

---

[12]*Buffalo Medical Journal* 13 (1875): 377–381.

[13]"Report on Charitable Institutions Eighth Judicial District," in *Eleventh Annual Report of the Board of State Charities* (Albany: Weed Parsons, 1878), p. 297.

[14]*Ibid.*, p. 298.

poorhouse looked almost inviting "with its open windows through which the summer air and sunshine is streaming, with the glimpse of the green fields without, or when it has been thoroughly renovated by the white-washing of its various apartments." By contrast, later in the year, the poor house was forbidding "when the foul air must be shut in to economize fuel, when the basement walls are streaked with trickling drops of moisture, when the institution is crowded with inmates, oftentimes sitting in the most listless idleness, their looks indicating a painful mental vacuity, without employment or amusement." [15]

Letchworth was reporting during a period of reform. During the year in which his report was published, Brooklyn abolished outdoor relief, and Buffalo established the first Charity Organization Society in the United States. As it applied to the very poor, the reform campaign had a number of components: eliminate or drastically reduce outdoor relief; introduce systematic visiting of the poor by representatives of the affluent; remove children from poorhouses; improve the classification of poorhouse inmates; eject the ablebodied from poorhouses and make any ablebodied person who remained within them work; and introduce better ventilation, construction, and diet. By 1893 some of these goals had been reached throughout the state, according to Oscar Craig, president of the State Board of Charities. The horrible conditions in poorhouses publicized by the second report of the state board in 1868, wrote Craig, largely had been eliminated. Over the "chaotic conditions" prevailing in 1868 "the brooding spirit of humanity, evoking order and reforms and remedies," had been generally successful. The one exception was the failure to classify inmates properly. For in most poorhouses only the sexes and the very sick were separated. This, however, was not so much the fault of "mal-admini-stration" as of the "bad construction of old buildings." What Craig wanted were regulations that would protect the "cleanly against the filthy . . . the morally clean against the defiled and the corrupting, and . . . the refined against the vulgar and the brutal." Still, the ablebodied pauper had "practically . . . been excluded from the poor-house"; children generally had been removed; and special institutions for the blind, deaf, feeble-minded, and insane had been founded. [16] State policy, in short, was attempting to reshape poorhouses into homes for the elderly and infirm.

---

[15]*Ibid.*, p. 315.

[16]Oscar Craig, "American Administration of Charity in Public Institutions," *Annual Report of the Stage Board of Charities* (Albany: James Lyon, 1893), pp. 14–15, 39.

| Name of Persons Committed | Age | Place of Nativity | Town or County pauper |
|---|---|---|---|
| Kenaz P | 45 | Albany N.Y. | County |
| Appahi P | 38 | Do. | Do. |
| Mary Ann P | 16 | Do. | Do |
| William P | 14 | Do | Do. |
| Henry P | 12 | Do. | Do. |
| Fredrick P | 10 | Do. | Do |
| Maria P | 8 | Do. | Do |
| Hency P | 6 | Do. | Do. |
| Philander P | 4 | Do. | Do. |
| Champion F | 32 | Michigan — | County |
| John F | 55 | Ireland — | " Do. |
| John D | 34 | Ireland — | Do |
| Joseph H | 39 | Saratoga Co. N.Y. | Do. |
| Walter F. Mc M | 21 | Herkimer Co. N.Y. | Do. |
| James H | 35 | Ireland — | Do. |
| Magnus F | 51 | Sweden | Do. |
| Peter L | 50 | Ireland — | Do. |
| Merit P | 35 | New Hampshire | Do. |
| Abigail P | 27 | Do. | Do. |
| Bathamia P | 11 | Do. | Do. |
| Martin P | 9 | Do. | Do |
| James P | 7 | Do. | Do. |
| Abigail P | 4 | Do. | Do. |
| Leonard H | 33 | Ontario Co. N.Y. | County |
| Olive H | 38 | Do. | Do |
| Emeline H | 2 | Do. | Do. |
| Amos B | 48 | Connecticut | Town |
| Alfred B | 6 | Do. | Do. |
| Wineford R | 27 | Wales | County — |
| Mary R | 10 | Oniodia Co. N.Y. | Do. |
| Cathrine R | 4 | Pensylvania | Do. |
| Emely R | 5 | Ditto | Do. |
| John R | 8 | Ditto | Do. |
| Joseph R | 2 | Buffalo | Do. |
| Joseph W | 62 | | Town |
| Pheobe S | 16 | Michigan | County |

**Plate 4.** First page of the register of the Erie County Poorhouse, 1829. Note the high proportion of family groups. (Inmates' surnames are not shown to maintain confidentiality.) (Courtesy of the Erie County Home and Infirmary.)

| From Whence sent | Time of Commitment | By whom Committed | Time Committed for | When discharg |
|---|---|---|---|---|
| | 1829 | | | 1829 |
| Buffalo | January 8 | A. Calender | | May 20 " |
| Do. | January 8 | Do. | | May 30 " |
| Do. | January 8 | Do. | | Jan.y 30 " 1829 |
| Do. | January 8 | Do. | | Jan.y 30 " |
| Do. | January 8 | Do. | | January 16 " " |
| Do. | January 8 | Do. | | May 31 " |
| Do. | January 8 | Do. | | Feb.y 13 N " |
| Do. | January 8 | Do | | May 30 " |
| Do. | January 8 | Do. | | May 31 " |
| Buffalo. | January 8 | A. Calender | | May 29 " |
| Do. | January 8 | Do. | | Died April 13 " |
| Do. | January 8 | Do. | | |
| Do. | January 8 | Do. | | Died Nov.r 30 " |
| Do. | January 8 | Do. | | March 31 - |
| Do. | January 8 | Do. | | April 30 " — |
| Do. | January 8 | Do. | | May 11 " |
| Do. | January 8 | Do. | | April 30 " — |
| Do. | January 8 | Do. | | Jan.y 30 " 1829 |
| Do. | January 8 | Do. | | January 30 " |
| Do. | January 8 | Do. | | Jan.y 16 " 1829 |
| Do | January 8 | Do. | | Jan.y 16 " 1829 |
| Do. | January 8 | Do. | | Jan.y 30 " " |
| Do. | January 8 | Do | | January 30 " |
| Buffalo. | January 8 | A. Calender | | January 27 " 182 |
| Do. | January 8 | Do | | January 27 " " |
| Do. | January 8 | Do. | | January 27 " " |
| Do. | January 8 | Do. | | |
| Do. | January 8 | Do. | | |
| Do. | January 9 | Do. | | Dec.r 16 " " |
| Do. | January 9 | Do | | Jan.y 23 " 1829 |
| Do. | January 9 | Do. | | Dec.r 16 " 183 |
| Do | January 9 | Do. | | August 30 183 |
| Do. | January 9 | Do. | | January 31 — |
| Do. | January 9 | Do. | Sent to Jail J. Reyno. &c | |
| Do. | January 9 | Do. | | Jan.y 18 " 1829 |
| Do. | January 9 | Do. | | Died June 14 |

*Plate 4* (continued)

71

To some extent the result of this policy can been seen in the demography of the Erie County Poorhouse.

## The Charactertistics of Poorhouse Inmates

There were four eras in the demographic history of the Erie County Poorhouse between 1829 and 1886. Until the 1840s the population included many families and a high proportion of native-born inmates. With the entrance of large numbers of Irish-born people in the 1840s, the poorhouse was used less often by families. During the Civil War the proportion of young men dropped sharply, and many more unmarried young women entered. After the war the proportion of children and women in the poorhouse began to decline, and the proportion of elderly people to rise. However, throughout these years a variety of types of people continued to use the poorhouse, which was a complex institution whose demography reflected the recurrent crises in the lives of the nineteenth-century poor. [17]

First consider the age-structure of the poorhouse (see Figure 2.4 and Table A.4). Note the drop in the proportion of inmates less than 14 years old. The proportion generally hovered around 30% until 1865–1869. Between those years and 1870–1974, it dropped from 32% to 13%. After the passage of the Children's Act in 1875, it dropped still further to 3% in 1875–1879, from which it rose to 6% between 1880 and 1886. The proportion of women (as will be noted) also increased slightly during the latter years. Together, the slight rise in the proportion of women and children points to the use of the poorhouse as a home for unmarried mothers and as a maternity home for single young women who were pregnant.

There never were very many inmates between 15 and 19 years old, only around 4–6%. The proportions in the most productive years of young and middle adulthood, 20–29 and 30–39, remained about 20%, and about 10–12% of the inmates during each period were in their 40s. Just why roughly 40% of the poorhouse population was between 20 and 39 is not clear. Very likely, many of them were unable to work because of physical or mental illness. Others probably were unable to find work. Certainly, the poorhouse sheltered many young men for short periods, especially during depressions. The number of 20–29-year-old men in the sample increased

[17]For an example of the role of crisis in the lives of the poor, see the case study in Chapter 1.

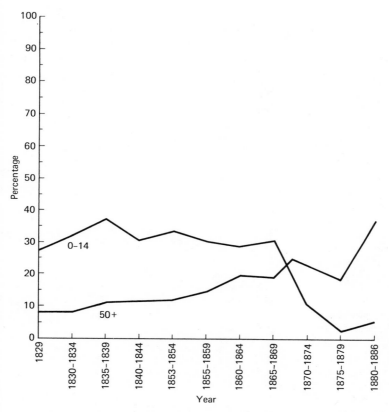

**Figure 2.4.** Proportion of inmates aged 0–14 and 50+: Erie County, New York, Poorhouse, 1829–1886.

from 122 in 1870–1874 to 541 in 1874–1879 and then dropped back to 89 between 1880 and 1886. Similarly, the number of 30–39-year-olds rose from 118 to 303 and then dropped to 69. The one group whose proportion of inmates rose steadily was the elderly. Their share of the poorhouse population rose from 9% in 1829 to 15% in 1855–1859; after the Civil War it hovered around 20% until 1880–1886, when it increased to 37%, a reflection of the partially successful policy of transforming poorhouses into old age homes.

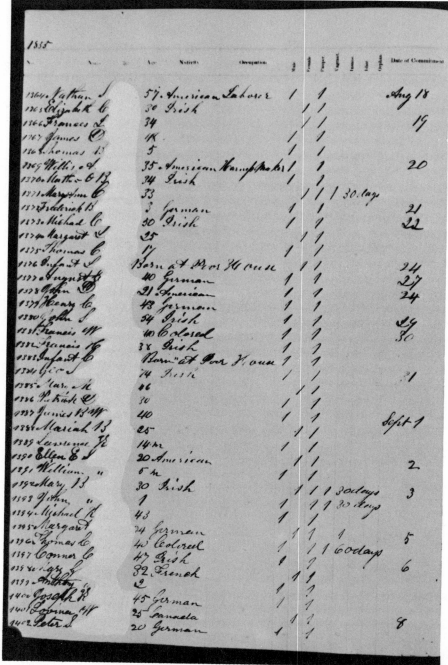

**Plate 5.** *A page from the register of the Erie County Poorhouse, 1855. Note the decline in the proportion of families since 1829. (Inmates' surnames are not shown to maintain confidentiality.) (Courtesy of the Erie County Home and Infirmary.)*

| By whom Committed. | Of what Town. | Direct Cause | Died | Asylum. | Date of Discharge |
|---|---|---|---|---|---|
| R. Nevitt | Buffalo | Rheumatism | | | Aug 24 |
| | | Intemperance | | | forward |
| | | Pregnant | | | Sept 25 |
| | | | | | forward |
| | | | | 1 | Aug 19 |
| | | Intemperate | | | " 28 |
| | | Broken Arm & General Life | | | forward |
| O.B. Bidwell | | Venereal & Intemperance | | | Abs Sept 10 |
| J. Johnson | West Seneca | | | 1 | Aug 21 |
| R. Nevitt | Buffalo | | | | " 24 |
| | | Pregnant | | | Sept 14 |
| | | Sore Eyes | | | Sept 11 |
| | | | | | " 25 |
| | | Rheumb Cut | | | Abs " 20 |
| | | Syphilis | | | Sept 8 |
| | | | | | Abs Aug 24 |
| | | One Arm | | | forward |
| | | | | | Sept 3 |
| | | Ague & Fever | | | " 24 |
| | | | | | Forward |
| C.S. Watchin | | Intemperate | | | Sept 10 |
| R. Nevitt | | Ague & Whiskey | | | forward |
| | | Heart Disease | | | " |
| | | Sore Eyes | | | " |
| | | Pregnant | | | " |
| | | | | 1 | Sept 1 |
| | | | | | " 14 |
| A.S. Merrill | | Intemperate | | | " Forward " |
| R. Nevitt | | Ague & Fever | | | Sept 11 |
| C.S. Watchin | | Insanity | | | Forward |
| O.D. Bidwell | | Syphilis | | | " |
| M. Hickel | Tonawanda | | | | " |
| R. Nevitt | Buffalo | | | | " |
| | | | | | " |
| | | | | | " |
| O.D. Bidwell | | 2 Black Eyes intemperate | | | " |
| R. Nevitt | | | | | Abs Sept 20 |

*Plate 5* (continued)

75

The proportion of women (see Figure 2.5 and Table A.5) rose from about 30% in the poorhouse's early years to 40% by the Civil War. On account of the problems of women during the war, it increased to about 47% between 1860 and 1864 but dropped back afterward to about 22% in 1870–1874, 12% in 1875–1879, and 28% in 1880–1886. Females were a substantial share, around 40%, of the inmates under 15 years old. Therefore when the proportion of child inmates declined, the share of women dropped as well. Before the Civil War a little over half of the adolescent inmates were women; that proportion rose to 71% during the war, probably because of increased pregnancy among unmarried women, the decreased availability of marriageable men, and the widowhood of soldiers' wives. Roughly the same pattern marked the share of 20–29-year-olds: During the war 66% were women, and until the 1870s at least half were women. Except for 1853–1854 and the war years, women were a minority among the 30–39- and 40–49-year-olds, and they always made up a relatively small share, 10–25%, of inmates 50 years old and over.

Thus the overall drop in the proportion of women was an artifact of the decline in the proportion of children. It had two components: first, the departure of young girls, and second, the departure of the mothers of children over 2 years old. We do not know where destitute women with families went for help. Perhaps they received outdoor relief or sent their children to orphanages. The question is important, but at this stage we can do little more than speculate about the answers. The rise in the proportion of women inmates during the Civil War also probably had two parts: The first was a combination of the number of men away at war and the increased availability of work for men; the second, which again is speculation, is a probable rise in illegitimacy. Finally, there always were more elderly men than women in the poorhouse. This is because children appear to have been more willing to take in their elderly mothers than their fathers and because public officials and private philanthropists gave outdoor relief more readily to women than to men. [18]

The nativity of poorhouse inmates reflected both the economic resources of different groups and changing patterns within Erie County (see Figure 2.6 and Table A.6). When Irish immigration increased in the 1840s, the proportion of native born declined. It dropped from over 55% in 1829 to 44% in 1835–1839, 40% during the 1840s, 10% between 1853 and 1854,

---

[18]On an explanation for the greater number of women in poorhouses, see Mary Roberts Smith, *Almshouse Women: A Study of Two Hundred and Twenty-eight Women in the City and County Almshouses of San Francisco*, Leland Stanford Junior University Publications in History and Economics, vol. 3 (Palo Alto, Calif.: Stanford University, 1896) p. 26.

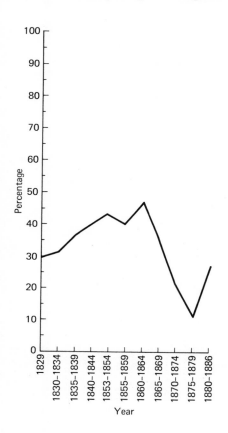

**Figure 2.5.** Proportion of females among inmates: Erie County, New York, Poorhouse, 1829–1886.

and 22% from 1855 to 1859. It rose slightly during the Civil War and, again, when the children of immigrants began to enter the poorhouse in the late 1870s. Of course, the proportion of Irish increased, rising from about 16% in 1835–1839 to 40% in the years before the Civil War. During these years the Irish born made up about 17% of Buffalo's population and a much lower proportion of the population of the rest of the county. After the Civil War the proportion dropped as immigration slowed. The proportion of Germans was high, around 35% only in 1853–1854 and in 1855–1859, 22%, when German-born people made up about 40% of household heads in Buffalo. Other immigrant groups made up smaller, shifting proportions of the inmate population.

Among all nativity groups the proportion of elderly (over 60 years old) increased (see Table A.7). However, it was especially low among the U.S. born: only about 10% in 1870–1886, compared with 24% among the Irish

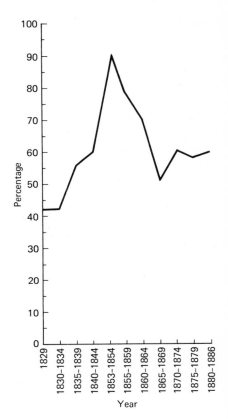

**Figure 2.6.** Proportion foreign born among inmates: Erie County, New York, Poorhouse, 1829–1886.

and 25% among the Germans. It was low, too, among the Canadian and British born. Natives and British immigrants, who had had better jobs, probably were more often able to support themselves in old age; the natives may have had more kin nearby and the Canadians may have returned home in old age. The proportion of young children in the poorhouse was especially low among the Irish and Germans. This is because many of the native-born children actually were the children of immigrants.

As the poorhouse residents became predominantly foreign born, families entered together much less often. Could it be that during its early history the poorhouse was more a communal institution, neither terrifying nor strange, a refuge during periods of crisis? Then, as it grew much larger and the nativity of its inmates changed, it became increasingly alien, a place for strangers who were, literally, starved to death. In this way, with the poorhouse the cycle of reform to custody that characterized mental hospitals, reformatories, and penitentiaries may have been transmuted into a shift from refuge to horror.

Two trends reflected the decline in families: the drop in both the number of children and in the number of inmates entering with relatives (see Figure 2.7 and Table A.8). The decline in relatives took place in stages. The proportion dropped from about 38% in 1839 to 10% in the 1850s. It rose slightly during the Civil War and dropped afterward to about 7% in 1865–1869 and 3% or 4% thereafter. Although this drop was due largely to the removal of children who had entered with their parents, it began prior to the decline in the proportion of young inmates. Thus it reflected the changing character of the poorhouse: its less frequent use as a family institution after the 1830s.

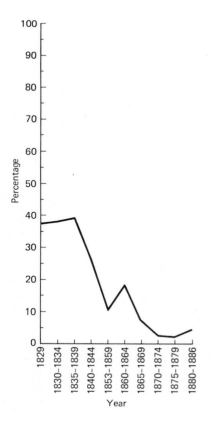

**Figure 2.7.** Percentage of inmates entering with relative: Erie County, New York, Poorhouse, 1829–1886.

From the earliest years men were less likely than women to enter the poorhouse accompanied by a relative (see Figure 2.8 and Table A.9). About 30% of men entered with a relative until the end of the 1830s and about 20% in the next decade. However, more than half of all women entered with a relative until the end of the 1830s. Again, the 1840s were the first major turning point in the demographic history of the poorhouse. Between 1853 and 1886 women continued to enter the poorhouse with relatives more often than did men (see Figure 2.9 and Table A.10). For example, 15% of women 60 years old or over, compared with 3% of men were accompanied by relatives. Differences were also striking among younger people. About 10% of the 15–19-year-old women and 3% of the men and 17% of the 20–29-year-old women and 1% of the men had relatives in the poorhouse. Among these younger women, the relatives, of course, most often were children. Their presence underscores the

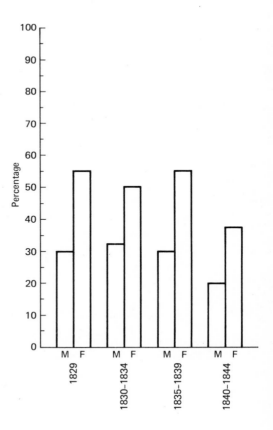

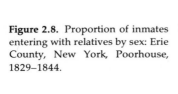

**Figure 2.8.** Proportion of inmates entering with relatives by sex: Erie County, New York, Poorhouse, 1829–1844.

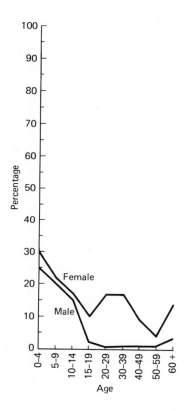

**Figure 2.9.** Proportion of inmates entering with relatives, by age and sex: Erie County, New York, Poorhouse, 1853–1886.

continued use of the poorhouse as a home for unmarried mothers and a maternity hospital. After the passage of the Children's Act a steep decline took place in the proportion of women entering with relatives until the 1880s, when it began to rise slightly. As noted already, this increase probably points to a rise in the use of the poorhouse as a maternity hospital. It may, in fact, reflect an increase in illegitimacy within the county.

When they made up a substantial share of the poorhouse population, native-born people often entered with relatives. For example, 46% of the New England born entered with relatives in the 1830–1834 period. As the poorhouse ceased to be a family institution and as the share of foreign born increased in the 1840s, native-born inmates began to enter with relatives much less often. In 1855–1859 only 19% of the native-born inmates were accompanied by kin.

After the 1820s and prior to the Civil War the Irish entered the poorhouse with relatives much more often than did the Germans. For example, in 1840–1844, 20% of the Irish and 11% of the Germans had kin in the poorhouse. In 1853–1854 only 5% of the Germans were accompanied by relatives. Perhaps the Germans were more able or willing to care for their dependent countrymen and women. With the exception of the Germans, there were few nativity differences in the proportion of women enterting the poorhouse with relatives (see Table A.11). The German share was characteristically low.

With multivariate analysis it is possible to sort out more precisely the characteristics of people entering the poorhouse with relatives (see Table A.12). [19] Between 1829 and 1844, when 35% of inmates entered with a relative, young children were especially likely to have been accompanied by kin. During the teen years the probability dropped to about 20%, and among people in their 20s and 30s women were more likely than men to enter with a relative, surely a reflection of the problems of young women: pregnancy without marriage, abandonment, and widowhood. No nativity differences had a significant effect on the likelihood that an inmate had entered with a relative. Nativity distinctions apparent in cross-sectional analysis reflect differences in other factors, notably age and sex.

The chances did vary, though, by year and month. They declined from 42% in 1830–1834 to 28% in 1840–1844. People were especially likely (52%) to enter with relatives in January, undoubtedly on account of seasonal unemployment among desperately poor families. Of course, in 1853–1886 the proportion of inmates who had entered with relatives dropped dramatically from 35% to 7%. Young children were the most likely to be accompanied by kin, but the odds had diminished sharply. Though fewer in number, young children now were likely to enter alone. They were, that is, more often orphaned or abandoned. This new pattern highlights the shift away from the poorhouse as a family institution. Women were still more likely than men to enter during their 20s and 30s, though the figures dropped dramatically from the earlier period. Even

---

[19]The Multiple Classification Analyses (MCAs) were done with the SPSS program. Norman H. Nie *et at., SPSS: Statistical Package for the Social Sciences* (New York: McGraw-Hill, 1975), pp. 409–410, 416–418. We used two MCAs, one for the 1829–1844 years and one for 1853–1886. The dependent variable was dichotomous: entrance with a relative. The factor or independent variables were age and sex (combined into one variable to account for interaction); birthplace; year of entrance; month of entrance; and, in the later period, cause of entrance.

elderly men were still much less likely than women to enter with relatives. The influence of place of birth on the likelihood that an inmate had entered with a relative remained insignificant, but the influence of year rose during the Civil War, for reasons that already have been discussed. Those who entered on account of "family disruption" had the greatest chance (19%) of entering with a relative, a finding that is not surprising.

No occupation was listed for most adults, and for those with an occupation most men were laborers and most women were domestics (see Table A.13). Unfortunately, the cause of entrance also was not an especially useful characteristic. It was not given at all prior to 1853, and after that time it was stated in a vague manner (see Table A.14). However, there were a few patterns. More men (41%) than women (28%) were recorded as destitute. However, the cause of entrance was not given for 47% of the women. Men more often than women were noted as suffering from a specific illness, and women more frequently were listed with a moral or criminal reason for entrance (10% compared with 2%). Moral causes were given especially often (in 18% of cases) during the Civil War, a reflection of problems already discussed. No cause for entrance was given for two-thirds of the inmates less than 5 years old; for 10% of them the reason was "family disruption." Among 20–29-year-olds, 42% were listed as destitute and 22% as sick. Moral causes were relatively high among them (7%), as well. By contrast, moral causes were given for only 3% of people over 60 years old. Of these, 39% were destitute, and 12% were noted as suffering from a chronic or general illness. Causes began to be recorded more specifically in the 1870s, when, on account of the depression, the proportion of "destitute" increased from 44% to 64%.

One of the most important questions is how long people stayed in the poorhouse. Was it a place where the old, sick, and helpless went to live until they died? Or was it a short-term refuge for people in trouble? To what extent did it combine both roles? The first observation to be made is that the proportion of short-term residents was very high (see Tables A.15 and A.16). Of the inmates, 20% between 1829 and 1844 and 29% between 1853 and 1866 remained in the poorhouse less than 1 week; in the same two periods, 20% and 15%, respectively, were there only between 1 and 3 weeks. Thus, 40% of the inmates between 1829 and 1844 and 44% between 1853 and 1886 were in the poorhouse for at most 3 weeks. In fact, during the earlier period 60% and in the latter 55% were there for 6 weeks or less. Clearly, for many people the poorhouse was a place of temporary refuge during crises or times of unemployment, not a permanent home.

However, about one-fifth to one-quarter remained there for a year or more, as best we can determine. [20] The elderly remained longest. About 30–33% were in the poorhouse more than a year. A substantial fraction of the youngest, between 20% and 30%, stayed for a year, too. Conversely, the youngest and oldest were the least likely to be short-term residents. Between 1829 and 1844 there was not much difference in the length of the residence of other age groups. However, in the 1853–1886 period 25–29-year-olds stayed at the poorhouse, by and large, briefly. Fifty-eight percent stayed less than 3 weeks. In the same years half of the 30-year-olds were there less than 6 weeks. In the earlier period no significant differences in length of residence separated nativity groups, but in the later period the native born were the most likely to be in the poorhouse for 3 weeks or less. Throughout both periods women were less likely than men to stay in the poorhouse for only 1 week or less (see Figure 2.10 and Table A.17). However, this is about the only difference of note between sexes. In the second period, 1853–1886, it was the people who entered with relatives who were more likely to remain for more than a week. Of those who entered with kin, 14% stayed 3–6 months, compared with 8% of those without relatives. Short-term residence (under 3 weeks) was highest during depression years, 52% between 1835 and 1839 and 56% from 1875 to 1879 (see Table A.18). The proportion of long-term (over 1 year) residents (who were, recall, often elderly) rose from 29% in 1840–1844 to 35% in 1880–1886. These relations between length of stay and time period point to both the use of the poorhouse as a temporary refuge during depressions and its increasing role as an old age home in the latter part of the century.

Once again, we can sort out the relative influence of various factors on length of residence with a multivariate analysis (see Table A.19). [21] As with the analysis of relatives, the influence of birthplace, apparent in cross-sectional analysis, disappears with other factors controlled. However, the influence of age remains very strong. People in their teen years were

---

[20]It is hard to be exact about this figure because length of residence could not be computed for some people. Each year the names of residents who had been inmates during the previous year were entered in a new register. Their date of departure was supposed to be recorded in the register for the year in which they had entered the poorhouse, but often it was not. However, everyone entered as a continuing resident had been in the poorhouse for at least some part of each of 2 years. Therefore, we have considered them long-term residents (a year or more) for purposes of this discussion, although their exact numbers are given in disaggregated form in the tables.

[21]In this instance, we partitioned length of residence into four categories: less than 3 weeks, 3 weeks to 6 months, over 6 months, and indeterminate.

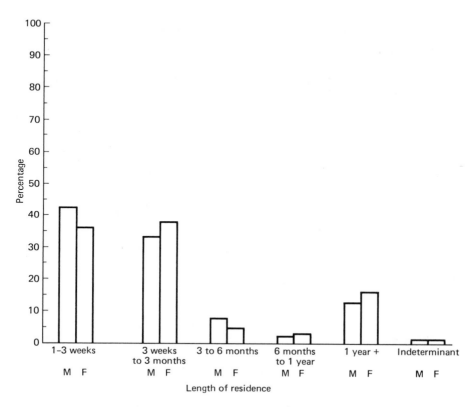

**Figure 2.10.**  Length of residence, by sex: Erie County, New York, Poorhouse, 1829–1844.

unlikely to have been long-term residents. In 1829–1844 young men were much more likely to have been in the poorhouse for 3 weeks or less than were women. The odds that a 20–24-year-old man would have been a short-term resident were 43%, compared with 23% for women. Despite the problems of underemployment, men could find work much more easily than could women, and this made it possible for them to stay in the poorhouse for shorter periods. [22]

People stayed in the poorhouse for short periods during depressions. The odds that someone would be there less than 3 weeks were 50% in 1835–1839 and 48% between 1875 and 1879. Between 1829 and 1844

---

[22]The proportion of employed women in Buffalo was quite low by comparison with other cities.

those people who entered the poorhouse in May were most likely (76%) to be short-term residents, as were those between 1853 and 1886 who entered in April (66%). Least likely to be short-term residents in either period were those people who entered in November and December. These figures show that young men looking for work stayed briefly at the poorhouse in the spring, whereas others, out of work for the season, entered in the winter.

Thus there were four major influences on length of residence: age, sex, year, and month. Those most likely to stay only a short time were young men temporarily out of work. Young women could leave less easily because they often had children and, as well, because it was more difficult for them to find work. During depression years more people than usual had to enter the poorhouse for short periods. Otherwise, length of residence varied with the season. Many people who were on the road looking for work stayed for a short time in the spring; others came to spend the winter. And the chronically sick and elderly often stayed until they died.

## CONCLUSION

The major trends in the demographic history of the Erie County Poorhouse are:

1. The shift away from the family institution associated with the changed nativity of the inmates. Natives not only used the poorhouse less but also less often used it as a family refuge in times of crisis.
2. The decline in the number of childen. This began prior to the Children's Act of 1875 and was a result of public policy. The relation of this shift to the development of orphanages in Buffalo should be studied.
3. The greater proportion of men among all inmates except children and, especially, the elderly. Families more often took care of their elderly female kin, which is a pattern that deserves much more exploration by historians of the family.
4. The effect of the Civil War. Young men went off to war or found jobs more easily. Therefore, they entered the poorhouse less often. Young women, by contrast, faced a number of problems that led more of them to the poorhouse than in any other period.
5. The effect of depressions. During periods when employment was scarce, larger numbers of young men entered the poorhouse.
6. The short-term residence of most inmates. Many people used the poorhouse as a temporary haven during periods of distress.

7. The increasing proportion of elderly inmates. The poorhouse was becoming an old age home.
8. The rise in the number of women and children in the 1880–1886 period. Even as it became an old age home, the poorhouse was also used more frequently as a home for unwed mothers and a maternity hospital. It is possible that this reflected a rise in illegitimacy.

Despite the wealth of data in this chapter, important questions about the poorhouse remain unanswered. It is not at all clear, first, just how people were admitted and discharged. Most, we presume, came and went voluntarily. But were there criteria for admission? Were some people refused? Did political patronage play a role? None of these questions can be answered at present. Second, we know relatively little about the internal routine and discipline practices within poorhouses. There are some hints in the descriptions given earlier in this chapter. But we have no systematic information on how they changed over time. Poorhouses were supposed to be unpleasant; the poor were supposed to dread them. But it is not clear whether inmates simply were given inadequate food and unhealthy surroundings or whether they were at some periods forced to work hard at jobs, such as breaking stone, as well. Nor is it clear what the poorhouse was like during its early family era. Whether the description of its horrors during the 1850s represents a degeneration from a better condition is not known. I suspect that a deterioration began with the increase in Irish inmates during the 1840s, but at the moment we have no way of confirming this supposition. Finally, we know very little about the people who ran poorhouses: Who were they, what were their careers like, how were they appointed?

Nonetheless, a number of important trends in the history of the poorhouse now are clear. If nothing else, this account makes clear that poorhouses have a history that should be studied and that poorhouse inmates do not match their stereotypes either in the past or present. The poorhouse was a complex institution. Its history reflected changing ethnic relations and the cyclical nature of the economy. Its occupants, in general, were not passive, degraded paupers who drifted into poorhouses, where they lived out their lives in dependent torpor. On the contrary, most remained only for a short period. Whatever the official purposes of the poorhouse, the poor themselves put it to their own uses: in its early years, as a short-term residence for native families in distress; and in later years, as a place to stay for a while during harsh seasons of the year, unemployment, or family crisis; as a hospital in which unmarried women could have their children; and, of course, as a place of last resort for the sick, helpless, and elderly. Although legislation created the poorhouse and, as with the Children's Act of 1875, partly shaped its development, its demographic history also was made by the poor themselves, who used it as a key life support amidst the harshness and unpredictability of existence in early industrial Erie County.

The demographic history of the Erie County Poorhouse also highlights important features of both poverty and policy in American history. Poverty was a complex condition and poor people a varied group, despite persistent ideological efforts to meld them into an undifferentiated class of the weak and undeserving. Some destitution resulted from the organization of the labor market: seasonal work, fluctuations in the demand for labor, periodic depressions. The poor people created by these conditions most often were men on the move in search of work either alone or with families and in need of short-term help. At the other extreme were people with some sort of disability—victims of industrial accidents, the mentally ill, or the chronically sick, for example—whose inability to care for themselves brought them to the poorhouse, where they remained for long periods of time. Other inmates of poorhouses were casualties of the life-course: widows with young children; young, pregnant women; orphans or children of paupers; and, especially, old people without spouses or kin to care for them. All of these people could be found together at the same time in most large poorhouses during the nineteenth century.

Public policy, however, sought to turn poorhouses into more specialized institutions. Indeed, the creation of poorhouses early in the century reflected the same impulse to specialize that prompted the creation of mental hospitals, reform schools, and age-graded public schools. After the establishment of poorhouses, the two major goals of the drive toward specialization were the removal of the insane and young children from poorhouses. The latter—which was largely successful by late in the century—had two other sources. One was genuine horror at the conditions that confronted children in poorhouses. The other, especially in the 1870s, was the hope of ending what were thought to be cycles of poverty by breaking up the families of the very poor. A similar mixture of compassion and harshness also ran through the general purposes that poorhouses were supposed to serve: deterrence of the ablebodied from seeking relief and shelter for the aged. By making relief available only inside poorhouses and by stigmatizing their inmates, public policy tried to discourage the ablebodied from seeking relief. At the same time, poorhouses were supposed to provide decent, if spartan, care for the elderly. These objectives conflicted, and, in the end, it was deterrence that won out. Even as poorhouses became old age homes, they retained their stigma, partly because of the degraded image of their inmates and partly because of their wretched conditions. The care that poorhouses gave always was the cheapest possible, and, in the end, it is its mean-spirited quality that most clearly marks policy toward poor and helpless people in America's past.

# PART II

# Early Social Science and the Causes of Pauperism

Scientific charity and professional social science appeared in America during the third quarter of the nineteenth century. Although usually considered separately, both were integral aspects of a new strategy for alleviating a social crisis with three major components: first, an alleged increase in social dependency manifested by rising poorhouse populations, an upsurge in admissions to mental hospitals, and the appearance of a new class of vagrants known as tramps; second, a breakdown in relations between social classes signaled by residential segregation, the withdrawal of the well-to-do from frequent contact with the poor, and, so it was thought, a crumbling of the deference that had served as a means of social control; and, third, the antagonistic relations between labor and capital, evident in the growth of trade unions and the frequency of strikes.[23]

Professional social science emerged from the quest for data with which to construct rational policies for ameliorating the social crisis. Early practitioners of social science, represented by members of the American Social Science Association, were administrators and professionals with practical concerns. They believed that the acquisition of hard data about social problems would point, ineluctably, to the policies for their resolution. Little interested in theory for its own sake, they wanted to know how to reduce the burden of dependence, what legislative changes to propose, how to administer social institutions more efficiently and effectively. What they lacked, they realized, was basic descriptive data

---

[23]Thomas L. Haskell, *The Emergence of Professional Social Science: The American Social Science Association and the Nineteenth-Century Crisis of Authority* (Urbana, Ill., University of Illinois Press, 1977); Mary Furner, *From Advocacy to Objectivity: A Crisis in the Professionalization of American Social Science, 1865–1905* (Lexington, Ky., University of Kentucky Press, 1975); Paul Boyer, *Urban Masses and Moral Order in America, 1820–1920* (Cambridge, Mass.: Harvard University Press, 1978), pp. 143–161; Gareth Stedman Jones, *Outcast London* pp. 268–280.

about the problems with which they were concerned. In fact, a failure to gather information about dependent populations, they believed, had contributed to the chaotic pattern of welfare administration in which misguided sentimentalists or corrupt local politicians gave relief indiscriminately, thereby demoralizing the poor and fueling the creation of a degraded pauper class.[24]

In this situation scientific charity emerged as the key strategy with which to curb the growing public expense and to reverse the demoralization of the poor that had resulted from lax welfare practice. Scientific charity was to be applied primarily through the formation of Charity Organization Societies (first established in America in Buffalo in 1878). The major tasks of these new organizations were to examine applicants for relief, to refer worthy cases to the appropriate agency, to maintain a citywide register of welfare recipients, and to undertake case work, or, as it was called at the time, friendly visiting, with individual families. In this way, the agents of Charity Organization Societies would detect fraud, rationalize welfare practice, promote the independence of the poor, and put the primary responsibility for welfare back in the private sector, thus ensuring that it would remain a charity rather than an entitlement, a political plum, or a source of demoralization.[25]

The ideals of scientific charity swept American welfare practice between about 1878 and 1893. In these years 10 of the nation's 40 largest cities abolished outdoor relief, whereas many other cities of varying size reduced the amount of relief they granted and tightened administrative regulations. The proponents of scientific charity worked closely with early social scientists. Indeed, frequently there was little distinction between the two groups. Early social science found its institutional home in the boards of state charities established in several states, starting with Massachusetts in 1863. The members and secretaries of these new agencies generally were vigorous supporters of scientific charity and advocates of Charity Organization Societies.[26]

Early social scientists and charity organizers contrasted their own honesty and objectivity with the self-interested manipulations of machine politicians who sustained expensive welfare practices for partisan pur-

---

[24]For a general criticism of outdoor relief, see Josephine Shaw Lowell, *Public Relief and Private Charity* (New York: Putnam's, 1884).

[25]On the history of the Charity Organization Societies, see Frank Dekker Watson, *The Charity Organization Movement in the United States* (New York: Macmillan, 1902).

[26]Schneider and Deutsch, *Public Welfare in New York* pp. 13–34; James Leiby, *A History of Social Welfare and Social Work in the United States* (New York: Columbia University Press, 1978), pp. 93–101.

poses. Yet it is apparent that the social scientists and charity organizers were themselves partisans. Protestations of objectivity and a concern for the general welfare aside, the formulation of research questions, the selection of topics for discussion at meetings or in reports, even the methods by which data were gathered—all of these revealed social science and charity organization as anything but neutral referees of the social crisis of their time. Their mantle of objectivity, their self-presentation as collectors of empirical data, proved useful, however, for it legitimated, indeed intensified, long-standing arguments that the source of pauperism and other forms of dependence resided within the characters of individual rather than within the social system. These arguments, in turn, were deployed successfully to advocate punitive and restrictive welfare policies.[27]

All of these strands had begun to come together even before the formal organization of Charity Organization Societies. Indeed, by the early 1870s the interweaving of social science and scientific charity, of research and public policy, and of the biases of early empiricism and popular attitudes had imprinted itself upon the texture of public and private philanthropy as the basis of progressive reform. The first great example of this new blend of theory, research, and policy was the remarkable examination of pauperism conducted by Dr. Charles S. Hoyt, secretary of the New York State Board of Charities in 1874 and 1875.[28]

In May 1873 a concurrent resolution of the New York State Senate and Assembly directed the secretary of the State Board of Charities, Charles S. Hoyt, to examine "the inmates of the various poor-houses and almshouses of the State, under the supervision of the commissioners of the several districts, with a view of determining, as far as practicable, the causes of the increase of pauperism." Hoyt compiled a schedule with 60 questions, which he and the district commissioners administered to every poorhouse and almshouse inmate in New York in 1874 and 1875. In "The Causes of Pauperism," an appendix to the tenth annual report of the board, Hoyt reported on the results of his survey of 12,614 paupers.[29]

According to Amos Warner, in his important and widely used book, *American Charities*, Hoyt's survey was "probably the completest picture of

---

[27]On the meaning and uses of objectivity, see the discussions throughout Furner, *From Advocacy to Objectivity*.

[28]Charles S. Hoyt, "The Causes of Pauperism," in *Tenth (1877) Annual Report of the State Board of Charities* (New York, 1978).

[29]Hoyt, "Causes of Pauperism," p. 97.

an American almshouse population ever presented." The report represented the "beginning of differentiation in that State, and gave the basis for the agitation which resulted in removing the children from New York almshouses, and has finally brought about the removal of the insane from those institutions."[30] The report also offered an apparently scientific confirmation of popular ideas about the moral origins of pauperism. As such, it helped legitimate the movement for charity reform—the attack on outdoor relief, the increased discrimination between worthy and unworthy poor, the establishment of Charity Organization Societies—that swept through American welfare practice between the late 1870s and the 1890s. As a result of Hoyt's survey, charity reformers could argue with increased confidence that most paupers either had inherited their defects or had brought their misery upon themselves. Indeed, within months of its publication Professor Francis Wayland of Yale cited Hoyt's conclusions to bolster his attack on tramps as lazy, degenerate, perhaps even genetically unfit, shirkers rather than unfortunate victims of technological change and the erratic demand for labor within American industry.[31]

Hoyt's survey is a useful document with which to undertake a close scrutiny of the personal interpretation of pauperism, one of the nineteenth century's enduring legacies to the present. How did Hoyt reach his conclusions? Can his data be interpreted differently? In part, answers can be found through studying the evidence in the remarkably detailed report itself and comparing it with other published aggregate data. Fortunately, however, all of the original schedules of Hoyt's survey exist, and these permit an individual-level reanalysis of his conclusions.[32]

Here I will examine Hoyt's report, first, by showing biases in the way in which it was compiled and presented. Then I will reexamine a sample of the schedules. Together, these reanalyses will show that Hoyt's methods of gathering and aggregating his data reinforced what I have called the personal interpretation of poverty. Other methods of analysis show quite a different picture.

---

[30] Amos G. Warner, *American Charities: a Study in Philanthropy and Economics* (New York and Boston: Thomas Y. Crowell, 1894), p. 146. Francis Wayland, "A Paper on Tramps Read at the Saratoga Meeting of the American Social Science Association before the Conference of State Charities: September 6, 1877," in *Proceedings of the Fourth Annual Conference of Charities* (1877), p. 111.

[31] Francis Wayland, "A Paper on Tramps Read at the Saratoga Meeting of the American Social Science Association before the Conference of State Charities: September 6, 1877," in *Proceedings of the Fourth Annual Conference of Charities* (1877), p. 111.

[32] The schedules are in the New York State Archives at Albany.

## THE DESIGN OF THE REPORT

Hoyt was a physician who developed an interest in public welfare during a distinguished career as a surgeon and hospital administrator in the Civil War. He was noted among his associates for his energy, efficiency, and concern with detail. Indeed, inattention and a lack of thoroughness are not grounds upon which Hoyt can be criticized. Commenting on the procedures of his study, he wrote that "no pains were spared to make the investigation as thorough and complete as possible." In most instances superintendents of the poor and poorhouse keepers accompanied Hoyt as he made his inquiries. Where inmates were unable to answer questions, officials, especially in rural areas where families were well known, supplied information. Hoyt, therefore, believed that "the statements recorded are as accurate and reliable as it is possible to obtain upon the subject."[33]

The 60 questions were divided into four groups: the first sought general demographic information: "name, sex, age, social condition, color, birthplace, etc." The second asked about "length of time a dependent" and attempted to find out how long people had received aid and from what sources. Third came the "personal and family history of the dependent," a section whose structure, reflecting the recent interest in hereditarian theory, asked questions about parents, grandparents, siblings, and aunts and uncles. Finally came a series of questions about "existing causes of dependence," which also asked about the prognosis for "recovery from the cause of dependence."

As Hoyt reported, not all aspects of the questionnaire could be filled out with equal ease or accuracy. Data on parental birthplace, for instance, were "in most cases, obtained with great difficulty," as was information about the age at which people became paupers. Especially hard to discover was "the full measure of relief which had been extended to these persons." However, by contrast, "the educational attainments of the persons examined were probably obtained with greater accuracy than any other matter connected with the inquiry" because in cases of uncertainty "the appropriate test was applied."[34]

Not surprisingly, inmates attempted to conceal "the practices of early life," and in most cases "the facts regarding the matter were given with

---

[33]Hoyt, "Causes of Pauperism," pp. 98, 107. On Hoyt, see Julia S. Hoag, "Memorial to Dr. Charles S. Hoyt ..." in *Thirty-second Annual Report of the State Board of Charities of the State of New York,* New York State Senate Document No. 19, January 16, 1899, pp. 165–184.

[34]Hoyt, "Causes of Pauperism," pp. 100–103.

great reluctance." Here, according to Hoyt, the opinions of the superintendents and keepers became crucial. If information regarding personal
habits was hard to establish, data on parents were even more elusive.
Many inmates tried to hide "the facts upon the subject, while others, owing
to their youth, or because of imbecility or mental infirmities, were wholly
incapable of giving any reliable testimony in the matter." Again, the
superintendents and overseers became a prime source. Hoyt was especially eager to learn whether relatives had been paupers, but only in rural
areas where families were well known could he gather any reliable
data.[35]

Some of the problems with Hoyt's data appear immediately. Much of the
information, especially about personal and parental habits and family
history, is based only on cases personally known to administrators. Some
of it surely was little more than gossip, and, as a whole, it was biased
toward families who had been relatively long term residents of the same
place. Indeed, the inadequacy of poorhouse records troubled Hoyt, who
argued that without an improvement in record keeping, it would be
impossible to gather the systematic data essential to the scientific study of
pauperism. As a result of Hoyt's experience, the state board began to
require almshouses to complete a detailed questionnaire on each entering
inmate and to forward the completed forms to it each year.[36]

Other major biases of the report are slightly less obvious but are at least
equally important. First, the examination did not include all of the inmates:
"This statement embraces the paupers coming from the fixed population
only. As other measures were being taken by the Board for the
examination and registration of transient paupers, this class was not
included in the inquiry." Hoyt did not define "fixed population," nor did
he describe how he discriminated between the fixed and the transient
population. But the result is clear enough. The survey included 12,614
persons. In Erie County he surveyed 462 inmates. However, in 1875,
57,077 people were "received" in the poorhouses of New York State. On
December 1, 1875, the population was 15,511. The reason for the
discrepancy is that 46,464 inmates were discharged during the year. In Erie
County 1725 persons entered the poorhouse in 1874 and 1291 in 1875. If
the lunatic asylum is included, the 1875 figure rises to 2413. Of these, 775
remained in the poorhouse on December 1, 1875.[37]

---

[35]*Ibid.*, pp. 104–107.

[36]For more comment on the subsequent registration requirements and an analysis of some
of the registers, see the latter section of this part as well as Part IV of this chapter.

[37]*Report of the Secretary of State upon Statistics of Pauperism for the Year 1875,* New York State
Senate Document No. 46, March 1, 1876, p. 5.

# STATE BOARD OF CHARITIES OF NEW YORK.

### SCHEDULE.

For the record of dependents examined by the State Board of Charities and its local Committees and agents, under and pursuant to the concurrent resolution of the Senate and Assembly, of May 27th and 29th, 1873. Each of these sheets is designed for the history of a single case. Examiners will be guided by the directions contained herein.

*Erie* .............COUNTY POOR-HOUSE.

*Examination No.* 5 .

I. NAME, SEX, AGE, SOCIAL CONDITION, COLOR, BIRTH-PLACE, Etc.

1. Name, *J. Brown*

2. Sex, (Male M. Female F.) *M*

3. Age at last birthday, 67 .......................years.
   (If under 1 year state the months).......................

4. Social condition, (Single, Married, Widow, Widower, divorced.)

5. Color (White, Black—if mixed, state degree),.......................

6. Birth Place (State or Country, *England*
   County,.......................Town,.......................
   City,.......................). (If born in a poor-house or other public institution, state the fact.)

   If of foreign birth, how long in the U. S. ? 26
   how long in this State ? 7 .......................at what
   port landed ? *New York*

7. Birth place of Father, (State or Country, *Eng*
   County,.......................Town,.......................
   City,.......................) (If born in a poor-house or other public institution, state the fact.)

8. Birth place of Mother, (State or Country, *Eng*
   County,.......................Town,.......................
   City,.......................) (If born in a poor-house or other public institution, state the fact.)

II. LENGTH OF TIME A DEPENDANT.

9. At what age did this person first become dependent upon public charity ?

10. What was the first mode of aid ? (State whether by neighborhood, church, organized society, temporary relief by public officials, or full support in a poor-house, or other public institution, the name of which should be given,)

11. If first aided outside of institutions, how long, was this continued ?

12. At what age did this person first become an inmate of a poor-house ? 62 years. (If under one year give the months.)

13. How long an inmate of this poor-house ? 5 years.
    (If less than one year give the months.)

14. Has this person been in other poor-houses ? *No*

15. If so, how many ?

16. How long in all has this person been an inmate of poor-houses ? 5 years. (If less than one year give the months.)

17. Has this person been an inmate of any insane asylum, blind asylum, idiot asylum, deaf and dumb asylum or refuge ? (If so, state which, and how long ?) *No*

18. Has this person been in Jails, Work-houses, Penitentiaries or Prisons, convicted of crime ? (If so state which, how long an inmate, and the nature of the offense.) *No*

III. PERSONAL AND FAMILY HISTORY OF THE DEPENDENT.

19. Is this person of legitimate or illegitimate birth ? (Write which.)

20. Is there consanguinity in the parents ? (If so, write what degree.)

21. Can this person read and write ? *Yes*

22. Did this person receive a fair school education ? *Yes*
    If not, why neglected ?

23. Had this person habits of idleness ? *No*
    "       "       "   thrift and saving ? *Yes*
    Was this person totally abstinent ?
    "       "       a moderate drinker ? *Yes*
    "       "       a periodical drinker ? *Yes*
    "       "       a constant drinker ?

24. Had the Father habits of idleness ?
    "       "       "   thrift and saving ?
    Was the Father temperate or intemperate ? (Write which.) *intemperate*

25. Had the Mother habits of idleness ?
    "       "       "   thrift and saving ?
    Was the Mother temperate or intemperate ? (Write which.) *temperate*

26. Was the Father immoral, sensual or otherwise debased ? (State facts.)
    Was the Mother immoral, sensual or otherwise debased ? (State facts.)

*Plate 6. An example of the schedule used in the examination of inmates of poorhouses by the New York State Board of Charities. Note the assumptions implicit in the questions about family background. (Courtesy of the New York State Archives.)*

27. Did this person receive moral and religious training in youth ? ....................

28. Did youthful habits of vagrancy and idleness exist ? (State facts.) ....................

29. Did this person have a fixed home, or lead a roving life before becoming dependent ? ....................

30. What trade did this person ever learn, or what occupation pursue ?   *Capenter*

31. Why was it abandoned ? ....................

32. What was the occupation of the father of this person ? ....................

   If a wife, what was the occupation of the husband ? ....................

33. Was the Father a pauper ? ....................
   "    Mother "
   "    Grandfather a pauper ?
   "    Grandmother "
   Were any of the Brothers of this person paupers ? ....................
   "    "    Sisters    "    "
   "    "    Uncles    "    "
   "    "    Aunts    "    "
   (Where there are two or more persons of the same family to be examined, questions 34 to 39, inclusive, should be put to one member only.)

34. Total number of persons in the above group of families (three generations living and dead), known to have been dependent on public charity ? ....................

35. Total number in the same group (living and dead), known to have been self-supporting ? ....................

36. Total number of insane (living and dead), in the same group ? ....................

37. Total number of idiots (living and dead), in the same group ? ....................

38. Total number of inebriates (living and dead), in the same group ?   /

39. Total number who have been in Penitentiaries or State Prisons (living and dead), in the same group ? ....................
   (Question No. 40 and 41 should be put to the Father only, if both parents are living and present ; if not, then to the only living parent.)

40. If a parent, how many children has this person now living ?   /

41. What is their condition ; are they in poor-houses, asylums, hospitals, refuges, etc., or are they self-supporting ? (Write the fact.)   *Self-Supporting*

IV. EXISTING CAUSES OF DEPENDENCE.

42. Homeless Childhood (illegitimate), ....................
   "    (abandoned), ....................
   "    (by death of father), ....................
   "    (by death of mother), ....................
   "    (by death of both parents), ....................
   "    (by pauperism of parents), ....................
   "    (by imprisonment of parents for crime), ....................

43. Homeless by abandonment of husband, ....................
   "    by death of husband, ....................

44. Old age and destitution, ....................

45. Permanent disabling disease (with the name of it.)   *Chronic Rheumatism*

46. Temporary disabling disease or sickness (write the name.) ....................

47. Crippled (how), ....................
   Deformed (how), ....................

48. Loss or impairment of any of the five special senses. (State which, and how.) ....................

49. Loss or impairment of any other natural faculty or bodily power ? (Write what faculty or power, and how lost or impaired.) ....................

50. Insanity ?    Idiocy ? ....................
   Epilepsy ?    Paralysis ? ....................

51. General feebleness of the mind ? ....................
   "    "    "    body ? ....................

52. Impairment or degeneration of the bodily powers, or mental faculties from inebriation ? (State the facts.) ....................

53. Is there proof of insanity, epilepsy, paralysis, special feebleness of mind or body, syphilis, or any other entailment of bodily or mental misfortune from parentage in this person's history ? (If so note the fact.) ....................

54. Is there mental or moral perversion, or morbid and debasing conditions of mind ? (If so state the fact and the causes to which attributed.)   *No*

55. Is this person capable of self-supporting labor without supervision ?   *No*

56. Is this person capable of self-support under direction and supervision ?   *No*

57. How is this person's time employed in this institution ? ....................

58. What is the chief cause of dependence in the case of this person, and what, if any, the remedies ? ....................

59. What appears to be the destiny of this person as respects recovery from the cause of dependence ?   *Wholly Dependent*

60. What family relatives of this generation, if any, have the pecuniary ability to suitably provide for, or take care of this person ? (State facts and evidence.) ....................

NOTE.—These Schedules should be numbered in the order of examination, and where there are two or more persons of the same family in any institution, they should be examined consecutively, commencing with the parents if present, if not, with the oldest representative. When the schedules are all filled out for any institution, they should be securely packed, and sent by express to the Secretary, at Albany. It is greatly desired to complete the examination and have the records in this office on or before the first day of October.
(Further remarks may be added by examiners, writing on the next page of this sheet.)

*Plate 6* (continued)

97

As a result of its restriction to the "fixed population," Hoyt reported that only 24.5% of the inmates had been in the poorhouses less than 1 year. However, in direct contrast, between 1853 and 1886 only 14% of the inmates in the Erie County Poorhouse had been there 6 months or more, and a plurality, 41%, had been inmates less than 3 weeks. By focusing only on the small proportion of inmates who remained in the poorhouse for a long period, Hoyt's survey distorted not only the length-of-residence patterns but also the age-structure of inmate populations. According to the survey, in the entire state 38% of inmates were 50 years old or over, and this figure includes the Randall's Island Infant Asylum in New York City, lowering the overall percentage. Yet in Erie County between 1870 and 1874 only 14.7% of inmates were at least 50 years old, a figure that dropped to 11.0% between 1875 and 1879. Hoyt's survey portrays poorhouse inmates as primarily old, long-term residents. A complete canvas of inmates, however, would have revealed that aside from the old, poorhouses sheltered large numbers of young inmates who used them for short periods, especially during times when work was hard to find. These younger, more temporary inmates, who did not match Hoyt's image, simply did not appear in his survey.[38]

Hoyt's statistics also are biased because they lump together paupers, inmates of insane asylums attached to poorhouses, and some children in orphanages. The inclusion of the insane (as will become clear shortly) dramatically increased the proportion of paupers whose condition appeared organic or hereditary. And since most cases of insanity were thought incurable, it increased the proportion of long-term residents and decreased the prospects for "recovery." Nor in his analysis did Hoyt make more than the most cursory distinctions between men and women. Yet the characteristics of poorhouse inmates, indeed the dynamics of pauperism, differed by sex, and any analysis that fails to differentiate poorhouse inmates by sex obscures about as much as it reveals.

## THE SAMPLE

The remainder of this chapter rests primarily on an analysis of a sample of the individual schedules collected by Hoyt. The sample contains 3689 cases, or 29.2% of all those included in the original survey. These cases are drawn from 23 different institutions in 20 counties. In 4 of the sample counties—Oneida, Monroe, Erie, and New York—the insane or lunatic

---

[38] See Part I of this chapter.

asylums attached to the poorhouses were enumerated separately. The sample also includes Randall's Island Infant Asylum in New York City. The counties were chosen to represent a variety of settings throughout the state: upstate, urban, rural, western, and so on. All of the schedules for each of the sampled counties were put into machine-readable form. Comments on the schedules by interviewers were recorded separately on cards indexed to the case number of the schedule.[39]

The sample represents Hoyt's survey reasonably well. First, consider nativity (see Table A.20). Somewhat more of Hoyt's group, 39.9%, had been born in New York State, compared with 31.3% of the sample. By contrast, 37.6% of the sample and 34.3% of the survey had been born in Ireland, and 11.7% and 8.9%, respectively, of each group in Germany. Only with young people aged 5–19 was there much difference in the two groups. In Hoyt's survey, 13.8% of the people were in these age categories, compared with 6.6% in the sample. However 5.9% of the sample and 6.2% of the survey were less than 5 years old; 13.2% of the sample and 11.2% of the survey were in their 20s; and 22% of the sample and 16.8% of the entire group were age 60 or over. In all, these age and nativity distributions were quite close.

More substantial differences in sex separated the two groups. Only a little over one-third, 35.3%, of the sample were males, compared with 50.6% of the entire survey. This difference reflects the greater proportion of young people in the survey, for, to foreshadow the argument, girls and young women were as likely as boys and young men to be found in almshouses, but among the elderly the sex ratio differed sharply.

The small differences between the sample and the survey should not bias the analysis of the former. That is, the sample provides an adequate body of data with which to test the major conclusions of Hoyt's survey. However, for most purposes the sample must be disaggregated because part of the bias in Hoyt's results stemmed from the combining of dissimilar institutions and populations. Thus most of the analyses here will distinguish between the 4 large (at least 185 inmates) poorhouses (Oneida, Monroe, Albany, Erie), the 15 small and medium-size (no more than 104

---

[39]The institutions in the sample were Monroe County Almshouse, Albany Abuse House, Oneida Poor House, Kingston Abuse House, Lewis County Poor House, Putnam County Poor House, Oswego County Abuse House, Poughkeepsie City Abuse House, Clinton County Poor House, Cayuga County Poor House, Monroe County Lunatic Asylum, Allegany County Poor House, Oneida County Poor House (insane asylum), Schoharie County Poor House, New York City Lunatic Asylum, Tioga County Poor House, Greene County Poor House, Essex County Poor House, Wayne County Poor House, Saint Lawrence County Poor House, Erie County Poorhouse, Erie County Poorhouse/Department of the Insane, and Randall's Island Infant Hospital.

inmates) ones, the 4 insane and lunatic asylums, and Randall's Island
Infant Asylum.

## INSTITUTIONAL DEMOGRAPHY:
## AGE, SEX, BIRTHPLACE

The populations in the various types of institutions differed from one
another (see Figure 2.11 and Table A.21). Indeed, even within categories,
especially among small and medium-size poorhouses, significant distinctions existed. However, a number of general points can be made about
institutional demography.

First the proportion of elderly inmates, age 60 or over, was substantially
lower in the insane asylums. Comparing the almshouse with the insane
asylum attached to it in three counties, we see these differences in the
proportion of inmates age 60 or more: Monroe, 15% to 45%; Erie 5% to
39%; Oneida 16% to 38%.

Conversely, the proportion of women in insane asylums was considerably higher than in the almshouses: in Monroe County, 63% compared
with 42%, in Oneida, 65% compared with 41%, and in Erie, 54% compared
with 43%. (The New York City Lunatic Asylum was for women only.) The
difference in sex composition between poorhouses and their attached
lunatic asylums did not result from differing age-structures. Among those
over the age of 60, more of the insane still were women: 56% compared
with 28% in Erie County; 70% compared with 23% in Oneida; and 72%
compared with 35% in Monroe.

By contrast, most of the elderly paupers in the poorhouses were men:
about 67% in Albany County, 72% in Erie County, 53% in Lewis County,
74% in Clinton County, 64% in Wayne County, and so on. There is no
question: Elderly women less often entered poorhouses.

In general, few people entered poorhouses with their kin. Of the entire
group surveyed by Hoyt, about 19% entered an almshouse or insane
asylum with relatives. In the sample virtually none of the insane and
relatively few people in the large poorhouses had kin with them. In the
latter the range entering with kin was 3.6–11.2%. In 3 of the smaller
almshouses few inmates entered with kin, but in 12 others the range varied
between 11.3% and 33.3%, generally higher than among the inmates of the
larger almshouses. Those kin most often were children who probably had
entered with their widowed or unmarried mothers. Officials in smaller
counties, where families were well known, may have been reluctant to
break up families by sending children to orphanages. In contrast, the

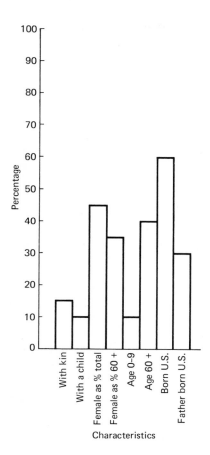

**Figure 2.11.** Selected demographic characteristics of New York State poorhouses, 1874–1875 (excludes insane departments and infant hospital).

officials in some of the cities, such as Buffalo, already had started to remove children from the poorhouses, an action mandated for the state as a whole in 1875.

Very few blacks could be found in either the poorhouses or the insane asylums. Blacks were 9.5% of the 42 inmates of the Lewis County poorhouse and 5% in Green County. Otherwise, their proportion of the total varied between nil and 3%.

The proportion of inmates born in the United States varied with the size and location of each institution more than with its type. Not surprisingly, only 15% of the inmates of the New York City Lunatic Asylum had been born in the United States, compared with 86% of the 49 in Schoharie County and 38% in Erie County.

However, most inmates had foreign-born parents. Indeed, the fathers of inmates in the large poorhouses overwhelmingly had been born outside of the United States: 89.2% in Monroe County, 91% in Albany, 75% in Oneida, 88% in Erie, and about 97% in the New York City Lunatic Asylum. Although the proportion of foreign-born fathers was lower in a number of the small and medium-size poorhouses, in only 5 of 15 of them had the fathers of at least half the inmates been born in the United States. As might be expected, the greatest discrepancy between the birthplaces of fathers and inmates occurred in the Randall's Island Infant Asylum. There 70.3% of the 229 children and only 9.2% of their fathers had been born in the United States.

Most of the children in Randall's Island were under 5 years old. Few of them, it should be noted, were actually orphans. Only about 9% of the boys and 11% of the girls had lost one of their parents through death. Mostly they were there because their parents were poor: About 20% were illegitimate; about 30% of the boys and 12% of the girls had been abandoned; approximately 6% of all parents were in prison; and the rest, 36% of the parents of boys and 50% of girls, were paupers.

With the exception of Randall's Island, poorhouses usually had a high proportion of elderly inmates, most of whom were men. The variation in the nativity of their inmates reflected their location, but in almost all of them either immigrants or their children comprised most of the populations. The insane, by and large, were less elderly as a group, and more of them were women. They, too, mainly had been born outside of the United States.

All of this raises some intriguing questions. Did the small and large poorhouses vary in their atmosphere and in the quality of their care? Did smaller country poorhouses, where, as Hoyt observed, families were well known, treat inmates better, more as unfortunate members of their community than as unworthy paupers? There was, in fact, a negative correlation between the size of counties and the average amount of both indoor and outdoor relief per recipient. To take another question, what was the significance of the sex ratios? Why were more elderly men in poorhouses? Was it because children were unwilling to take in their elderly fathers or because women more often received outdoor relief? Conversely, why were more of the insane women? What kind of behavior led to incarceration in a county insane asylum? Aside from the question of sex, nativity remains a puzzling issue. Were immigrants and their children more likely to become insane? Was their behavior more easily misunderstood? Did they have less resources when in need of help? If any of the answers to these questions is positive, it becomes easier to understand why such a high proportion of poorhouse and insane asylum inmates were immigrants or their children.[40]

## HOYT AND THE CAUSES OF PAUPERISM

Hoyt's primary conclusion was unambiguous:

> By far the greater number of paupers have reached that condition by idleness, improvidence, drunkedness, or some form of vicious indulgence.... These vices and weaknesses are very frequently, if not universally, the result of tendencies which are to a greater or less degree hereditary. The number of persons in our poor-houses who have been reduced to poverty by causes outside of their own acts is ... surprisingly small.[41]

In other words, pauperism was a character defect, often inherited. Hoyt's conclusions about the role of drunkenness in the creation of paupers rested on the survey's questions about drinking habits. Paupers were to be classified into four groups: abstinent, moderate drinkers, periodic drinkers, and constant drinkers. Of course, the categories themselves are vague and there is no indication of how they were interpreted. When he reported on the survey's results, however, Hoyt classified everyone who drank at all—that is, everyone but the completely abstinent—as intemperate. On that basis he found, not surprisingly, that 81.36% of men and 41.97% of women were intemperate. But suppose we take a less stringest criterion and classify as intemperate only those called constant drinkers. After all, not everyone who drinks now and then, or even everyone who has an occasional spree, can be called a drunk. On that basis, the proportion of intemperate among men drops to 27.3% and among women to 13.5%.[42]

If one uses the same criterion, the proportion of intemperate fathers drops as well (see Figure 2.12 and Table A.22). Mothers, it should be noted, were not a problem, even to Hoyt, for he considered only 17.2% of them intemperate. However, he does assert that 44.59% of fathers were

---

[40]There is some fragmentary evidence that points to the better treatment of paupers in rural counties and in smaller poorhouses. An initial correlation shows a negative relation between county size and per capita expenses on relief. Also see the evidence in Katz, "New York's Poorhouses."

[41]Hoyt, "Causes of Pauperism," pp. 287–288.

[42]*Ibid.*, pp. 104–105.

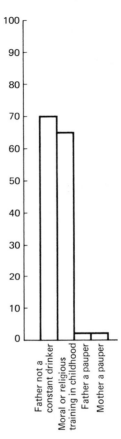

**Figure 2.12.** Selected family characteristics of inmates aged 18 and over in large poorhouses: New York State, 1874–1875 (average percentage for four poorhouses).

intemperate. It should be pointed out that this figure, which is less than half, certainly is not conclusive evidence by itself of the impact of heredity upon pauperism through drink. The figures for fathers, moreover, must be treated with caution because, as Hoyt himself observed, information about parental habits could not be gathered for most inmates. Nonetheless, using once again a less stringent definition of intemperance, the proportion of temperate fathers rises sharply. It was lowest, 49.6%, in Monroe County, rising to 73.1% in Albany, 77.6% in Oneida, and 79.8% in Erie County.

Even more devastating to Hoyt's assertion was the lack of connection between the drinking habits of paupers and those of their fathers. No significant difference existed between the proportion of temperate and intemperate fathers among temperate and intemperate paupers. The share of intemperate fathers among nondrinkers was 38.8%; among moderate drinkers, 37.6%; among periodic drinkers, 40.6%; and among constant drinkers it was, contrary to theory, lowest of all, 34.1%.

Nor do the data support Hoyt's argument about the widespread existence of idleness and "vicious indulgence." Only 22.4% of answers to the question, "Had this person habits of idleness?" were positive. Moreover, to the question, "Did this person receive moral and religious training in youth?" 73.4% of answers were positive. True, only 26.5% had "habits of thrift and saving," but one wonders if this was very much lower than it was among the entire working-class population. As a sidelight on ethnic stereotypes, the only ethnic variation in habits separated out the Germans, who had a slightly lower proportion of previously idle, 18.3%, and a substantially higher share who had been thrifty, 47.3%.

For only a small minority of inmates could information be gleaned about some of the nastier causes of dependence. For example, in 84.8% of cases in large poorhouses answers were blank to the question, "Impairment or degeneration of the bodily powers, or mental faculties from inebriation?" Among those who answered, only 28.3% of the replies were yes. Again, in the large poorhouses, of the 16% with answers to the question, "Is there proof of insanity, epilepsy, paralysis, special feebleness of mind or body, syphillis, or any other entailment of bodily or mental misfortune from parentage in this person's history?" the answer was positive in only 7.1% of the cases. Rather more answers, about 29%, were given to the question, "Is there mental or moral perversion, or morbid or debasing conditions of mind?" Only in 13.6% of instances was the answer here yes. Even these relatively low figures probably are too high for two reasons: First, some of the blanks may have been negative answers. Second, the people collecting the information were biased toward positive answers and, most likely, would have interpreted questionable replies as affirmative.

Questions about the moral and hereditary origins of dependence were left unanswered for almost all the insane, too. However, the few answers given reflected quite a different pattern: Of those for whom information was available, 69.2% allegedly had impaired or degenerate powers and faculties on account of inebriation; 19.3% had inherited some debilitating disease from parents; and 89.7% showed evidence of "mental or moral perversion, or morbid or debasing conditions of the mind." Although the evidence is fragmentary at best, it does point to at least a difference in appearance among the insane, a hint that the definition of mental illness and immorality overlapped.

Nor did pauperism itself, as Hoyt claimed in his report, frequently appear a hereditary condition (see Figure 2.12 and Table A.22). Hoyt argued that about 3.2% of the inmates were children of pauper fathers, and

10.8%, of pauper mothers. Those proportions by themselves do not sound alarming considering the enormous handicaps faced by children of extremely poor parents. They are, however, biased upward, for Hoyt included in his sample children who had entered poorhouses with their parents and the homeless children in Randall's Island Infant Asylum. (Indeed, of all inmates with pauper mothers, 54.3% were children of women in the same institutions.) If one looks, instead, only at adults age 18 or over, the proportions drop sharply. Within some of the small and medium-size poorhouses the share of inmates with pauper fathers was nil, and in the large poorhouses it was small: 1.1% in Monroe County, 2.8% in Albany, 3.8% in Oneida, and 1.2% in Erie. The figures for mothers were almost identical. For instance, in Erie County, 3.3% of male paupers and 1.5% of women had mothers who also had been paupers. Nor, as Hoyt implied, was pauperism almost invariably transmitted to their children by the current inmates of poorhouses. In both large and small poorhouses about 80% of the known living children of inmates were self-supporting. Clearly the hereditarian image of pauperism cannot be sustained by Hoyt's survey.[43]

It is probably true, as Hoyt claimed, that inmates were not as well educated as the rest of the population, though whether they were less educated than others of similar social background is not at all clear. However, they were not nearly as ignorant as Hoyt implied when he called them "generally uneducated." Although only between about 50% and 60% had received a "fair schooling," within each age group between 6 and 7 out of 10 were literate. For the most part, men were a few percentage points more literate than women.[44]

None of this should imply, however, that most of the inmates surveyed by Hoyt could hope to leave the poorhouse or to work. In most poorhouses from 80% to over 90% of the inmates examined were considered permanently dependent. This is not to say, recall, that 80% or 90% of all poorhouse inmates were permanently dependent, since the group surveyed by Hoyt was chosen precisely because it consisted of paupers who were not "transient."

Given the evidence already presented, it is clear that Hoyt's data do not sustain his second general conclusion: "The degraded, vicious, and idle, who, when in good health, are always on the verge of pauperism, and who, at the approach of old age and illness, inevitably become paupers, are continually rearing a progeny who, both by hereditary tendencies and the

---

[43]*Ibid.*, pp. 107–108.

[44]*Ibid.*, p. 104.

associations of early life, are likely to follow in the footsteps of their parents."[45]

If people usually lived on the edge of pauperism, the fault rested mainly in an economic system that paid unskilled labor poorly, employed it irregularly, and offered no form of security for old age or sickness. Paupers, it is no surprise, originated by and large in the most vulnerable sections of the working class.

Most paupers had lived their entire lives within the working class: Of the men, 41% in the larger poorhouses and 27% in the smaller had been laborers, proportions far higher than in the entire population (see Table A.23). Of the former 9.7% and of the latter 18.6% had been employed in agriculture, usually as farmers. Only 1.8% and 2.3%, respectively, had occupations that could be classed as white collar. In 14.8% and 25.4% of the two types of poorhouses, respectively, the occupations of men were unknown. Even more women, 40.5% in the large and 71.8% in the small poorhouses, listed no occupation. In the former 35.4% and in the latter 13.0% had been domestics. A significant proportion, 21.6% in the large compared with 5.4% in the small almshouses, had worked in textiles and apparel.

A substantial share of inmates had the same occupations as their fathers: Of laborers' fathers 42.2% had themselves been laborers, 22.3% were in agriculture, the occupations of 22.5% were unknown, and the other 13% were in miscellaneous trades (see Table A.23). In a parallel way, 59.2% of the inmates who had worked in agriculture had fathers employed in agriculture, too. Family background, of course, varied with location. Inmates in the larger urban poorhouses more often came from working-class and laboring backgrounds, and those in the smaller poorhouses, from agriculture. There is, thus, no evidence that any more than a handful of inmates ever had the economic resources necessary to live very far away from "the verge of pauperism."

Hoyt believed that the welfare system itself had played a key role in the perpetuation of pauperism. "It appeared," he wrote, "that large numbers of those examined had been trained and educated for the poor-house by out-door relief administered by law or by private charity." It is impossible to know on what evidence Hoyt based this claim. The examination asked, "What was the first mode of aid?" and "If first aided outside of institutions, how long was this continued?" But these questions almost always were left blank. No conclusions about outdoor relief can be drawn directly from them. However, some evidence on the question can be teased out by

---

[45] *Ibid.*, p. 288.

comparing the aggregate figures for the number of years dependent, the total time in poorhouses, and the total time in the poorhouse where examined. If outdoor relief had been an important source of aid, then the number of years dependent should exceed the time spent in poorhouses.[46]

The number of years dependent could not be calculated reliably for the large poorhouses. For the small and medium-size ones, however, it was quite close to total time in poorhouses and total time in the poorhouse where examined (see Table A.24). For example, 17.1% of men had been dependent 6–9 years; 19.4% had been in poorhouses for the same length of time; and 19.9% had spent that span of years in the poorhouses where they were examined. Clearly few could have been long-term recipients of outdoor relief. Most had spent the entire span of their dependent years in the same poorhouse.

Because of their exclusion from the labor market, women became dependent much earlier than men, especially when their husbands died. Thus in large poorhouses nearly twice as many 60-year-old women, about 39%, had been dependent for 10 or more years as had men, about 20%. Indeed, 41.7% of women had been dependent 10 or more years, but only 27.6% had been in poorhouses that long. Women were more likely to receive outside aid, especially when they had children. In many cases the cause of their dependency was not the aid itself but their increasing age. As widows they probably had received some assistance when they had children at home or when they could take care of themselves. When their children left home or when they became sick and infirm, they entered poorhouses.[47]

The experiences of women and men in poorhouses differed notably: First, women entered poorhouses earlier than men (see Figure 2.13 and Table A.25). The women aged 60 or more usually had been in poorhouses much longer than men of the same age. For example, in Monroe County 18.3% of the men and 25% of the women over 60 had been in the poorhouse 6–10 years. In Erie County, 5.4% of the men and 22.6% of the women over 60 had been in the poorhouse 10 years or more. Women, quite obviously, became dependent earlier than men, the result, as already noted, of the earlier death of men and the problems of widows.

Among the insane, by contrast, little difference in age separated the age at which men and women became insane. Of those dependent 10 or more

---

[46]Ibid.

[47]Many of the first major charitable organizations in nineteenth-century cities were Ladies Benevolent Societies.

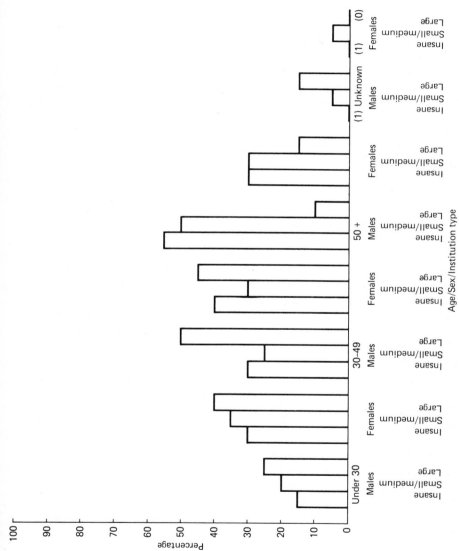

**Figure 2.13.** Age of entrance to New York poorhouses and insane asylums by sex, 1874–1875.

years, 23.5% of the men and 29.1% of the women had become dependent in their 20s, and 27.5% and 31.5%, in their 30s. Thus inmates entered poorhouses at a later age than they entered insane asylums. For example, consider the proportion entering at the age of 60 or over. Among men, it was 38.1% in large poorhouses and 39.0% in smaller ones; among women, 16.8% in the larger and 17.2% in the smaller. For the insane, the same proportions were 2.6% and .6% for men and women, respectively. Roughly one-quarter of women inmates entered poorhouses in their 20s and another quarter in their 30s, and between 25% and 30% entered between the ages of 40 and 59. However, over half of the women entered insane asylums in their 20s and 30s, and about another fifth, in their 40s. In Erie County's insane asylum, 37% of the women had entered in their 20s.

Thus it is clear that differences existed between the insane and other paupers. Although the groups shared similar social and ethnic backgrounds, the onset of their dependency occurred at different ages. It happened earliest to the insane, both men and women, next to women paupers, and, latest of all, to the men who entered poorhouses.

Among poorhouse inmates more than 30 years old, there were relatively few short-term residents. However, the group with the lowest proportion of short-term inmates was, not surprisingly, the insane. For instance, among men in their 40s, the proportion who had been inmates between 1 and 3 months was 17.9% in large poorhouses, 17.1% in smaller ones, and 2% in insane asylums. Among the more elderly, insane males had been resident longest. Of the 50–59-year-olds, 72.6% of the insane men had been inmates 5 or more years, as had 81.8% of the insane males age 60 or more. For women, the same proportions were markedly lower, 52.2% and 47.3%, respectively. The proportions for paupers were quite close to the ones for the female insane. Perhaps insane men proved especially troublesome or inconvenient. At any rate, they were institutionalized sooner.

Thus the dynamics of institutionalization were the opposite for the sane and insane poor of each sex. Poor men were able to support themselves until relatively late in their lives, and, hence, avoided the poorhouse longer than did women. Women, by and large, were more successful in avoiding the poorhouse altogether than were men. But those who did enter became dependent at an earlier age largely because of their vulnerability and lack of employment opportunity. Among the insane poor, however, men unable to support themselves found little assistance outside institutions and were incarcerated earlier than were women. Overall, though, more women than men ended up in insane asylums.

If children were more willing to care for their aged mothers than for their fathers, if women entered poorhouses when they lacked children to care for them, then the married and widowed women in poorhouses should have had fewer living children than did the men. To some extent this was so (see Figure 2.14 and Table A.26). For example, in the small and medium-size poorhouses 46% of married women, compared with 29% of married men, had no living children.

What stands out for both men and women in poorhouses, however, is their relative lack of children. Among widowed paupers, 75.6% of the men and 78.0% of the women in large poorhouses had either no living children or only one. In the smaller poorhouses the same figures were 76.3% and 80.3%, respectively. Even more striking was the situation among the insane: 82.9% of the widowed men and 96.5% of the widowed women had no living children or only one. Clearly these are numbers vastly lower than those in the population of widowed persons taken as a whole in New York State.[48]

Equally striking, a very high proportion of paupers never had married. The proportion of single men in the large poorhouses was 53.0%, 41.0%, and 25.3% among the 40–49, 50–59, and over-60-year-old cohorts, respectively. For women of the same ages, the proportions unmarried were 50.9%, 30.8%, and 18.3%, respectively—proportions much higher, of course, than those in the entire population.[49]

Therefore, one major reason why people entered poorhouses was that they lacked a family to provide them with a home. It was not, as Hoyt argued, because these poor people had been especially spendthrift, idle, and debauched that they lacked any resources when old age or the death of a working spouse pushed them over the "verge of pauperism." Rather, they had been unlucky enough to lack grown children.

Of course, one might speculate that the reasons for some people not marrying and the disabilities that brought them to the poorhouse were, in fact, the same. There is no way to tell if unmarried paupers were especially

---

[48]In Buffalo in 1900 there were 784 children age 0–5 for every 1000 married women between the ages of 23 and 25. Families with children age 15–19 had, on the average, six or seven children. Figures for the mid-1870s would be higher since fertility was declining. Michael B. Katz and Mark J. Stern, "Fertility, Class, and Industrial Capitalism: Erie County, New York, 1855–1915," *American Quarterly* 33 (1981): 89, 91.

[49]In Erie County in 1880 the proportion of single men among 40–44-and 55–59-year-old males was 11.6% and 3.4%, respectively. Among women the same proportions were 9.9% and 3.8%, respectively. These figures are derived from a sample of the 1880 manuscript census of Erie County.

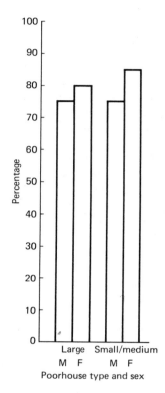

**Figure 2.14.** Proportion of inmates aged 18 and over with 0–1 living children by poorhouse type and sex: New York State, 1874–1875.

unappealing or unattractive, especially in their youth and early adulthood. However, no special association between any sort of disability and marital status emerges from Hoyt's questionnaires, and, as the next part will show, there were relatively few cases of overlapping disabilities among New York's institutionalized population in the late nineteenth century. More important, the major point is that the absence of a spouse or children—for whatever reason—deprived working class people of the key support they required in times of unemployment, sickness, or old age.

The comments occasionally appended to the examination schedules reinforce the image of poorhouse inmates as pathetic. Comments were made on only a minority of cases, with no apparent system. By no means do they represent a reliable sample of the population. Rather, they appear to have been chosen to provide Hoyt with evidence to show the moral causes of pauperism or because particular cases were especially interesting or colorful. "This man lived alone for 12 years. He resembles Rip Van Winkle." "This man has a huge head and is almost totally devoid of intelligence." "Though deaf–dumb–blind, and an idiot, this woman had a son."

Mostly the cases described have three themes. The first was moral failing: "This woman is a bold, bad one, is said to have led a disreputable life. She is brazen." "This woman is dissolute. She is undoubtedly of a respectable family, though now badly drunken." "This woman left her husband at age 17 and led a disreputable life. She is dying of venereal disease." The second was a physical or mental illness: "This man became helpless and dependent from the loss of the most important natural faculties." "Blind and consequently helpless." "This woman came here due to spells of fever. She is kept under restraint, but now has a tumor in her side." The third was abandonment: wives abandoned by husbands, children abandoned by parents, parents abandoned in old age by children. "Her first husband deserted her, returned and then deserted her again. This caused her to lose her sanity." "This man's wife ran off with another man over 6 years ago. He will end his days here." "His son brought him to America and then deserted him. He is a broken down drunkard." Even through the filter of Hoyt's selection the helplessness and pathos of New York's paupers cannot be missed.

Despite its reinforcement of the personal interpretation of poverty, Hoyt's report had some redeeming positive aspects.[50] He pointed forcefully to the defective poorhouse management that mingled young and old, sane and insane, sick and well, and he highlighted the lack of attention to health, the failure to care for wounds and illness, and the lack of work for inmates within the poorhouses. No one could quarrel with his attempts to get the children out of the poorhouses or to obtain better care for the paupers who remained. For his role in these achievements, he should receive his full measure of credit.

But it cannot be doubted that he found among the paupers what he expected. He structured his inquiry and interpreted his data in a way that reinforced the conclusions with which he began. In this way his report had an unfortunate influence. It provided an allegedly objective, even scientific, confirmation of what everyone believed: Pauperism was the result of individual behavior. Often inherited, pauperism was the offspring of bad drink and bad habits. Thus, by definition, paupers were immoral. It is striking that nowhere in his report of more than 300 pages did Hoyt mention the severe economic depression that continued even as he wrote.

---

[50]For some good insights into what I call one personal interpretation of poverty, see Piven and Cloward, *Regulating the Poor*, p. 149.

## TABLE 30.

STATE OF NEW YORK—OFFICE OF STATE BOARD OF CHARITIES, }
ALBANY, *September* 20, 1875.

*To keepers and other proper officers of poor-houses and alms-houses:*

The following instructions are hereby furnished to keepers and other proper officers of poor-houses and alms-houses for the record of inmates, as provided by Act Chapter 140 of the Laws of 1875:

### I. GENERAL INSTRUCTIONS.

The book for the record of inmates of poor-houses and alms-houses herewith provided, is not to be substituted for the general register now kept in these institutions, but is to be maintained in addition to such register. It is required of superintendents and overseers of the poor, to give such information as practicable regarding each person brought or sent by them to poor-houses or alms-houses, and such information is be to recorded by the keeper or other proper officer. No record of Statepaupers or of tramps need be kept in this book, as the registration of these classes is otherwise provided for. The book should be carefully preserved in the institution, and copies of the record made and forwarded to this office on the first day of each month, in the manner hereinafter directed.

### II. THE RECORD.

The names of the paupers in the institution October 1, 1875, should be first entered in the book and numbered in the order in which they were admitted. The entries thereafter should be made at the time the person is received in the institution. The name of each person should also be alphabetically entered in the index with the record number. The blanks should be filled out in their order. Readmissions and discharges should be entered in the left-hand margin. In case of death, the cause to which it is attributed should be stated. The sample sheet herewith furnished, will assist keepers in their labors, and its careful study is earnestly requested. In order to secure uniformity in the record, throughout the State, special attention is called to the following questions, viz.:

1. *Birth-place.*— If the person or ancestors or other relatives were born in poor-houses or alms-houses, or in other public institutions, the fact should be stated.

2. *Education.*— The answers to this inquiry should be as follows, in accordance with the facts in each case.

    Unable to read or write.
    Can read only.
    Can read and write.
    Received a common-school education.
    Received an academic education.
    Received a collegiate education.

If the person be blind, a deaf-mute or a teachable idiot, educated in institutions for these classes, the fact should be stated.

3. *Existing cause of dependence.*— Under this heading the immediate cause of dependence, or in other words, *the condition of the person at the time of admission,* should be stated. The following are enumerated as the most probable causes of dependence, and it is desired that the classification here given, as far as practicable, be adhered to:

    Homeless childhood, illegitimate.
    Homeless childhood, abandoned.
    Homeless childhood, by death of father.
    Homeless childhood by death of mother.
    Homeless childhood, by death of both parents.
    Homeless childhood, by pauperism of parents.

*Plate 7. A copy of the Act of 1875 by which the New York State Legislature required poorhouses to keep records of their inmates.*

Homeless childhood, by imprisonment of parents.
Homeless, by abandonment of husband.
Homeless, by death of husband.
Old age and destitution.
Diseased (the name of the disease should be given).
Crippled (how and to what extent should be stated).
Deformed (the nature of the deformity should be noted).
Loss or impairment of any of the special senses, as blind, deaf and dumb, etc.
Insanity.
Idiocy.
Epilepsy.
Paralysis.
General feebleness of mind, as imbecility.
Impairment of the bodily powers, or mental faculties, from inebriation.
Vagrancy and idleness.

4. *Probable future of the person as respects recovery from the cause of dependence.* — The following should be noted under his question, as, in the opinion of the keeper, the condition of the person may seem to warrant:

Permanently dependent.
Will probably recover from dependence.
May recover under certain conditions, which should be stated.
Future doubtful.

### III. SPECIAL INQUIRIES.

There are many special matters in the keeping of the record upon which it is desirable to collect and record all the information possible. Among these may be stated the following:

1. *Entailment of disease, or bodily or mental misfortune from parentage.* — In case the person admitted is suffering from insanity, epilepsy, paralysis, special feebleness of mind or body, etc., the condition of the ancestors, and other relatives, should be carefully inquired into, and if it is learned that any of these, as grandparents, parents, brothers, sisters, uncles, aunts or other relatives were thus diseased, the facts should be stated in the column for remarks, with full particulars. The condition of the offspring of consanguineous marriages should also be noted.

2. *Relations of pauperism to crime* — Where there is reason to believe that the person admitted has been in jails, work-houses, penitentiaries or State prisons, the matter should be inquired into and the facts stated.

3. *Moral character.* — The moral character of the person, if an adult and of proper intellect, , should also be inquired into. If there is mental or moral perversion, or morbid and debasing conditions of mind, the fact should be stated and the causes to which attributed.

4. *Pecuniary ability of ancestors and family relatives.* — The pecuniary ability of ancestors and family relatives should be learned as far as practicable, and noted.

[Any other information of importance that may be obtaind regarding individual cases, should also be recorded.]

### IV. COPIES OF THE RECORD.

Copies of the record as provided for by the act, should be made on the blanks herewith forwarded. Great care should be exercised in making these copies. No copies will be required in case of readmissions. The copies should be forwarded to this office on the first day of each month in the addressed envelopes herewith furnished. In case the postage does not exceed thirty cents, the package may be sent by mail in the light envelope, otherwise, by express in the heavy envelope. Requisitions for books, blanks or other matter for use under the act, should be timely made to this office.

By direction of the Board.

CHAS. S. HOYT, *Secretary.*

*Plate 7* (continued)

## THE ACT OF 1875 AND THE CREATION OF POORHOUSE RECORDS

Hoyt's examination of poorhouses showed how poorly almshouse records were kept. "The failure heretofore to keep and preserve proper records in the poor-houses and alms-houses of the State," reported John L. Pruyn, president of the New York State Board of Charities in 1876, "has . . . been one of the greatest defects in the administration of their affairs." Although most institutions kept a "general register of the inmates for business purposes," none had preserved any records of their "personal or family history before becoming dependent, or of any changes" that occurred "in their condition after admission." The board had been aware of the lack of adequate records for some time, but it was the study of the causes of pauperism that most forcefully "revealed their defects."[51]

The inquiry discovered that poorhouse administrators had "acquired a large amount of valuable information" about "those under their care" and, more generally, about dependency within their local areas. But they had made no record of their knowledge, "and it was, therefore, of no value to the public." Poorhouse keepers realized the importance of the data that they could provide and were willing to record it "but in the absence of proper statutory directions were at a loss how best to accomplish the object." The problem. Pruyn believed, was solved by an act of 1875 requiring poorhouse administrators to record data on inmates on a standard form.[52]

In order to design a form, the board sponsored a conference "with a committee of superintendents of the poor appointed by the State convention of superintendents, and their views were obtained." The "proper officers" then were given "substantially bound books," accompanied by "full instructions." The records were to be preserved and copies made and forwarded to the board on the last day of each month.[53]

The board was eager "to secure uniformity and accuracy" in the records. For this reason, "personal conferences were had, as far as practicable, with the keepers of the poor-houses and alms-houses throughout the State, by members of the Board." Local officials generally showed "great interest" in the work and, despite the labor it required, "entered upon the work with earnestness and zeal." Indeed, Pruyn reflected, the timing of the new

---

[51] *Tenth Annual Report*, p. 14.

[52] *Ibid.*

[53] *Ibid.*, p. 15.

procedure was appropriate because most of the poorhouse administrators were "intelligent and capable officers, many of whom" had "the advantages of large experience."[54]

Hoyt administered the new record-keeping procedure, and his instructions to local poorhouse officials reflected his characteristic concern for administrative detail. What is particularly revealing is that Hoyt instructed local officials not to keep records of all their inmates. "No record of State paupers or of tramps need be kept in this book, as the registration of these classes is otherwise provided for." Although the advice sounds innocuous, it systematically skewed the image of poorhouses produced by the new records, for Hoyt gave no definition of "tramp." Although many tramps stopped at poorhouses to seek outdoor relief, many others sought shelter for a night, a few days, perhaps even a month or two in the winter. These short-term inmates composed a large fraction, in some cases a majority, of the actual population of poorhouses during each year. By excluding them from the official records, Hoyt fostered the creation of a partial demography of poorhouse populations. Paupers appeared helpless, sick, and often old, a permanently degraded and dependent class, if Hoyt was to be believed. The young, active men who needed food and shelter for short periods when they were out of work did not fit Hoyt's conception of paupers, and he therefore excluded them by definition from the records of poorhouse inmates that he compiled.[55]

Even with this limitation, the records gathered by the state board after 1875 are an exceptionally interesting historical source. Like Hoyt's survey of 1874–1875, they offer an opportunity to test prevailing ideas about the more permanent inmates of poorhouses against their actual demography. At the same time, they give a comprehensive view of the pauper population of the state during the last decades of the nineteenth century. Because they were compiled with unusual care at the time of admission, questions about previous experience and family background were filled out better than on Hoyt's survey. Thus, it is possible to draw some conclusions from the records about the connections between indoor and outdoor relief, recidivism within poorhouses, and family background.[56]

---

[54]*Ibid.*

[55]*Ibid.*, p. 91; see also Part I of this chapter.

[56]The counties and years in the sample are Allegany, 1880, 1885, 1890; Albany, 1874–1875, 1880, 1885, 1890; Erie, 1880, 1885, 1890, 1893; Greene, 1885–1891; Kingston (city), 1876, 1882; Lewis, 1875–1882, 1883–1889; Monroe 1875, 1880, 1887, 1890, 1894; Oswego, 1875, 1880, 1885, 1890–1894; Poughkeepsie (city), 1876–1883; Schoharie, 1884–1893; Saint Lawrence, 1876, 1880, 1885, 1890, 1895; and Wayne, 1876, 1880, 1885.

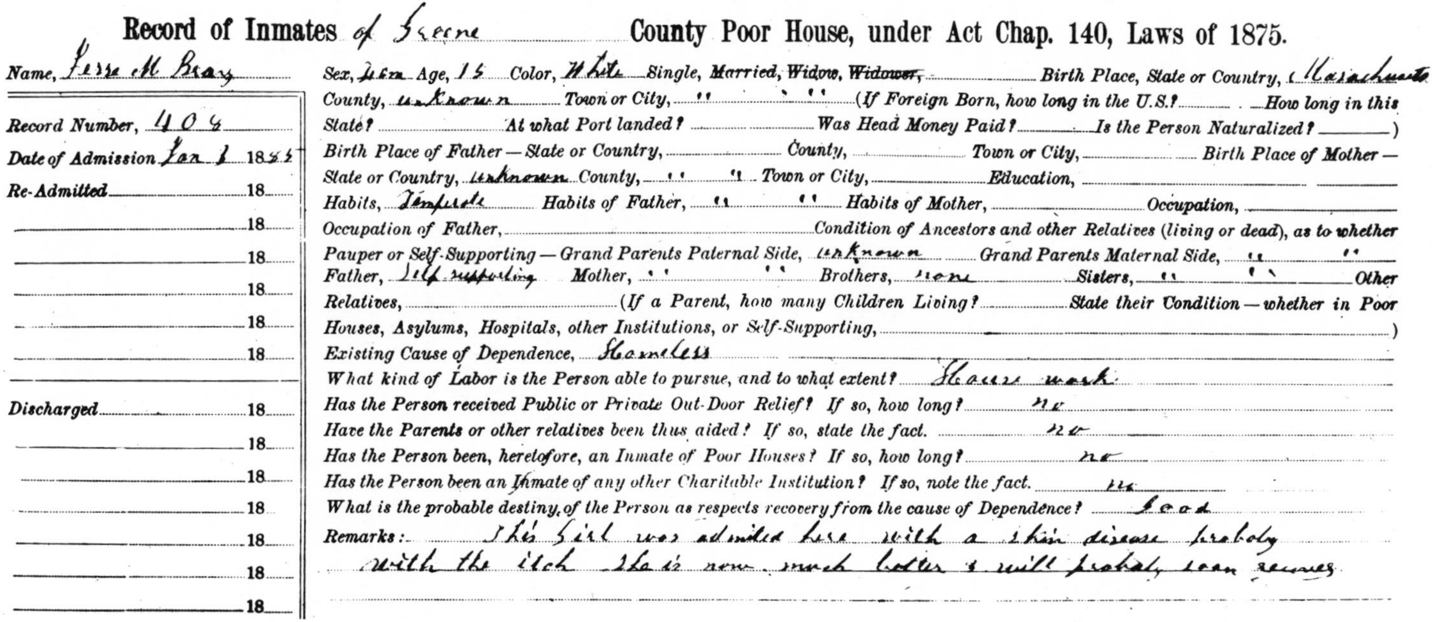

## Record of Inmates of *Keene*

**County Poor House, under Act Chap. 140, Laws of 1875.**

Name, *Lizzie M. Bray*

Sex, *Female* Age, *15* Color, *White* Single, Married, Widow, Widower, ————— Birth Place, State or Country, *Massachusetts*

County, *unknown* Town or City, *"* *"* *"* (If Foreign Born, how long in the U.S.? ————— How long in this

State? ————— At what Port landed? ————— Was Head Money Paid? ————— Is the Person Naturalized? ——— )

Birth Place of Father — State or Country, ————— County, ————— Town or City, ————— Birth Place of Mother —

State or Country, *unknown* County, *"* *"* Town or City, ————— 

Habits, *Temperate* Habits of Father, *"* *"* Habits of Mother, ————— Occupation,

Occupation of Father, ————— Condition of Ancestors and other Relatives (living or dead), as to whether

Pauper or Self-Supporting — Grand Parents Paternal Side, *unknown* Grand Parents Maternal Side, *"* *"*

Father, *self supporting* Mother, *" "* Brothers, *none* Sisters, *" "* Other

Relatives, ————— (If a Parent, how many Children Living? ————— State their Condition — whether in Poor

Houses, Asylums, Hospitals, other Institutions, or Self-Supporting, ————— )

Existing Cause of Dependence, *Harmless*

What kind of Labor is the Person able to pursue, and to what extent? *Harmless work*

Has the Person received Public or Private Out-Door Relief? If so, how long? *no*

Have the Parents or other relatives been thus aided? If so, state the fact. *no*

Has the Person been, heretofore, an Inmate of Poor Houses? If so, how long? *no*

Has the Person been an Inmate of any other Charitable Institution? If so, note the fact. *no*

What is the probable destiny of the Person as respects recovery from the cause of Dependence? *Good*

Remarks: *The girl was admitted here with a chair disease probably*
*with the itch. She is now much better & will probably soon recover*

Record Number, *409*

Date of Admission *Jan. 1 1855*

Re-Admitted ————— 18——

————— 18——

————— 18——

————— 18——

————— 18——

Discharged ————— 18——

————— 18——

————— 18——

————— 18——

————— 18——

*Plate 8. An example of the inmate records kept by New York poorhouses subsequent to the Act of 1875. (Courtesy of the New York State Archives.)*

## POORHOUSE DEMOGRAPHY

Poorhouses had more male than female inmates, and sex ratios were more unbalanced in the large than in the small and medium-size ones. In the larger poorhouses between 30% and 33% of inmates were women, and in the smaller ones, 40–45%. No significant shifts in these proportions took place between 1875 and 1894. In both types of poorhouses many of the inmates were elderly. In the larger ones, the share of the elderly was highest, 52%, between 1875 and 1879. It then dropped to between 37% and 40%. There were no trends in the smaller poorhouses, where between 30% and 33% of the women were over the age of 50 and 20–25% over 60. The proportion of elderly men was about the same in large poorhouses and was larger in small and medium-size ones. Even before the passage of the Children's Act of 1875, the State Board of Charities had begun to encourage poorhouse officials to send young children either to families or to special institutions. Thus, the act ordering the removal of children between the ages of 2 and 16 continued a process that already had begun. However, the process was more complete in the large than in the small and medium-size poorhouses (see Figure 2.15 and Table A.27).[57]

A substantial share of paupers had been born in New York State. The proportion, not surprisingly, was higher in the small and medium-size poorhouses, which were located in areas that had fewer immigrants. Throughout the last 2 decades of the nineteenth century between about 30% and 33% of the men in large poorhouses were native New Yorkers; in the small and medium-size ones the figure rose from about half to over 70% in the mid-1890s. Most inmates, wherever they were born, had parents born outside of the United States (see Figure 2.16 and Table A.28). In large poorhouses only around 10% of male inmates' fathers had been born in the United States, as had between 14% and 17% in smaller ones. The proportion of native fathers among women in larger poorhouses also was about 10%, and in smaller ones, 16% to 24% throughout the period. (It should be pointed out that in over 90% of cases birthplaces of fathers and mothers were the same.) The proportion of those of Irish background remained substantial in large poorhouses, but relatively few inmates were the native-born children of German immigrants. Although poorhouse inmates overwhelmingly were immigrants or their children, they were not recent arrivals: Of the foreign-born inmates, both men and women, 73% had lived in the United States for at least 10 years and only 8% of the men and 6% of the women had been in the United States for 1 year or less.

---

[57]For figures, see tables in *Tenth Annual Report.*

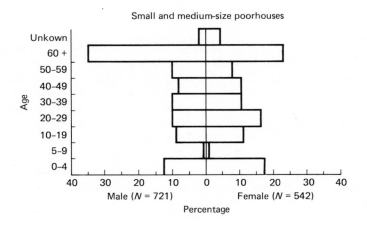

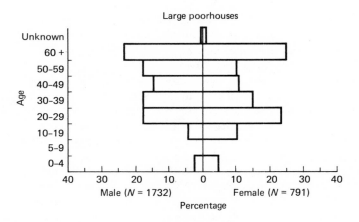

**Figure 2.15.** Age and sex by poorhouse type: New York State, 1878–1894.

Clearly, complaints that pauperism was the result of European countries dumping their poor and disabled on American shores ring hollow (see Figure 2.17 and Table A.29).

Throughout the period a large share of inmates were unmarried. The only difference between poorhouses of different sizes was the larger proportion of single women in the smaller ones. (Perhaps widows in smaller or more rural areas more often had children or kin who could care for them.) In all, about half of the adult men and 40% of the women were single, and many of the elderly had been widowed: 52% of men in their

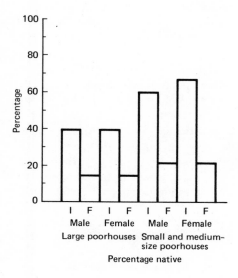

**Figure 2.16.** Percentage native born among inmates of poorhouses and their fathers: New York State, 1878–1894. (I = inmate; F = father.)

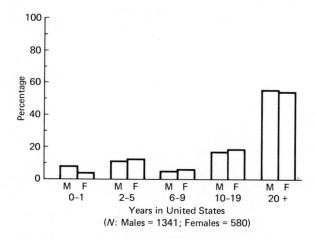

**Figure 2.17.** Time in United States by foreign-born inmates of poorhouses: New York State, 1875–1894.

60s and 70% of women. Adding the proportion single to the proportion widowed, it is clear that the overwhelming share of elderly people in poorhouses—74% of men and 83% of women—lacked a spouse. Thus, it is important to ask if they had children who might have cared for them (see Figure 2.18 and Table A.30).

Apparently, a great many did not. Here an ambiguity in the records makes it difficult to determine whether people lacked children. The question read, "If a parent, how many children living?" In many cases the answer was left blank. This probably indicated no living children, but it also may have reflected a failure to ask the question or to receive an answer. Assuming that most blank answers among married people reflected a lack of children, 59% of the men and 69% of the women had either no living children or only one. Among men the proportion with none or one living children was lowest among those over 60, 57%, whereas among women of the same age it was highest, 72%. Elderly people, all of this points to, only entered poorhouses when they lacked a spouse or children who could care for them (see Figure 2.19 and Table A.31).

The question, however, remains: Why did poorhouses have more men than women? One answer may be that children were more willing to take in their widowed mothers than their fathers. Indeed, in Hamilton, Ontario (where I have studied family arrangements closely), elderly women were much more likely to live with their kin than were elderly men, who when

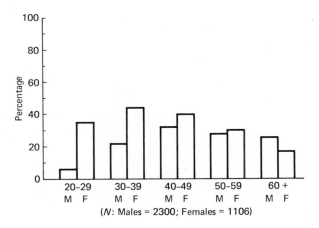

**Figure 2.18.** Proportion of currently married inmates by age and sex: New York State poorhouses, 1875–1894.

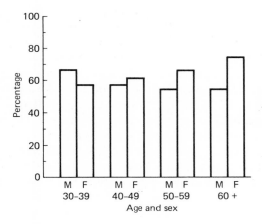

**Figure 2.19.** Proportions of married inmates with 0–1 living children: New York State poorhouses, 1875–1894.

widowed more often lived as boarders. Children might have been more ready to provide a home for their mothers for either instrumental or sentimental reasons, or some combination of the two. Elderly women, after all, could be useful around the house and helpful with children. Perhaps, too, bonds between mothers and children were stronger than those between fathers and children. One thinks, for instance, of the relation between sons and mothers in D. H. Lawrence's evocation of life in a mining town in *Sons and Lovers*. The other reason why women were less often in poorhouses is that they more often received outdoor relief. Widows with children, after all, were the clearest examples of the worthy poor. Indeed, they often were the objects of much nineteenth-century philanthropy. For example, in late nineteenth-century Buffalo, New York, several charitable organizations aided women, but not one was devoted solely to the relief of destitute men.[58]

In her study of almshouse women in 1892 Mary Roberts Smith, an assistant professor of social science at Stanford University, argued that the greater number of men in poorhouses reflected different popular responses to dependence among men and women. Although women were less often in poorhouses, they were, Roberts argued, more often dependent. "Domestic occupations," she observed, "unfit women for self support." The lives of uneducated, married women were "consumed" with "the most exhausting of duties—child bearing," which often resulted in "lack of ambition, and in a round of small routine duties and petty details

---

[58]Katz, Doucet, and Stern, *Early Industrial Capitalism*, chap. 8; Buffalo, New York, Charity Organization Society, *Twenty-Third Annual Report* (Buffalo, 1900), p. 29.

of the most unsystematic sort." All their "cleverness and ambition" were "worn away in domestic processes." Widowhood, thus, left them with "domestic service" as their only "resource, and even for that" their "home life" had "unfitted" them. The almshouse women Roberts interviewed "frankly" regarded "marriage as a means of escape from self-dependence, and many of them" grieved for "dead husbands and children chiefly because support" was "no longer forthcoming." Although more often dependent than men, women less often ended their lives in poorhouses because "the world recognizes the inevitable dependence of women by considering it a most disgraceful thing for relatives or children to allow an old woman to go to the almshouse." By contrast, "men are supposed to have had their chance to lay up money, and if they have not done so they must take the consequences. This one-sided filial obligation keeps large numbers of women out of the almshouse who are wholly dependent."[59]

A fairly low proportion of poorhouse inmates had received outdoor relief: 11% of the men and 24% of the women. The proportion, though, varied by sex, type of poorhouse, and time period. The smallest proportion who had received outdoor relief were men in large poorhouses: 15% in 1875–1879 and 2% in 1890–1894. Next came men in the small and medium-size poorhouses, among whom previous recipients of outdoor relief declined from 26% to 7%. The proportions among women were much higher. They declined from 47% to 33% in large poorhouses and from 66% to 33% in small and medium-size ones. There are two possible explanations (not mutually exclusive) for the decline in the proportion over time. First, the earlier group included people who had just lived through the depression of the early and mid-1870s; the other groups entered poorhouses in more prosperous times (the sample stops before the depression of the 1890s). Second, an attack on outdoor relief began in the late 1870s. Some cities abolished outdoor relief, and others reduced it drastically. Thus those inmates who entered prior to 1879 may have been able to obtain outdoor relief a good deal more easily than ones who entered later.

In the large poorhouses 52% of the men in 1875–1879 and 27% in 1890–1894 had been inmates of poorhouses before, compared with 33% of men in the small and medium-size poorhouses at the start of the period and 4% at it close. Among women in large poorhouses the proportions were 31% and 17%, respectively, at the two points in time; the share among women in smaller poorhouses was similar. The nativity group most likely to have been in poorhouses before was the Irish: Of the Irish born, 19% of men

[59]Smith, *Almshouse Women*, p. 26.

and 21% of women had previously been inmates of poorhouses. Some overlap existed between people who had previously been inmates and those who had received outdoor relief (see Figure 2.20 and Table A.32). Of the men who had been inmates before, 30% also had received outdoor relief, compared with 7% of those who had not spent time in poorhouses. Among women the same proportions were 45% and 17%, respectively. Again, the combination of the depression of the 1870s with more lenient relief practices probably produced the higher figures for the earlier years. However, throughout the period men in need of aid more often were forced to use poorhouses, either because local officials were less willing to give them outdoor relief or because they could not find a home with kin (see Table A.33).

Paupers by and large were not illiterate. Only 7% of men and 6% of women had an "academic" or "good" education, but only 4% of men and 10% of women could "read only" and 8% of men and 12% of women had received a "poor" education. The majority of both sexes had a "common" or "ordinary" education. What these terms mean is far from clear other than that the poorhouse inmates, overwhelmingly, were a literate group, and many of them, furthermore, had worked. Fewer than half of the men (46%) had been laborers. The rest were scattered through a variety of occupations, of which the next largest share, 7%, were in agriculture. A very sizable proportion of the women, 61%, were known to have been domestics. Only 1% of the entire group had been employed in white-collar occupations (see Table A.34). The proportion of laborers, 65%, was

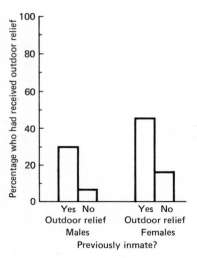

**Figure 2.20.** Proportion of inmates who had received outdoor relief by former residence in poorhouse: New York State poorhouses, 1875–1894.

highest among the Irish, next highest, 49%, among the Germans, and lowest, 35%, among the native born. The proportion of women who had been domestics also was highest, 81%, among the Irish. These, of course, are the same occupational biases found in the entire population.

Most paupers came from working-class families; 39% of the fathers of men and 41% of those of women were laborers. Only about 1% were white-collar. However, a much higher proportion of fathers than in-mates—about 20%—had agricultural occupations, and among poorhouse inmates whose fathers had agricultural occupations, only 15% had themselves worked in agriculture, 28% were laborers, and 28% were domestics. Thus many poorhouse inmates appear to have been men and women caught in the transition from agriculture to industry. Among the inmates whose fathers were laborers, 42% were laborers and 28% were domestics. Because these figures include both men and women, they mean that almost all the sons of laborers were themselves laborers (see Table A.35).

Although from working-class backgrounds, most inmates did not come from pauper families. If Hoyt had hoped that the new system of record keeping would offer sound support for his theories about the heredita-bility of pauperism, he was disappointed. Again, the presence of blanks on the record form makes the interpretation of answers to questions about relatives and siblings difficult. Among those who responded to questions about relatives, 66 had pauper fathers and 2671 had fathers who were self-supporting; 83 had pauper brothers and 1961 had brothers who were self-supporting; the size of the two groups among paternal grandparents was 20 and 2187, respectively. Of all relatives, only 3% were known to be paupers (see Table A.36).

The reasons why people were in poorhouses also were difficult to interpret since they were stated vaguely. Of the men, about two-thirds listed some form of illness, compared with 52% of the women. About 10% of the men and 16% of the women were homeless or deserted; about 10% and 12%, respectively, cited old age; and 9% and 13%, insanity. These, of course, are not mutually exclusive categories. What they amount to is a picture of a weak, sickly population. That image is reinforced by the observations of superintendents that 70% of the men and 60% of the women were unable to pursue any work and 20% of the men and 28% of the women could do only "light work." Still, and it seems a contradiction, 48% of the men and 42% of the women were expected "probably" to recover, according to those who filled out the records.

Had pauperism been brought on by excessive drinking, as most commentators at the time believed? Fewer than half the men, 45%, were listed as intemperate, even by the stringent standards of the period. The proportion of intemperate women, 21%, was substantially lower. Intemperance, by and large, had not been inherited, as many believed, for the proportion of intemperate fathers among men was much lower, 21%, although about the same, 23%, among women. A striking 91% of temperate sons, compared with 57% of intemperate sons, had temperate fathers; among daughters the corresponding figures were 83% and 57%, respectively. Clearly, although associations existed, the connection between intemperance in parents and children was far from universal (see Table A.37). Nor was there very much association between intemperance and outdoor relief. The proportion of intemperate men among those inmates who had received outdoor relief was 48% and among those who had not, 47% (see Figure 2.21 and Table A.38).

Three aspects of the experience of poorhouse inmates can be better understood through multivariate analysis: prior receipt of outdoor relief, previous residence in a poorhouse, and chances of recovery. In the analyses that follow I will refer to the probability that people with certain characteristics had received outdoor relief, lived in poorhouses, or were likely to remain permanently dependent. The probability figures, stated as proportions, are approximations of the likelihood of an outcome with other factors held constant. Although they are not exact (indeed, because all factors are never really constant, precision is not possible), the figures point to the general range of the probability and should be interpreted in that way.[60]

First consider the analysis of prospects for recovery. In all, 38% of both men and women were not expected to recover. Age had a direct impact. As might be expected, the youngest group were more likely (72%) to recover, and the elderly were least likely (17%). Among women the likelihood of permanent dependence increased in their 50s to 63%, and for the group age 60 and over reached 81%. Birthplace, however, had no independent influence whatever among either men or women. Marital status, likewise, made no difference among men, although married women were very slightly more likely to recover. Those men who had received outdoor relief and who were intemperate were the least likely (47%) to recover. But by itself intemperance did not affect chances of recovery, for the odds of permanent dependence among intemperate men who had not received outdoor relief were 34%. Among women the two factors had no impact. Nor did the size category of the poorhouse have any impact upon either men or women.

---

[60]For a complete discussion of the MCA results and the tables, see Working Paper No. 5, Michael B. Katz and Associates, Appendix to Final Report NIMH Grant No. RO1MH32520.

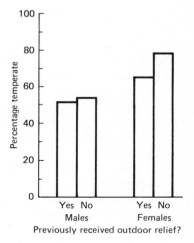

**Figure 2.21.** Proportion of inmates who were temperate by former receipt of outdoor relief: New York State poorhouses, 1875–1894.

Thus, the chances of permanent dependence were primarily a function of age. Prior to old age they probably reflected physical or mental debility. Nonetheles, there was a small group of intemperate men who had lived for some time on welfare.

There was little difference in the proportions of men and women who had been in poorhouses before: 11% and 13%, respectively. Those men and women under the age of 40 were a bit less likely to have been inmates before, and among men only the native born were a bit less likely than others to have been in poorhouses before. Among women, to the contrary, the natives of native parentage were the most likely (21%) to have been in poorhouses previously. Marital status, however, made no difference among either men or women. Men who had received outdoor relief were the most likely to be in poorhouses. Drinking habits, however, had no impact. The probability among the temperate who had received outdoor relief was 33%, compared with 9% among the temperate who had not received outdoor relief. Among women the probability was highest (44%) among the temperate who had received outdoor relief. Similarly, among those who had not received outdoor relief, the temperate were more likely—24% compared with 6%—than the intemperate to have been poorhouse inmates. In the small and medium-size poorhouses the chances that a man had been an inmate before were nil; in the larger ones, 13%. Among women poorhouse type made little difference.

Thus, once again there appears to have been a class that lived continually at the edge of destitution: within rural areas, women, and within larger areas, both men and women, who alternated between outdoor relief and sometime residence in a poorhouse. What is striking about them is that neither age nor drinking habits appeared to define their existence. They were not by and large drunks, as contemporaries would have had one believe; nor were they only the elderly; and the precise factors that made them particularly vulnerable remain elusive.

To some extent an examination of outdoor relief highlights the people who lived at the margin of subsistence. Among women age was a more important factor than it was among men. Women under 30 years old were least likely to have received outdoor relief. After that, not much difference separated age groups. The men most likely to have received outdoor relief (15%) were the native-born children of natives. The likelihood for the Irish was 11% and the Germans 8%. Among women the German-born children of Germans were the least likely to have received outdoor relief; little difference existed among the other nativity groups. Sex and marital status also affected the probability that a poorhouse inmate had received outdoor relief. The probability for a single male was lowest, 11%, for a single woman next lowest, 17%, for a married male, 20%, and for a married woman, 28%. By contrast, habits had little influence. As we should expect by now, those who had been inmates of poorhouses before also were most likely to have received outdoor relief. But there were no differences between the temperate and intemperate.

Real differences, however, existed among inmates in different types of poorhouses. The probability of having received outdoor relief was much higher among the inmates of the small and medium-size poorhouses: for men, 32%, compared with 6% in the larger ones, and for women, 41%, compared with 15%.

Poorhouse size stands as a rough surrogate for urbanism. Those inmates who lived in rural areas or towns were much more likely to have received outdoor relief. Women everywhere, especially those who were married, were more likely than men to receive outdoor relief, but both more often were relieved outside poorhouses in towns and rural areas than in cities. Although relief in the countryside and in small towns remained both more casual and a bit more generous, in both town and city outdoor relief was given more freely to those who appeared most worthy, and these were primarily women with families.

## CONCLUSION

Both the experience and treatment of dependence were complex and varied. Some children of farmers, either squeezed off the land or seeking opportunity in cities, ended up in poorhouses. Women, often left widows with young children, faced special hardships but were more often given outdoor relief than were men. Healthy men only entered poorhouses when they could no longer work. They ended their lives in poorhouses more often than did women because children were more willing to take in their elderly mothers than their fathers and because public and private authorities were more willing to give aid to women than to men. Most paupers grew up in the working class but not in pauper families. They reached the poorhouse on account of neither inherited tendencies to pauperism nor drunkenness but through a variety of circumstances that left them destitute and helpless. Of these, the worst was to be without a spouse or children in old age. Again, prior to pensions and Social Security, the importance of families as supports in old age is unmistakable. It was those working-class men and women lacking family support, not the particularly feckless or degraded, who ended their days in poorhouses. How they were treated, however, depended partly on where they lived. In small towns and rural areas communal obligation toward the poor may have remained stronger, for officials appeared more willing to give outdoor assistance, and the amount itself may have been a bit larger. Even the style may have been modestly less degrading. Within cities, therefore, the organization of larger poorhouses and the systematization of relief did not emerge from or encourage humanitarian concerns for the very poor. In fact, the very size of institutions and formality of practice created sharper distinctions within the working class itself. Welfare reform was mainly a synonym for reducing the number of people on relief. In this respect, welfare reformers succeeded, for public officials trimmed relief rolls in cities between the 1870s and the early 1890s, and the poorhouse population decreased proportionally as well.

Thus, welfare reform and the bureaucratic style of relief that it sponsored served the purposes of industrial capitalism in three ways: They made relief increasingly humiliating and unpleasant and so provided an incentive to labor; they emphasized the parasitic and degraded qualities of the very poor, thereby reducing popular sympathy and justifying retrenchment and repression; and they divided the working class against itself at the very moment when labor militancy was growing.

In his report on the causes of pauperism, Charles Hoyt argued that either heredity or a weak character had led most inmates to almshouses. Paupers, by and large the drunk offspring of drunk parents, were idle, degenerate, and ignorant people whose weaknesses kept them always on the verge of destitution. They proved a menace to society for two reasons: They caused a great tax burden, and they spawned more paupers and so multiplied their influence. The other factor that filled almshouses was the nature of the welfare system itself. Through outdoor relief the welfare system encouraged dependence and trained people to be paupers. In its misguided generosity the public supported both the unworthy and worthy poor and perpetuated the very problems it hoped to solve.

None of Hoyt's major assertions were accurate. He reached them by limiting his study to permanent residents of the almshouses. In this way he avoided poorhouses' dual function as short-term resting places for the temporarily destitute and as long-term homes for the sick and elderly poor. Nor did he differentiate between the subpopulations in his examination: inmates of large urban and smaller rural almshouses, insane asylums, institutions for children, men and women. He overlooked the absence of hard data on the role of outdoor relief and the contrary evidence hinted at by comparing length of dependence with time spent in poorhouses. He neglected to examine the role of children in providing homes for elderly parents and to compare the number of adult children among inmates with that usually found among people of a similar age and background. He also completely ignored the socioeconomic context of pauperism: the plight of widows and the labor market for women, the insecurity of industrial work, the decline of wages during old age, and the severe problems created by the depression. He even perpetuated the image of pauperism in his report by instructing poorhouse superintendents not to enter short-term inmates and tramps on the poorhouse registers sent to the State Board of Charities after 1874.

Thus the images that emerge from a reanalysis of Hoyt's data and from the registers of poorhouses in the next 2 decades differ from the one in his report and from contemporary ideas about paupers. The permanent residents of the poorhouses largely were working-class men who had entered when they were too old or sick to work any more and women who came in when younger because they could not support themselves. Among the elderly, men were inmates more often because women had other sources of support, either outdoor relief or children. In cities people ended up in poorhouses more often than in the country, partly because they had fewer kin and partly because outdoor relief was given less often. Behavior classified as mental illness appeared earlier in life, and most people entered insane asylums earlier than they entered poorhouses. In direct contrast with the situation in poorhouses, women formed the majority of inmates of insane asylums. Exactly why women more often than men appeared insane remains unknown—a key question for social history. However, it is clear that both the ordinary paupers and the insane had relatively few children. Indeed, the absence of children may have been the principal reason why many people ended their lives in poorhouses.

Paupers in general were not old drunks, the debased offspring of defective parents. A small share had lived for a long time at the margin of destitution, both intemperate and on relief, but mostly they were old, sick, friendless, and helpless, brought to destitution by the vicissitudes of life among the very poor.

Still the question remains: How are we to account for Hoyt's image? Why was he blind to the dual role of poorhouses? How could he ignore the factors that affected the earning ability of women? How could he miss the impact of the depression? The answers to these questions must be sought for a group much wider than Hoyt and his associates because their conclusions reflected views widely shared among commentators on poverty and social institutions. It would be wrong to cast Hoyt as a villain. Rather, he articulated a conventional view with an unusual amount of data. The belief that poverty was a personal responsibility, a fault of the individual more than the social system, was widely shared during the nineteenth century, although articulated with particular ferocity in the 1870s. Hoyt's report testifies to the hold of the idea upon social thought, its capacity to shape even an allegedly objective evaluaton.

To explore the source of the individualistic or personal interpretation of poverty would take us beyond the scope of this section, deep into one of the central questions in American social history. It raises the problem of relating a view that clearly was functional to the personal motivation of individuals and groups. To argue, as do Piven and Cloward, that stigmatizing the poor served to maintain labor discipline undoubtedly is true. But the argument hardly can be left at that point unless one is willing to accept a crudely functional or cynical explanation of individual behavior. The role that a belief plays within a social system tells only something about the way in which it is transmitted across time and space or the role it plays in the lives of particular people.

One point is clear, though, and it is the relation of Hoyt's conclusions to public policy. Hoyt's intent, after all, was not to discredit the inmates of poorhouses. Rather, his target was outdoor relief. He was an active participant in the campaign to reform public welfare by eliminating or greatly reducing the amount of relief given outside of poorhouses. To accomplish this purpose it was necessary to argue that outdoor relief perpetuated, even aggravated, the problem of pauperism and that most applicants for relief did not merit help. Alarmed by the increase in both outdoor and indoor relief during the 1870s, Hoyt and people like him tried to stop the drain on public resources by turning off the tap. It was the misguided generosity of the public itself, not the great depression, that had caused the problem, they argued. Given this goal, Hoyt's report could not have been more useful or timely. Perhaps it did contribute to the removal of children from almshouses, but it also preceded the concerted and often successful attempt to abolish or reduce outdoor relief not only in New York State but also throughout the country. If the story sounds familiar, it should.

# PART III

"The Morphology of Evil"

## THE PROBLEM OF SOCIAL CATEGORIES

In 1880 seven special schedules of the federal census enumerated the "dependent, defective, and delinquent" population of the United States. These were the blind, insane, prisoners, deaf-mutes, idiots, paupers, and homeless children. Frederic Howard Wines, who supervised the enumeration, used two major arguments to defend treating the seven classes in one inquiry. The first was their essential similarity: "The causes at work in modern society, with its high degree of organization and development, which tend to hasten the growth of either of the forms of misfortune," observed Wines, "affect the growth of all of them." It was, really, a matter of accident whether a disposition toward deviance appeared in one guise or another. "The physical and moral causes which are the occasion of insanity in one man excite another to crime. The connection between crime and pauperism is exceedingly close; so is that between crime and imbecility; but not more intimate than that between insanity and idiocy." In fact, claimed Wines, his report showed a "correlation between idiocy, blindness, and deaf-mutism."[61]

Confident about the conclusions of early social and behavioral sciences, Wines, despite his bow in the direction of social causation, turned for his explanation to heredity. "It is a well-ascertained fact that, in the operation of that mysterious but potent factor in the production of defective types of humanity which we call heredity, insanity in an ancestor may become idiocy or crime in a descendant, and vice versa."

The implication of his analysis was ominous. "There is a morphology of

---

[61]Frederick Howard Wines, *Report on the Defective, Dependent, and Delinquent Classes of the United States as Returned at the Tenth Census (June 1, 1880)* (Washington, D.C.: U.S. Government Printing Office, 1888), p. x. Issued as vol. 21 of the Tenth Census.

evil which requires to be studied," wrote Wines. "How far it may extend, or what may be its ramifications, no one can yet say." Like a malignant growth, the spread of "defective types of humanity" threatened to overwhelm the social body. All "forms of misfortune are often a cause of pauperization of individuals and of entire families," asserted Wines. "Preventive work among children is calculated to check the growth of them all, or to alleviate the condition of their hapless victims. They strike those whom they assail at a very tender age, even before birth."[62]

Thus, Wines's second reason for combining all seven conditions into one study related to public policy. "This branch of the census," he said, "may be likened to the wrong side of the balance-sheet in making up the national account." Other censuses had enumerated "our wealth of men, of money, of property of every description." These accounts of America's advance "in all the material elements of progress" should be balanced by "a glance at the increasing burdens which civilization has to bear." After all, a large share of state tax money was being "absorbed in the care of the criminal and the unfortunate; in some states more than half of the general revenue is devoted to this specific end." Given the size of the problem, it was important for legislatures to know "the whole extent of the evil to be contended against" and to have the data "accessible in a single report."[63]

In order to make rational plans legislators needed an accurate account of the extent of the problem. Although Wines wanted to further the scientific study of social problems, his key metaphor, "morphology of evil," had both a scientific and a moral component, testimony to the ambivalence with which he viewed the populations he enumerated. Despite his emphasis on the collection of hard data, Wines began with the assumption that all seven classes really were branches of the same class. They were not only unfortunate but also inferior; their problems were not merely physical but also moral. Wines believed that the collection of data about these seven classes would help legislators and others formulate better policies for treating them. Yet because of his emphasis on heredity, he was essentially pessimistic, in the end relying, as did so many others, on capturing children at a formative stage. Thus, Wines's legalistic defense of his use of the term *defective* rings somewhat hollow. His seven classes were defective not only in a specific sense but also in a more general one as well. They were, in his view, the faulty offspring of faulty parents.

Wines's argument raises two important problems. One is the accuracy of his statement. To what extent were the seven classes he enumerated

---

[62] *Ibid.*

[63] *Ibid.*

similar? I will return to this issue shortly. The other question concerns perception and the creation of social categories. Social categories are constructions, choices among many ways of representing the physical characteristics, behavior, and interaction of people. How those categories are created and the features used to classify people as members of a common group show at least as much about social values, about the aspirations and anxieties of observers, as they do about actual human behavior and social organization.

Few, if any, social categories reveal more about those who construct them than do ones used to define and label some people as deviant. Deviance is an evaluative as much as a descriptive concept. It implies not only difference but also inferiority, and the many synonyms for deviance all serve to stigmatize some behaviors or conditions. One way in which ordinary or causally complex conditions are stigmatized is by assimilating them into behavior already labeled pathological or deviant. Thus, in America the association of poverty with crime, insanity, and other "defective types of humanity" has translated the lack of money into a condition of moral weakness. Although differences in behavior cannot be completely ignored, social constructions of deviance usually combine disparate activities or conditions into a metaclass that is despised. By its inattention to differences between individuals and groups, the social construction of deviance turns the victims of misfortune and exploitation into objects that deserve, at best, pity and charity rather than respect, dignity, and an equitable share of social resources. This was the function of assembling the blind, insane, criminal, deaf-mute, idiot, pauper, insane, and homeless children into a metaclass of the "defective, dependent, and delinquent" population whose analysis outlined the "morphology of evil."

The question remains, though, just why these groups were selected and combined, how each group was itself defined, and how Wines (who was, after all, reasonably representative of social administrators and scientists of his day) manipulated data to construct his "morphology of evil." This is why the first task is unraveling the categories themselves, teasing out what can be learned about the demographic differences as well as the similarities between each group. Even if Wines turns out to be wrong, we are left with the problem of understanding exactly how various forms of misfortune affected people, of how the life-course, gender, class, and family intersected with the operation of industrial capitalism. We are left, too, with interpreting the response to misfortune, for the "defective, delinquent, and dependent" population was not only despised or pitied; it also, frequently, was locked up. Why some people rather than others with the same nominal condition managed to avoid the institutions that brooded over America in the Gilded Age remains far from clear. Although he did not answer the question himself, this is one issue that Wines's data can illuminate at least a little.

According to Wines, the "most striking result of the investigations ... respecting the insane, the idiotic, the blind, and the deaf in the United States is the apparent increase in their number." However, Wines distrusted the increase because it "has always been the opinion of experts that" previous censuses "failed to show the actual number of these several classes."[64]

Wines, by contrast, took great care to obtain as accurate a count as possible. Here is his description of his method:

> The basis of the present investigation was a list of institutions throughout the United States, prepared with great care in advance of the actual taking of the census, so that it is demonstrable that few, if any, of the important charitable and correctional institutions of the country failed to be accurately reported. Second, a system of special schedules was devised, one for each separate class; and every enumerator was required not merely to enter upon the general population schedule the name of every defective person enumerated by him, but also to transfer the name of every such person to its appropriate special schedule, and upon that schedule to answer certain definite questions, applicable to him as a member of the class to which he was supposed to belong. For this extra service the enumerator was offered additional compensation; and it was impressed upon him that he should exert himself to find these defective persons, and make a full report of each case. He was instructed to counsel with physicians upon this point, to make inquiries of neighbors, and to report all defectives, whether the information respecting them should be derived from the family to which they belonged or from other sources, if in his judgment it was worthy of confidence. By this method it was sought to obtain approximately as complete an enumeration of defectives outside of institutions as of the inmates of such institutions. Third, with respect to the idiots and the insane, the work of the enumerators was supplemented by correspondence with physicians, in all parts of the United States, to the number of nearly 100,000 all of whom were furnished with blank forms to return, and were invited and urged to report to the Census Office all idiots and lunatics within the sphere of their personal knowledge. Four-fifths of them responded to this invitation .... The information thus obtained supplemented to a very considerable extent that derived from the enumerators.[65]

---

[64] *Ibid.*, p. ix.

[65] *Ibid.*, pp. ix–x.

Not content with merely reporting the information on the schedules, Wines employed a "large force of clerks" to transcribe the data on the manuscripts and to locate all duplicates. Although the Census Office closed before he could complete his tabulations, Wines published a remarkable account of the special schedules as Volume 21 of the Tenth Census. In some cases he was able to tabulate the number and some characteristics of populations by county within states. With homeless children he was able only to compile one long table. In order to supplement the statistics on prisoners, he wrote to the police in each city of more than 5000 people and asked them to report on the size and composition of the police force and the number of brothels, saloons, and arrests and on related topics. Thus, even in its incomplete form, Wines's volume represents a magnificent compendium of information about the dependent and criminal population in the United States in 1880, including a comparison of handicapped people inside and outside of institutions. It is remarkable that it has been so little used by historians.[66]

It is comforting that at the time Wines wrote some people objected to his use of the term *defective* as a derogatory reference. Although Wines appreciated their discomfort, he argued that he lacked an alternative and, anyway, that defective was a precise description.

> I would have preferred some other term, had I been able to think of a better, but no one has suggested a better. The deaf and the blind lack the sense of hearing or the sense of sight; the idiots lack the full development of their mental powers; and the insane have lost, to a greater or less extent, the faculty of reason or the balance between the intellectual powers of which, before becoming insane, they were possessed, and which the most of them still partially retain. In the case of each of these four classes, their claim to the protecting care of the government is, therefore, based upon a physical or mental defect.

---

[66]*Ibid.*, pp. v. x. Wines was the son of Enoch Wines, an ordained minister and an important early and mid-nineteenth-century prison reformer who was secretary to the New York Prison Association, one of the founders of the National Prison Congresses, and chairman of an international prison congress. Frederick, also an ordained minister, was first secretary (1869) of the Illinois State Board of Charities, which became a "model for most of the other states." He was one of the "principal organizers" of the "National Conference of Charities and Corrections and was responsible for keeping its work separate from that of the American Social Science Association, so that it remained a clearinghouse for state boards alone." He also carried on his father's work in prison reform and was appointed "special adviser on the defective and delinquent" classes to the Tenth Census and was in charge of the "crime, pauperism, and benevolence figures" in the Eleventh Census. *Encyclopedia of Social Work*, 16th issue (New York: National Association of Social Workers, 1971), 2:1538–1539.

Of course, Wines admitted, these were not the only defective classes, but they were the only ones for which government made provision for "their maintenance, tutition, or medical treatment, in institutions created by law and supported at the expense of the public treasury." It was because of their "peculiar relation" to the public that they were enumerated "in order that the governments referred to may know the precise extent of the claim which may justly be made in their behalf and the amount of provision to be made for them."[67]

Although Wines realized that his enumeration still remained incomplete, especially for paupers who received outdoor relief, he felt that the schedules came close to estimating the total number in the seven special classes. If the true number were known, he argued, there would be an increase in the total enumerated from 466,958 to about 500,000. The latter, he stressed, represented about 1 in 100 of the total population.[68]

The problem for policymakers, therefore, was very real. The dependent, defective, and delinquent classes put a great and unavoidable burden on the public treasury. It was not, though, one distributed evenly throughout the country. Wines tried to provide the data with which to study the differential distribution of the seven classes, and in some cases, most notably paupers, he began the analysis himself. His research, in fact, led him to formulate a "law which governs the distribution of pauperism in the United States." It was that "the ratio of paupers to the total population diminishes alike from north to south and from east to west." In other words, the situation was worst in New England, especially Massachusetts. The reason for the distribution, he hastened to point out, had little to do with the moral caliber of the various regions of the country, for "nature is more bountiful to the poor in warm climates than cold; and newer communities may be expected to have a less proportion of paupers than older ones. This is a complete explanation of the fact . . . but . . . is none the less worthy of note."[69]

The interpretation of the statistics of pauperism was complicated by the failure of enumerators to record many recipients of outdoor relief and by the varied provisions within different states. Even where the law was similar, there was "always the difficulty of deciding whether the amount of relief extended is governed by the actual demand for it, or by the generosity or favor of those by whom it is administered." The problem observed by Wines, it might be noted, has not disappeared, and no one has

---

[67] Wines, *Report*, p. viii.

[68] *Ibid.*, p. xi.

[69] *Ibid.*, pp. xix–xx.

yet formulated a satisfactory explanation of the distribution of welfare in America.[70]

One problem affected virtually all the statistics: namely, age heaping. Wines pointed out the abnormally large proportion of people in most categories who listed their ages with a number ending in 5 or 0. "This is because, when the age of an individual is asked, the answer given to the enumerator represents his age approximately, and not with exactness." Wines reserved special criticism for those people who erroneously claimed to be 100 years old. According to the enumeration, there were were 784 "centarians enumerated among these special classes. The statement, of course, is preposterous." In fact, the "colored race," which had the smallest number within these classes, contributed "578 of the mythical" centenarians. Nearly "all of these cases," Wines believed,

> are destitute of any more substantial basis than the lively imagination of people who are too ignorant to know their own age, and who are sufficiently self-important to value themselves upon this cheap and impalpable distinction. In fact, most of them are said to be illiterate upon the population schedules. The census of every country presents the same feature of large numbers of poor and ignorant persons reported as a hundred years of age and over.[71]

Herein is the perspective of the bureaucrat, already well developed.

It was the perspective of the incipient social scientist rather than of the bureaucrat that guided Wines's attempt to show the interconnection between the various forms of handicap represented by the seven schedules. His evidence was clearest, he felt, for the relation between the blind, idiots, and deaf-mutes. "If the tendency to any given form of misfortune in the population at large is taken as normal," he wrote,

> then the number of the blind who are also idiots is twelve times, and of the blind who are also deaf-mutes it is fifteen times as large as it should be according to the normal standard. Similarly, the number of idiots who are also blind is eighteen times too great, and that of idiots who are also deaf is forty-five times too great. The number of deaf-mutes who are also blind is fifteen times too great, and that of the deaf who are also idiots is forty-five times too great.

---

[70]*Ibid.*, p. xxi; Gilbert Y. Steiner, *Social Insecurity: The Politics of Welfare* (Chicago: Rand McNally; 1966), pp. 29–30.

[71]Wines, *Report*, p. xxvi.

Had he organized his figures somewhat differently, Wines speculated, he would have been able to show that the tendency toward double or treble misfortune would have been greater among "congenital" than among noncongenital cases. "This would be almost certain to be so, if congenital deafness and congenital blindness are due to the operation of the same or like causes which produce congenital idiocy." There are, he thought, "degrees of arrested development . . . . The point of the physical structure at which the arrest takes place may be the eye or the ear; and this may be concurrent with arrested development of the intellect." However, there was another, more sinister reason, pointed out to Wines by the superintendent of a training school for idiots, who stated:

> There is little reason to doubt that abortions and attempts at abortion must be included. Where abortion does not occur, the child upon those life an assault has been made in utero comes into the world a wreck. And investigation would perhaps show that an attack upon the life of one child affects the development of every child subsequently born to the same mother.[72]

There were connections, as well, between blindness, deaf-muteness and insanity. According to Wines, "the liability of deaf-mutes to become insane appears to be four times as great and of the blind six times as great as of persons not afflicted with either of these forms of misfortune." The reason, he felt, was the "isolation occasioned by deafness and blindness," which was "calculated to depress the nervous system, and these infirmities are apt to be found in conjunction with a nervous temperament."[73]

Yet, for all his attempts to show the similarity between populations, Wines was forced to admit that the deaf, blind, and idiots were found much less often in institutions than were the insane and that the deaf and the blind were found much less often in their native states than were the insane and idiots. One reason was that there were far fewer institutions for the deaf, blind, and idiots than for the mentally ill. The proportion institutionalized, therefore, reflected the provision of facilities as much as the severity of various handicaps. Even more,

> It may be presumed that the blind are, to a greater or less extent, wanderers in search of a livelihood; while the deaf are active, energetic, inquisitive, and they move easily from one place to another. Another reason for the large

---

[72]*Ibid.*, pp. xxxviii–xxxix; James Mohr, *Abortion in America: The Origins and Evolution of National Policy* (New York: Oxford, 1978).

[73]Wines, *Report*, p. xxxix.

proportion of blind and deaf away from the state in which they were educated is the large number of blind educated in the institutions at Boston and Philadelphia, and of deaf educated at Hartford and Washington.[74]

Wines's own evidence, thus, calls into serious question his assertion about the similarity between groups. Exactly how they differed remains to be explored.

## THE DEMOGRAPHY OF DEPENDENCE

The statistics that follow are based upon the seven special schedules for several counties in New York chosen to represent the different regions of the state. All the information on each schedule was coded, and they were linked to the population schedules, to which they were indexed.[75]

Clearly, differences in age and sex separated the seven special classes from one another (see Figures 2.22 and 2.23 and Table A.39). First consider the prisoners. They were, as should be expected, overwhelmingly male. Of those in the sample, 1601 were male and 96 female. The reason for the discrepancy, said Wines, "is partly because women are better than men, and partly because they are more timorous and less aggressive; if a wicked woman wants a crime committed, she can usually get a man to do it for her. Partly, too, the smaller proportion of women who are prisoners is due to the leniency of the officers of the law in dealing with them."[76] The age distribution of male and female prisoners, however, was quite similar; they were both primarily young. About half of the men, for instance, were in their 20s, and about a quarter were in their 30s; few were elderly.

The sex ratio among paupers was more even than among prisoners. Of those enumerated, 877 were men and 843 were women. This is in contrast with the actual population of the Erie County Poorhouse, described in Part I of this chapter. The proportion of women is inflated by the inclusion of

---

[74]*Ibid.*, p. xxxvii.

[75]All of the schedules have not survived. By comparing the number coded on each schedule with the number in each county recorded by Wines, it became apparent that in some cases, such as the insane in Monroe County, whole categories are missing. In other cases, the numbers are below those actually enumerated. Since it is not possible to differentiate accurately between the counties on the basis of the statistics in this analysis, they are treated together. The counties in the sample are Albany, Cayuga, Dutchess, Erie, Essex, Greene, Lewis, Oneida, Oswego, Putnam, Saint Lawrence, Schoharie, Tioga, Ulster, and Wayne.

[76]Wines, *Report*, p. xlviii.

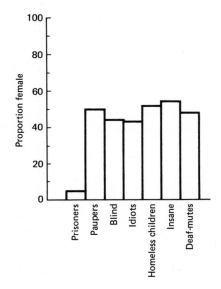

**Figure 2.22.** Proportion of females among seven special classes: New York State, 1880.

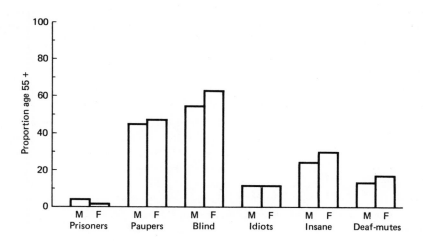

**Figure 2.23.** Proportion of six special classes aged 55+ by sex: New York State, 1880.

people who received outdoor relief, among whom women were more numerous than they were among poorhouse inmates. It also reflects the date of the taking of the census, June 1, which was the season of the year in which the fewest young men entered poorhouses. As among the prisoners, the sex ratio of the paupers was roughly the same at each age. However, paupers were much more likely to be elderly. Nearly half of them, in fact, were more than 55 years old.

Idiots were fairly evenly divided between the sexes, 410 males and 351 females, and the sex ratio was about the same at each age. They were, largely, young. Recall that insane children were automatically classified by Wines as idiots, and he clearly considered idiocy to be a congenital condition. Thus nearly a third of the idiots were less than 20 years old. The homeless children, too, had similar sex ratios, 408 boys and 450 girls. By definition they were young. Most, however, were not infants. Only 14% of the boys and 11% of the girls were less than 5 years old.

There were more men than women among the blind, 425 to 334, although the age distribution among the blind of each sex was similar. Because some people had been born blind, about 11% of the males and 10% of the females were less than 20 years old. However, blindness increased considerably with old age. More than half, 54% of the men and 63% of the blind women, were more than 55 years old.

Among the insane there were, as is to be expected, more women than men, 1045 compared with 926. Among them, too, there were similar proportions of males and females at each age. A high proportion of the insane, 53% of the men and 50% of the women, were less than 20 years old. There was also a substantial proportion among the elderly: 14% of the men and 18% of the women were 55 years or over.

Distinctions between the seven groups existed in terms of their origins as well (see Figure 2.24 and Table A.40). Wines compared the proportions of natives and foreign born, but that comparison is inadequate because it does not distinguish the native-born children of foreign-born parents.[77] The lowest proportion of foreign origin was found among those people with presumably physical or congenital infirmities, those whose problems were least apt to be defined by social norms, custom, or law. By contrast, foreigners, or the native-born offspring of foreign-born parents, more often were found among groups whose status was defined by social misfortune, such as poverty, or by behavior considered deviant. For

---

[77]Given the small numbers, the discussion that follows distinguishes between the native-born children of native parents, the native-born children of foreign-born parents, and the foreign-born children of foreign-born parents. These show trends more clearly than finer breakdowns by regions within the United States or by individual countries.

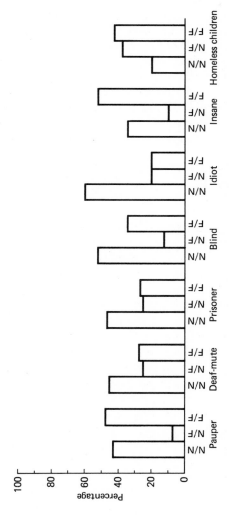

**Figure 2.24.** Nativity of seven special classes: New York State, 1880. (N/N = native born of native parents; N/F = native born of foreign parents; F/F = foreign born of foreign parents.)

Page K.

Supervisor's Dist. No. 1

Enumeration Dist. No. 29

1793  A.

The object of this Supplemental Schedule is to furnish material not only for a complete enumeration of children in institutions, but for an account of their condition. It is important that every inquiry respecting each one be answered as fully as possible. Enumerators will, therefore, after making the proper entries upon the Population Schedule in regard to the members of poor or abandoned children, copy the same (with Schedule page and number) of every child found in any institution designed for the care of poor or abandoned children, or in any poor-house, or under the name of the institution. In addition to this inquiry, special attention is called to the several additional columns indicated in the headings of the several columns. Special attention is called to the questions respecting the child's antecedents, which are designed to bring out the proportion of children in institutions who belong to the respectable and to the vicious classes severally.

SUPPLEMENTAL SCHEDULE No. 5.—HOMELESS CHILDREN (in Institutions) in Saint James Home, New York City, in the County of New York, State of New York, enumerated by me June, 1880.

Robert L. Andrews, Enumerator.

| NAME | Residence when at home. City or Town | Residence when at home. County | | | | | | | | | | | | | | | | |
|------|------|------|---|---|---|---|---|---|---|---|---|---|---|---|---|---|---|---|

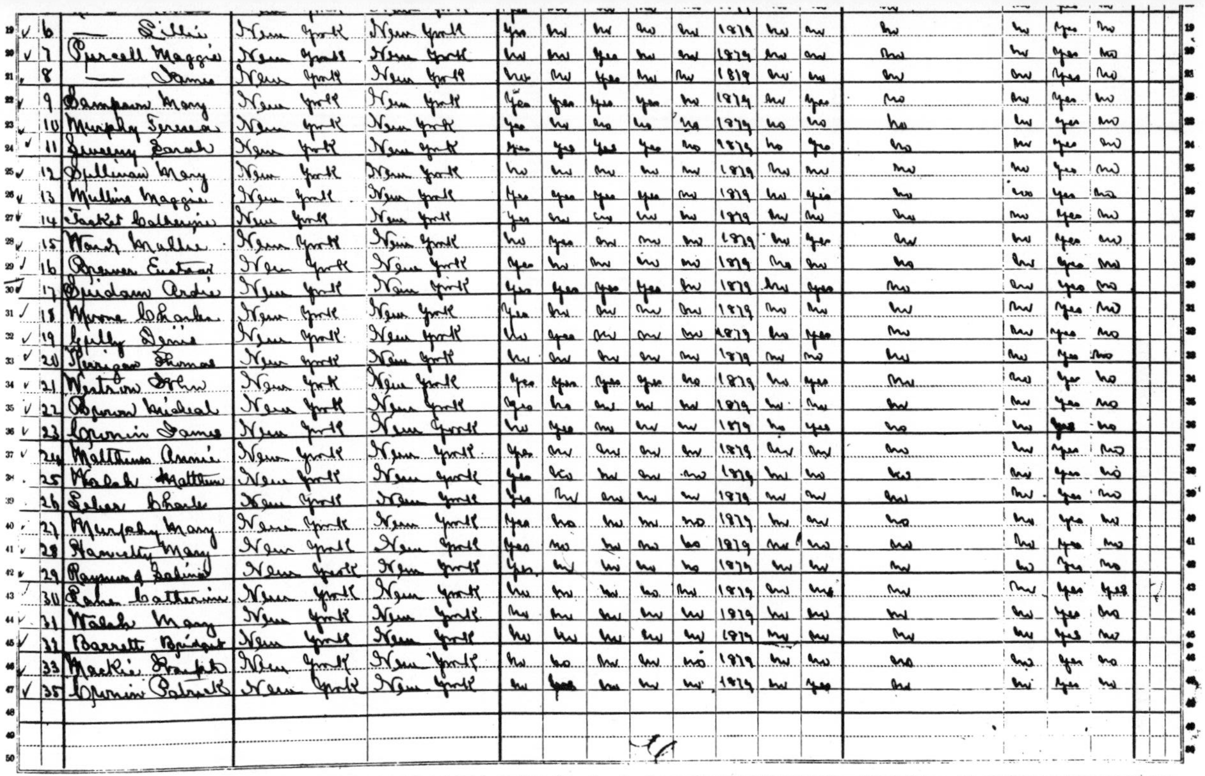

NOTE A.—Children in institutions may not be residents of the county or State in which the institution is situated, and in that case their residence when at home should be stated, in order that they may be accredited to the State or county to which they properly belong, and that the county in which the institution is situated may not be charged with more than its due proportion of dependent children.

NOTE B.—In making entries in columns 18, 19, and 20 an affirmative mark only will be used, thus: /.

***Plate 9.*** *An example of a schedule enumerating Homeless Children from the Schedules of the Dependent, Defective and Delinquent Populations in the 1880 U.S. Census. Note how each entry is indexed back to the main population census.*

example, 47% of paupers and 53% of the insane, the highest proportion of any group, were foreign born of foreign parents. By contrast, over half of the blind and idiots were natives of native origin.

Although different proportions of each group had married, in each case the share married was substantially lower than among the population as a whole. Moreover, widowhood was high among groups that contained substantial proportions of married people. Among paupers over the age of 50, 62.5% of the women and 47.2% of the men had been widowed, compared with 16% of the male prisoners of the same age and 17% of the insane men and 29% of the women. Widowhood, undoubtedly, was much more often a direct cause of entrance to a poorhouse than to an insane asylum or prison (see Table A.41).[78]

Not very many inmates of institutions listed their previous occupations, but the fragmentary data that do exist point to some interesting variations between the insane, paupers, and prisoners (see Figure 2.25 and Table A.42). The highest proportion of men reporting skilled trades, 25%, was among the prisoners, compared with 14% of the insane and 9% of the paupers. The proportion of laborers was lowest, 20%, among the insane, followed by 25% among the prisoners and 60% among the paupers. More similar proportions had followed agricultural occupations: 15% of the prisoners, 19% of the paupers, and 27% of the insane. By contrast, few prisoners (4%) or paupers (1%) had been in white-collar occupations, compared with 15% of the insane. So a sort of social structure existed among the three groups, with the insane highest and paupers at the bottom.[79]

Within some of the groups interesting differences separated the institutionalized and noninstitutionalized men. (see Table A.43). Among paupers, 19.5% of the household heads and 7.4% of the poorhouse inmates had skilled trades, and, conversely, 24% and 42%, respectively, were laborers, and 34% and 10%, respectively, had followed agricultural occupations. Among the deaf-mutes there were few differences among those in and out of institutions in the proportion following skilled trades (13% and 10%, respectively), but there were large differences in the proportion of laborers, 9% and 31%, and also in agriculture, 26% and 38%. There was little difference in occupation among the blind in and out of

---

[78]This point also is supported by the analysis of poorhouse populations in Part I of this chapter.

[79]Distinctions between paupers and criminals are made by Monkkonen in *Dangerous Class.*

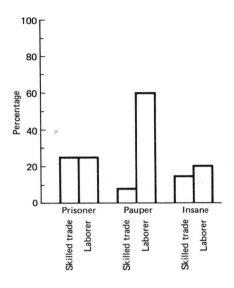

**Figure 2.25.** Proportion of skilled trades-men and laborers among male prisoners, paupers, and insane: New York State, 1880.

institutions, and among the idiots the difference was most marked in agriculture: 44% of the household heads and 21% of the inmates.

Not surprisingly, too, the noninstitutionalized were more likely to be married (see Table A.44). Among paupers 50% of the inmates and 77% of the household heads were married; among deaf-mutes the proportions were 65% and 83%; among the blind, 31% and 78%; and among the insane, 57% and 81%.

The variation in the proportion in institutions should be noted as well (see Figure 2.26 and Table A.45). Of those enumerated, 69% of the paupers, 37% of the deaf-mutes, 22% of the blind, 23% of the idiots, and 76% of the insane were inmates. Most of the rest lived at home with their families. Indeed, a substantial share were living with their parents, even when adult. Just how one is to account for the uneven rate of institution-alization, which reflects the uneven state of institutional development, is not at all clear. Part of the answer, in the case of the idiots, blind, and deaf, may rest in the youthfulness of the populations. Because the handicap affected children, most had parents who could care for them and, perhaps, were unwilling to surrender them to institutions. Even more, because they had homes with parents, it was unnecessary for the state to supply expensive institutions on anything like the scale it did for criminals, the insane, or paupers. Thus, among the blind and idiots children were institutionalized much less often than adults. The figures for deaf-mutes work in exactly the opposite direction. The proportion in institutions dropped after the age of 30 because of differences in the nature of the institutions for deaf-mutes, which were schools where the deaf learned how to live by themselves. Thus, parents may have been more willing to send their children for special training, and the schools probably were unwilling to retain adults.

The closer one looks at each group the less support there is for Wines's argument about their essential similarity. Most of the prisoners were in state or county jails, and most (63%) were considered state prisoners. The length of their sentences were not well recorded, but almost all of the women had been admitted in 1879 or 1880, compared with only half of the men, which shows that women were receiving shorter sentences. Part of the reason is that they were arrested more often for nonserious crimes, that is, for drunkenness, vagrancy, or disturbing the peace.

Most of the idiots were supported by public funds, not by their families. Very important as evidence against Wines's argument, few of them had what he would term a double affliction. Only 1.3% were also insane and 5% epileptic. Most, confirming the age statistics cited earlier, had developed their handicap early: 551 before the age of 20, 9 between 20 and 34, and 2 between 35 and 49.

Most of the blind outside of institutions, 80 of 115, were self-supporting, compared with 55 of the 112 within them. A substantial number had been blinded earlier in life, but the largest number had been blinded at the age of 50 or over: 42% of the household heads and spouses and 39% of the inmates. Again, almost none reported any other handicap, and few had ever been in any institution: 8% of the household heads, 6% of the spouses, and 24% of the children. Of the inmates, 90% were in an institution for the first time.

Although it was common for deaf-mutes to spend some time in residential schools, two-thirds lived outside of institutions. More than half of the deaf-mute household heads, 59%, were self-supporting, compared with 14% of the inmates. Most had become deaf before they were 20 years old. Thus, in direct contrast with blindness, the onset of deaf-mutism seldom occurred in adults or the elderly. However, as in the case of the blind and idiots, very few deaf-mutes had any other handicap.

Nor did any but a tiny number of insane have any other handicap. Nonetheless, only 144 of the 1388 institutionalized insane were not kept at least some of the time in a cell, and 228 of 931 for whom information is available were kept at least some of the time in straps. These numbers reinforce a point made by Wines. Insane asylums had lost their earlier rehabilitative character. Increasingly, they had become custodial institu-

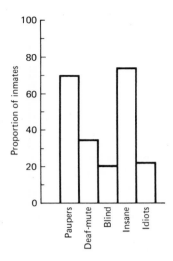

**Figure 2.26.** Proportion of five special classes who were inmates of institutions: New York State, 1880.

tions for chronic patients, large in size, too often brutal in their methods.[80] Of the insane, a plurality had had their first "attack" between the ages of 20 and 24, with the next highest number between 35 and 49 years old. (The word *attack* points to the somatic bias that still characterized ideas about mental illness in this period.)[81] A substantial fraction of the insane had been in institutions before, but the proportion of inmates was highest among the foreign born: Of the insane born in New York State to native parents 59% were institutionalized, compared with 87% of those born in the United States to Irish parents, for instance. Also, the foreign born were the most likely to be put in cells; compare the 51% among New York natives with the 83% among those born in the United States to Irish parents. Thus, the foreign-born insane were incarcerated more frequently than the natives and when in an asylum were treated more harshly. These trends reflect both the biases within the social structure and the greater likelihood that native insane with native parents would have families present and able to care for them.

The support of paupers in poorhouses was divided roughly evenly between city, county, and institutional funds. With only .1% supported by

---

[80]Wines, *Report*, pp. xlii, xliv.

[81]For a good discussion of the somatic basis of American ideas about mental health, see Nathan Hale, Jr., *Freud and the Americans: The Beginnings of Psychoanalysis in the United States, 1875–1917* (London: Oxford University Press, 1971), pp. xi–xiii.

state funds, the local base of welfare stands out unmistakably. About 60% of those people who received outdoor relief were supported by the city or town rather than by the county. By and large, adult paupers were not lazy and intemperate men and women avoiding work. Most, first of all, were not ablebodied. In fact, only 38% of the household heads and 41% of the inmates were listed as ablebodied. Even more striking, only 19% of the household heads and 13% of the inmates were considered intemperate, a proportion quite low given the usual account of the reasons for pauperism. Intemperance, however, varied with age and sex: Of the men 30–49 23% and 10% of the women were listed as intemperate; for those over the age of 50 the proportions were 25% of men and 5% of women. (These figures are much lower than those that emerge from the analysis of poorhouse registers, reported in Part II of this chapter. The higher figures there probably resulted from the definition of intemperance applied by Charles Hoyt, who, it will be recalled, classified everyone who drank at all as intemperate. The census takers may have used a less stringent criterion.)

Again, as in the case of the other groups, very few paupers had any other form of disability. Only 8.2% of paupers in poorhouses had relatives there with them. Nor surprisingly, the proportion was highest among children (20% of those under the age of 15) and lowest among the elderly (5% for both men and women). Of those with relatives more were accompanied by mothers (98) than by fathers (44). Few of the paupers in poorhouses appeared to be short-term residents. Only 33% had entered in 1879 or 1880; 34% had been there before 1875, that is, at least 5 years. More of the young those under 15, had, of course, been there for a shorter time. But the question remains: How is one to reconcile these figures with the large number of short-term residents who appear on the registers of the Erie County Poorhouse, described in Part I of this chapter? The answer probably is, first, that few short-term inmates would be present at any one time since most of them were in the poorhouse only for a few weeks or months. Second, as noted earlier, the census was taken June 1, the time of year when the fewest transients needed the shelter that poorhouses offered. Thus, these statistics, like those reported in Hoyt's survey or those that appeared on the forms he designed, actually distort the nature of poorhouse populations.

The homeless children by and large were not orphans in the modern sense. Only 20% of their parents had died. About 16% had been abandoned by their parents and 21% surrendered. Nearly half, 48%, had been "separated" from their mothers, though exactly what this phrase means is unclear. (Probably it means that either through death, divorce, desertion, or accident they no longer lived with their mothers at the time they were taken into institutions.) Only a few, 2%, had been born in institutions, and a bare majority, somewhat surprisingly, came from "respectable backgrounds." Indeed, only 9% had been "rescued from a bad environment," and very few had any physical or mental handicaps. A plurality, 46%, had been in an institution for 3–5 years, and 28%, for about a year or less. There were no differences in these trends between boys and girls. It was the few native-born children of native parents whose fathers and mothers least often were dead and who, moreover, were the most likely to have been abandoned or surrendered. A striking 42% of native boys and 68% of native girls had been abandoned, compared with 4% of the native born of Irish parents, none of the Irish born, 4% of the native born of German parents, and none of the Germans. The natives also came least often from "respectable backgrounds": 38% of the New York–born natives, compared with 58% of the U.S.-born Irish and 56% of the Germans, for example. Foreign-born parents, it appears, were especially reluctant to surrender or abandon their children. The greater number of their children in institutions probably reflected the accidents and early death that accompanied their poverty and the lack of kin who would care for their children during family crises.

## CONCLUSION

Several general conclusions emerge from this demographic overview of the seven classes of "dependent, defective, and delinquent" people in New York counties:

1. The groups had different age and sex structures. In some cases, notably deaf-mutes and idiots, problems appeared at birth. Most homeless children had not entered institutions until they were 4 our 5 years old. The insane and prisoners usually were young adults, and blindness and pauperism much more often accompanied old age. With the exception of prisoners and paupers, sex ratios were relatively balanced between the groups. Most out of balance were sex ratios among prisoners, who were overwhelmingly men.
2. The native born formed a greater share of those groups with physical or genetic disabilities. There was a higher proportion of foreign born among those whose conditions were related to poverty or defined by social conventions and laws.
3. The proportion of people in institutions varied between the groups,

even excluding those groups, prisoners and homeless children, who were institutionalized by definition. The variations reflected the provision of public facilities and, as well, the age at which people acquired disabilities. Those people who acquired their disabilities at birth or in early childhood least often were in institutions, or if they were, as with the deaf-mutes, were there for relatively short periods to acquire training.

4.  The noninstitutionalized were more likely to be married, though marriage was very low among all of the groups, albeit probably for different reasons. They also had better occupations. This is one reason why they were able to stay out of institutions.

5.  Some differences existed between the occupations of the various groups, particularly the insane, prisoners, and paupers. The insane had the most favorable occupational structure, and the paupers the worst.

6.  There was little overlap between the groups. Only a tiny number of people had any sort of "multiple affliction."

Clearly, the "morphology of evil" did not conform to Wines's assumptions. The seven classes of "dependent, defective, and delinquent" people were, by and large, distinct from one another. Only by assuming that all handicaps or behaviors were the result of bad genes, that a general tendency toward a defective body, mind, or character was inherited, popping out at birth or later in life in one or another guise mainly by accident, could one consider these seven classes of unfortunate people to be but branches of one metaclass. As in every other instance examined in this book, the demography of dependence and its rhetoric differed sharply.

The "massive growth of institutions," wrote Harry Braverman, "stretching all the way from schools and hospitals on the one side to prisons and madhouses on the other represents not just the progress of medicine, education, or crime prevention, but the clearing of the marketplace for all but the 'economically active' and 'functioning' members of society." As Wines's enumeration makes clear, by the latter part of the nineteenth century the marketplace had been swept relatively clean because most of those people unable to work within it had been relegated to an institution. In general, those institutions had been created after 1820. Mental hospitals, reformed penitentiaries, reform schools, poorhouses, special schools for the blind and deaf, even public schools—all were nineteenth-century inventions. The creation of what Braverman calls the "universal market"—

the substitution of "market relations" for "individual and community relations"—meant an increase in

> the human detritus of urban civilization . . . not just because the aged population, its life prolonged by the progress of medicine grows ever larger; those who need care include children—not only those who cannot "function" smoothly but even the "normal" ones whose only defect is their tender age. Whole new strata of the helpless and dependent are created, or familiar old ones enlarged enormously.

This is why Wines could so easily and automatically lump together his seven classes of "dependendent, defective, and delinquent" people and why he saw them all as but different branches of a "defective humanity" with a common origin. They did not meet what Christopher Lasch has called the "single standard of honor" of capitalist America. Because they were dependent, they consumed resources; they had no productive role; they not only remained outside the universal market but drained it as well.[82]

The characteristics that differentiated those aged, poor, or handicapped people who managed to avoid institutions from those who spent years in custody highlight, once more, the critical role of kin before the era of pensions and Social Security. It was, by and large, only those who could eke out a living or who had kin able and willing to care for them that remained on the outside. The problem of the late nineteenth century, however, was the escalation of strains and pressures that made families and communities reluctant or unwilling to care for their helpless members. As Braverman observed, "Since no care is forthcoming from an atomized community, and since the family cannot bear all such encumbrances if it is to strip for action in order to survive and 'succeed' in the market society . . . care . . . becomes institutionalized, often in the most barbarous and oppressive forms."[83]

Wines's amalgamation of the seven classes of "dependent, defective, and delinquent" people into one metaclass of "defective types of humanity"

---

[82]Harry Braverman, *Labor and Monopoly Capital: The Degradation of Work in the Twentieth Century* (New York: Monthly Review Press, 1974), pp. 280–281; Christopher Lasch, "Origins of the Asylum," in *The World of Nations: Reflections on American History, Politics, and Culture* by Christopher Lasch (New York: 1973); Katz, Doucet, and Stern, *Early Industrial Capitalism*, pp. 349–391.

[83]Braverman, *Labor and Monopoly Capital*, pp. 280–281.

did more than reflect the values of the universal market. It also served an important role in the formulation of public policy, for it justified the cheap and custodial quality of institutional care by defining dependence as the manifestation of an inferior and hopeless condition. At the same time, its one thin ray of hope was children. In this way, Wines's portrait helped set the stage for the intense concentration of reform and social uplift that, as the child saving movement, soon captured meliorist energies in Progressive America.

# PART IV

# New York's Tramps and the Problem
# of Causal Attribution in the 1870s

## THE TRAMP PROBLEM

During the 1870s American social commentators invented the noun *tramp* to describe the groups of men suddenly roving through towns and cities, begging alms, asking for outdoor relief, and crowding the floors of police stations at night. Vagrants, of course, hardly were new, but it was the size and pervasiveness of the wanderers that both appalled and frightened the respectable classes, evoking—what one observer called "a happy innovation in language"—the new name.[84]

Mobility, of course, had been a characteristic of the American working class for a long time. Indeed, the extraordinary rate of population turnover in nineteenth-century towns and cities has been a dramatic and consistent discovery of social historians in recent years. Although all sorts of people were on the move, young, propertyless men were the most mobile. As wage laborers buffeted by business cycles and irregular work, they were a reserve army of the underemployed on the road in search of a job. Prior to the third quarter of the nineteenth century almost no one commented on this massive population turnover that was so ubiquitous a feature of social life. It was a great, quiet, almost underground stream, accepted, without doubt, as part of the landscape, a feature so well known it scarcely deserved comment. However, by the mid-1870s the stream had become a torrent, threatening to engulf American life. Clearly, by throwing many more men than usual out of work the depression of 1873 had added to the volume of mobility. But it was the context as well as the quantity of

---

[84]Paul T. Ringenbach, *Tramps and Reformers 1873–1916: The Discovery of Unemployment in New York* (Westport, Conn.: Greenwood Press, 1973), p. 3; Francis Wayland, "Paper on Tramps," p. 11; Edward E. Hale, "Report on Tramps," in *Proceedings of the Fourth Annual Conference of Charities* (1877), p. 102.

population movement—increased labor militancy and the unmistakable emergence of an industrial proletariat—that prompted respectable citizens to transform unemployed, wandering, hungry, and perhaps often angry men into a new and menacing class called tramps.

Certainly, in the years after the onset of the depression of the 1870s social commentators, philanthropists, and administrators wrote almost endlessly about tramps. Because most discussions assumed the causes of tramping to be straightforward, rooted in individual weakness and immorality, discussion centered on responses. How could tramps be discouraged from entering local communities? How could tramping itself be reduced? One historian of tramps in New York State, Paul T. Ringenbach, has observed that discussions of tramping were remarkable for their omissions. Almost none of them attempted to relate the upsurge of tramping to the dislocations caused by rapid industrial development or, even, to unemployment. Indeed, claims Ringenbach, not until the depression of the 1890s was unemployment discovered by public policymakers and philanthropists in New York State.[85]

Two examples illustrate the characteristics usually attributed to tramps during the 1870s. First are the remarks made by Edward Everett Hale as he reported on the deliberations of a committee on tramps to the Conference of Boards of Public Charities in 1877. As Hale sought to account for the "tramp epidemic," he almost touched on its real origins. When "any considerable change in the industry of a nation, or any considerable over-supply of labor in one or more branches of industry has, for the time, removed many unskilled laborers from the places where they had made their homes," asserted Hale, an upsurge of tramping would follow. It was, he was careful to point out, not the entire working class that furnished the tramps. Rather, they originated among unskilled laborers. Indeed, it was "the laborer least skilled who suffers. In proportion as the workingman has craft, or resource, does he secure employment in the midst of change."[86]

In the United States two factors had contributed to the increase in tramping. One was the Civil War, which "taught, to a large number of laboring men, the methods of the bivouac, and its comforts." To an exsoldier, "the hardships of a tramp's life," were "not more severe than he has borne, perhaps cheerfully, in the line of his duty." War had taught

---

[85]Ringenbach, *Tramps and Reformers*, pp. 17–18; Howard Green, "It's Easier to Beg than Dig": The Tramp as Mendicant and Laborer in Victorian America" (Paper delivered at the Annual Meeting of the American Historical Association, December 12, 1979). Discussion of tramps is a common theme in almost all of the *proceedings* of the Annual Conventions of the County Superintendents of the Poor in the late nineteenth century.

[86]Hale, "Report on Tramps."

laboring men the art of marching, of finding food and shelter, "the habit of living off the country,—and the disposition to trust tomorrow to take care of tomorrow." Besides the war, American generosity contributed to tramping. To refuse to give food to a wayfarer, wrote Hale, had been "for centuries, regarded here a sign of utter meanness,—almost unheard of." In America food was so abundant that "habits" had "come into existence, which show . . . that, in the popular estimation, the meanest man has almost a right to food without work."[87]

The habits learned in war and American generosity had fueled the "rapid increase" in tramping, which "attracted attention, and excited alarm through the whole country." The situation had become so bad that one of the committee's correspondents from Massachusetts reported that "twenty years ago any woman within two miles of his church would have been willing to come, without escort, to any evening service in it, and to return home in the same way." Now, however, "no woman in the town would willingly go alone after dark a quarter of a mile from home."[88]

Those who aided tramps realized that some of them actually were traveling from one place to another in search of work. But they were a small minority. "For one such person . . . there are twenty, not to say one hundred 'professionals' . . . men who make travelling and begging a business." Even those men who started out looking for work probably had succumbed to the lure of the road, for "mere companionship" with professional tramps was "to the last degree demoralizing." At any rate, even the so-called honest laborers had weak characters. "No man of much force of character, or with an established handicraft, is likely to be found in such travel for work." Indeed, "between the skilled workman and the professional tramp" there yawned a "gulf as wide as that between a courtly nobleman and the beggar to whom he throws a penny."[89]

Hale concluded his report with some suggestions for tightening the administration of relief. Then the principal spokesman for Hale's committee, Professor Francis Wayland of Yale, delivered his own report on tramps.

Wayland began systematically by dividing paupers into three groups: first, people reduced to pauperism by some physical disability or mental illness; second, persons fairly entitled to outdoor relief because of temporary destitution or other causes truly beyond their control; third, "able-bodied persons without homes and without regular occupation, who

---

[87] *Ibid.*

[88] *Ibid.*

[89] *Ibid.*

*Plate 10.* *An example of the menacing image of the tramp from the Exhibition of the Philadelphia Society for Organizing Charity in Philadelphia, 1916. (Courtesy of the Historical Society of Pennsylvania.)*

are either unable to find employment or unwilling to labor." Those people in the second division of the third group—persons unwilling to labor—were tramps. Wayland had no sympathy for tramps. Indeed, his description of tramps could not have been harsher:

> a lazy, shiftless, incorrigible, cowardly, utterly depraved savage . . . he seems to have wholly lost all the better instincts and attributes of manhood. He will outrage an unprotected female, or rob a defenceless child, or burn an

isolated barn, or girdle fruit trees, or wreck a railway train, or set fire to a railway bridge, or murder a cripple, or pilfer an umbrella, with equal indifference . . . . Having no moral sense, he knows no gradations in crime. He dreads detection and punishment, and he dreads nothing else . . . . Practically, he has come to consider himself at war with society and all social institutions . . . . He has only one aim,—to be supported in idleness.[90]

Rehabilitation was even less likely to work with tramps than with criminals, for often "hardened criminals" could be reached by "the strength and sacredness of family ties, the love of mother or wife, or child." But "this possible refuge of respectability" was lacking for the tramp, who had "no home, no family ties," and had "cut himself off from all influences which can minister to his improvement or elevation."[91]

Again, the theme of danger on the streets pervaded Wayland's report as well as Hale's. The tramp's "frequent presence in our village communities has again and again transformed their quiet, peaceful life into a reign of terror." The state detective force in Massachusetts believed that the "great body of tramps" were "professional thieves," formed "into organized gangs, under the direction of skilful leaders, with general headquarters in the western part of the State, where their plunder is divided." Not content with terrorizing women and children or with organized robbery, tramps fomented labor discontent as well. "The inner history of the recent disgraceful and disastrous riots in some of our principal cities," claimed Wayland, revealed the major culprits to be tramps and not strikers. "It is, indeed, a significant circumstance, that Pittsburg, which, doubtless from some good or bad reason, had long been the favorite rendezvous of these wandering hordes, was the principal sufferer from the reckless outrages."[92]

Any policy for reducing the number of tramps, according to Wayland, should be based on four premises: First, "in this country, it is, fortunately, very rare that employment furnishing some remuneration cannot be obtained by all who are really anxious to secure work." Second, the truly worthy poor all had friends or family willing to aid them or, if unable, to recommend them as "worthy objects of private charity." Third, in his appendix to the *Tenth Annual Report of the Board of State Charities*, Charles Hoyt had demonstrated that " 'by far the greater number of paupers have reached that condition by idleness, improvidence, drunkenness, or some

---

[90]Wayland, "Paper on Tramps."

[91]*Ibid.*

[92]*Ibid.*

form of vicious indulgence.' " Fourth, every "sound principle" of "moral and political economy" demonstrated that "the habit of begging should be promptly and effectually discouraged." Thus Wayland offered a series of recommendations for dealing with tramps. First, "provide for their necessities"; second, force them to "perform useful work"; third, "prevent them from comitting crime"; and, ominously, fourth, "render it impossible for them to propagate paupers." The latter, Wayland emphasized, implied "confinement, with enforced labor and separation of sexes."[93]

The image of tramps in the 1870s had a cluster of components. First, men tramped because they were lazy. They did not want to find work. Anyone who wanted work in America only had to look diligently for a job. Those who had most difficulty finding work were unskilled laborers. Men with crafts almost never were on the tramp.

A host of undesirable moral qualities accompanied laziness, most notably heavy drinking. Tramps also cheated, lied, stole, and murdered.

Tramps, some observers thought, had been born with weak characters. The idea that a reluctance to work was innate received confirmation by the hereditarian theories that had surfaced by the 1870s. Hereditarian theory, in turn, was reinforced by Richard Dugdale's work on the Jukes, research inspired by visits to poorhouses in New York State.[94]

If it need be said, tramps usually, though not always, were male. The literature often is silent about the existence of women tramps. Instead it portrays tramps as primarily young or middle-aged males, usually white. By definition, as Ringenbach notes, tramps were homeless. In an age when respectable thought presented family life as the source of moral culture and social stability, the homelessness of tramps appeared particularly menacing.[95]

When social commentators attempted to link tramping to social conditions, they usually pointed to immigration. Although the number of native American tramps worried some observers, most were believed to be immigrants. Thus one proposed response was to tighten immigration laws and ship friendless paupers back to the countries from which they had come.[96]

Given their questionable antecedents, worthless character, and degenerate habits, it should be expected that tramps appeared dangerous. The

---

[93] Ibid.

[94] Ringenbach, *Tramps and Reformers*, pp. 18–19.

[95] Ibid., p. 4.

[96] Proposals to tighten immigration laws were made regularly by the county super-intendents of the poor at their annual conventions.

danger they posed, in fact, had three components. First, tramps were thought to be violent, especially when not aided. Second, they were labor agitators. Although the latter image does not coincide with the assumption that tramps were lazy and self-centered, Ringenbach documents the belief that they stirred up discontent among workers, preached revolution, and, especially in the aftermath of the great strikes of 1877, threatened the political and social stability of American life. Third, tramps were dangerous because of the bad example they set. Their very existence spread the notion that it was not necessary to work in order to live. They were, thus, a disease, a virus of demoralization infecting the will of the working class.[97]

Tramping, commentators either stated or implied, was a way of life, not a temporary passage between jobs or a phase in the life-course. Some observers, such as Josiah Flynt Willard, drawn to tramps even as they criticized them, wrote about their distinctive subculture, language, pastimes, and social code. However, most of the more sympathetic writing about the subculture of tramps starts in the 1890s; I have found none 2 decades earlier.[98]

Thus tramps emerge from the literature of social observation and social administration as a class by themselves. Tramps were not unfortunate members of the working class. They were, rather, a classic lumpen proletariat. As a summary image of tramps, consider the observations of John V.L. Pruyn, president of the New York State Board of Charities, in the board's *Tenth Annual Report*:

> Very much worse . . . than the pecuniary burden entailed on the people of this State, by their negligence in dealing with this great evil, are the moral consequences. These men and women are generally debased, and exercise a deteriorating influence on all with whom they associate. As they pass from town to town, and lodge at the house of the Overseers of the Poor, or elsewhere, they spread moral contagion, and when they seek a rest in the county poorhouse, they corrupt all those who are better than they when committed . . . . Two significant facts have lately been noted in regard to tramps—that they are generally young men, and that the number of native Americans is increasing to an alarming extent . . . . The evil is a growing one . . . this army of tramps naturally attracts to itself the young and idle . . . the life once entered on is seldom abandoned . . . all public and private action at present has little tendency to overcome the evil . . . all these

---

[97] On social anxiety in the 1870s, see Boyer, *Urban Masses*, 123–131.

[98] Josiah Flynt (Josiah Flynt Willard), *Tramping with Tramps: Studies and Sketches of Vagabond Life* (New York: Century, 1899).

young and vigorous men will transmit to their children their own debased habits of life and character.[99]

Pruyn's comments oozed fear, loathing, and impotence. They could be pushed to support arrest, repression, the suspension of habeas corpus, and, most menacing, sterilization. They also reflected his puzzlement and desire for more data. After all, he was not exactly sure who the tramps were. For this reason the board, under the leadership of its secretary, Charles Hoyt, had started an inquiry "regarding the number and condition of 'tramps' applying for public aid, and also as to the expenditure in connection with their relief." Pruyn explained:

> In view of the growing and serious evils resulting from this condition of things, the Board, in the past year, determined to institute an inquiry regarding the number and condition of tramps applying for public aid during the six months commencing October 1, 1875, and also as to the kind and amount of relief furnished. Accordingly appropriate forms in blank were issued throughout the State, to the keepers of the poor-houses and alms-houses, and to the police of cities (excepting New York and Brooklyn) with the request to register and forward monthly to the office of the Board the names of all tramps applying for relief, their ages, places of birth, habits, education, civil condition and occupation, as far as the same could be ascertained, with full descriptions of their persons, the places from which they commenced "tramping", the length of time so engaged, the point where last aided, the place of destination, the reasons given why aid was required, and also as to the amount expended.[100]

Pruyn argued that the early returns by and large supported his image of tramps:

> The greater portion of them are unmarried and generally able-bodied men, in the prime of life. Most of them are returned as uneducated, intemperate and classed by occupation as laborers. A small portion of them have had settled residences in this State, but the mass, it appears, are the waste population of this and other States and countries, and a considerable number of them are foreigners, not naturalized. It is generally claimed by these persons that they commenced "tramping" during the year, but many of them admit they have led this mode of life for a long period. The reason usually assigned for asking relief is lack of employment; in fact the returns show that the plea for aid in nearly every instance is, "want of work."[101]

---

[99]John V.L. Pruyn in *Tenth (1877) Annual Report*, pp. 31–32.

[100]*Ibid.*, p. 27.

[101]*Ibid.*, p. 28.

It remains to be seen whether Pruyn reported accurately on the data. Despite his assertion that most local authorities completed the questionnaires, many did not, and those that did often filled them out either incompletely or illegibly. The board never published a tabulation of the results. Perhaps Hoyt felt they were too incomplete to be reliable. Or, it could be that they so contradicted prevailing stereotypes that he felt them best ignored. However, returns with over 5000 fairly well completed entries did reach Hoyt. Although he did not analyze them, they do constitute probably the largest and most complete body of information about the tramp population in the 1870s. The major problem with utilizing the returns, of course, is estimating their reliability. Some questions were answered by those recording the information, that is by people observing the individual tramps requesting aid. Others were answered directly by the tramps themselves. There is no way to check how accurately they replied. However, the tramps had little incentive to lie. It is hard to see why they would have been dishonest, unless on principle. Moreover, the results show consistent and sensible patterns unlikely to have emerged from a series of randomly offered falsehoods.

In the rest of this part, I analyze all of the usable questionnaires, which lay untouched in the bowels of the New York State Archives for over a century. My first purpose is to compare the standard image of tramps in the late 1870s with their demographic characteristics as they appeared on the questionnaires. My second object is to use the contrast between image and demography to raise the issue of causal attribution in history, particularly to challenge Thomas Haskell's argument that the problem that this book explores—the relation between image or belief and social fact—is both uninteresting and wrongly framed. [102]

One initial word about the population. It seemed reasonable to suppose that there might be recidivists among the tramps, that is, people aided more than once during the period when the questionnaires were compiled. For this reason I had the file sorted alphabetically and tried to identify repeaters. In fact, I was quite sure that I had found the same person more than once in about 10% of the cases. Therefore, I created a new file in which each individual appears only once. I thought it would be interesting to compare the repeaters and nonrepeaters on various measures. In fact, it was not interesting; there were no differences between the groups. This is because probably nearly all of the sample were repeaters. The spotty, scattered quality of the records accounts for why they appear only once during this period.

---

[102]Haskell, *Emergence of Professional Social Science*. Haskell's interpretation is discussed later in this part.

## THE CHARACTERISTICS OF TRAMPS

First, their birthplace: Most tramps were, indeed, immigrants (see Figure 2.27 and Table A.46). Almost half (44.8%) had been born in America, about 28.4% in New York State. In this respect tramps were almost identical to almshouse inmates. Whether their parents were as frequently immigrants cannot be known with certainty, but there is no reason to suspect otherwise. Among the foreign born the Irish, of course, were the largest group (26.3% of the total); the Germans, 5.5%, were a very small segment. There were fewer Irish and Germans among the tramps than among the almshouse inmates surveyed by Hoyt. In fact, among tramps immigrants from Great Britain made up a more substantial share, 10.1%, undoubtedly a result of the migration of poor British artisans in the late 1860s and early 1870s.

Even more than the elderly inmates of the almshouses, the tramps were male, as commentators implied (see Figure 2.28 and Table A.46) Indeed, 93.7% were men, compared with about two-thirds of the elderly or 35.3% of all almshouse inmates. However, like the poorhouse inmates, they were almost all, 97.7%, white.

Although tramps were much younger than the almshouse inmates, there were differences in the age-structure of tramps born in different places (see Figure 2.29 and Table A.46). Using an index of representation we find that the natives were substantially underrepresented among the elderly and the New England (80) and New York (57) born, whereas the index for the Irish was 147 and for both the Germans and British, 109 (see Table A.46). Among teenagers, New York born, 183, were greatly overrepresented, as they were among the few younger children, 223. The latter figures probably represent nothing more than the birth of children to the foreign-born poor. However teenagers were not underrepresented among the Irish, although they were among the German and British, the result, perhaps, of some differences in immigration patterns. Among the 20–40-year-olds, all groups were represented in a roughly proportional way.

Thus tramps most often were young men, half of them under 30. This stands in striking contrast to the poorhouses, where only 30% of the inmates were similarly young and about three-quarters of the inmates over 40. What needs most explaining among tramps is the high proportion of elderly among the Germans and Irish. This may have reflected special hardship during old age among immigrants who had smaller kin networks on which to draw for assistance.

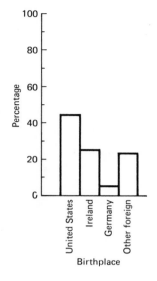

**Figure 2.27.** Birthplace of tramps: New York State, 1875–1876.

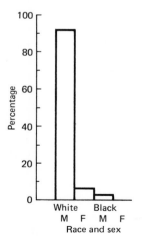

**Figure 2.28.** Race and sex of tramps: New York State, 1875–1876. ($N = 4310$.)

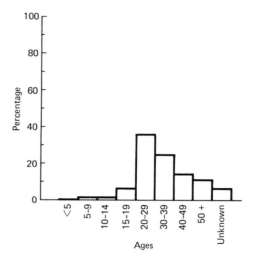

**Figure 2.29.** Ages of tramps: New York State, 1875–1876. ($N = 4310$.)

   Most of the tramps, 75.6%, were unmarried, strong confirmation of their "homeless" condition (see Table A.46) The proportion widowed or divorced, 8.7%, was especially low. Even those tramps in the age groups when people usually married were largely single. Of 30–39-year-old men, 71.8% were single, as were 55.4% of the 40–49-year-olds and 44.6% of those over the age of 50.

   Some important differences separated the men from the few women tramps. Women, first, were older; 36.2% were over 40, compared with 25.3% of the men. And only 19.9% of the women were unmarried, compared with 79.2% of the men. Conversely, 28.3% were either widowed or divorced, compared with 8.6% among men. Women, too, more often were considered temperate (79.2%) than were men (57.2%) (see Table A.47). Again, as with the almshouse inmates, it is not clear what temperate meant. If the same criteria were applied, if the intemperate included everyone who drank at all, then the actual share of drunks would be much lower. At any rate it is remarkable that superintendents and overseers of the poor and local police officers actually reported well over half of the male tramps as temperate. Though more temperate, women were less educated; 34.3% of them reported no education, compared with 16.1% among men. Also, women were more likely to be sick: 29.6%, compared with 19.6% among men.

   Some of the characteristics of women surely reflected the fact that they were tramping with their husbands. Few, probably, were on the road by themselves. Thus it is to be expected that most women would be married.

Many of the older married male tamps also, without doubt, were on the road with their wives. Clearly, then, there existed a group of married couples on the road that was overlooked in contemporary commentary.

Contrary to much contemporary opinion, few tramps were recent immigrants (see Figure 2.30 and Table A.48). About 83% of the Irish had been in the United States at least 5 years, as had 72% of the Germans and 67% of the British. Of those whose length of residence was known, 60% of the Irish, 43% of the British, and 32% of the Germans had been here a decade or longer. Despite their prolonged residence, only about 40% of the Irish had been naturalized, compared with higher figures for the British (60.3%) and Germans (68.1%), who, by and large, had been here for shorter periods. The significance of the lower rate of naturalization among the Irish, a group with a low rate of return migration, is not at all clear. In fact, the distinction between immigrant groups becomes more striking when one observes that the proportion of German and British immigrants who had been naturalized quite closely matched the proportion in America for 5 or more years. Had recent immigrants been recruited directly by employers? Did they work for lower wages and hence find work more easily? Were longer term immigrants fired when new waves of men willing to work for lower wages entered the country? These are important issues, but ones about which the data permit only speculation. Here the major point is that tramps were not recent immigrants, and social commentators who tried to blame the tramp

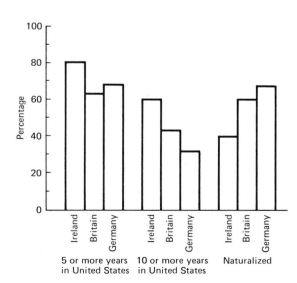

Figure 2.30. Years in United States and naturalization for selected immigrant tramps (known cases only): New York State, 1875–1876.

problem on countries that shipped their paupers to America clearly erred.

No difference in rates of temperance separated foreign-born and native tramps (see Table A.47). Most immigrants, moreover, like the natives, had received some education (see Table A.47). The proportion without any education was, among New England born, 9.1%, New York 15.4%, Germany, 5.7%, and Britain, 9.7%. Only the Irish stand out: 26.5% with no education. Whatever their moral failing, tramps were not in general illiterate. Nor, it might be added, had literacy by itself proved much of a preventive against tramping.

Tramps frequently claimed to have specific craft skills, a characteristic inconsistent with their popular image (see Table A.49).Only among the Irish did most tramps (about 60%) call themselves laborers. Among tramps born in other places the proportion of laborers was New England, 36.1%; New York, 41.7%; Great Britain, 36.2%; and Germany, 42.5%. Nonetheless, among groups other than the Irish the proportion of laborers probably exceeded the proportion in the nontramping population by a factor of two to four times. Such was not the situation among the Irish, where the proportion of laborers among tramps probably did not substantially exceed the proportion of laborers in the work force. Aside from their concentration in laboring, tramps practiced a wide variety of trades, although only a small proportion had followed agricultural occupations. In each nativity group, between 6% and 8% claimed skills in the building trades; the proportion of British born in metal trades, 15.6%, was particularly high; otherwise, distinctions are not noteworthy. Clearly, the tramps did not differ sharply from the rest of the working class. Were they less a lumpen proletariat than a group of particularly unfortunate, or unemployed, workers?

The most important statistic to emerge from this survey of tramps supports the thesis that tramps should be viewed more as casualties of working-class life than as a degenerate stratum outside the class structure. To Pruyn and other observers the essential feature of tramping was that it was a way of life. The tramp was not a man on the road in search of work; rather, he had rejected work for a life spent begging and stealing as he wandered, carefree and well fed, from place to place. "Tramp" was a permanent condition; it placed a man outside the class structure, indeed outside of civilized social life. It was not an accidental status, a result of misfortune, but a freely chosen alternative whose voluntary nature placed the tramp beyond the legitimate boundaries of compassion and philan-thropy. However, the board's survey showed that during these 6 months men and women had been on the tramp only a very short time (see Figure

2.31 and Table A.50). Between 85% and 90% of tramps born in any region of the United States or other countries had been on the road for 1 month or less. For these men and women tramping was a recent, probably temporary, activity, not a way of life.

Most of them were tramping around within New York State, moving from one city to another, stopping in country towns along the way (see Table A.51). A large proportion, 45.6%, had started in a city within the state; 42% were headed to one. If one includes those people whose origins were unknown, 63.7% had started tramping within New York State. Because nearly 30% did not give their destination, the share heading toward a city within New York was probably even larger. Conversely, the share of the tramps sent by neighboring states was very small: 3.7% from New England and 5.7% from the West. Contrary to what Pruyn claimed, New York's tramp problem began within its own borders.

In general, the movement of tramps from place to place resembled a flow in and out of cities in roughly the same proportions (see Table A.51). This shows most clearly using the raw numbers: 650 began tramping in downstate cities, 188 had last been aided in one, and 667 were headed there; 495 had started in western New York cities, 357 were last aided in one, and 294 were going there. Conversely, 82 people had started

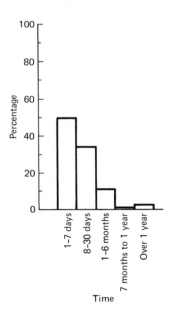

**Figure 2.31.** Time tramping (known cases only): New York State, 1875–1876.

tramping in noncity areas of western New York, 172 had last been aided there, and for 81 they formed a destination.[103]

Indeed, more people frequently received their last aid outside of cities within particular regions (see Table A.51). For example, in New York's Southern Tier of counties, 38 tramps had started in noncities, 70 had last been aided there, and 28 were going to the same area; in the Finger Lakes region, the three numbers were 79, 372, and 66, respectively, compared with 176, 68, and 189 in Finger Lakes cities. The area where most were aided was outside of cities in the Catskills, which was the place of origination for 131, the last place aided for 430, and the destination for 91. These figures hint strongly that tramps found it easier to obtain aid in towns and villages than in cities. [104]

Note that for most men and women the last place aided was not the place where they had begun tramping (see Table A.51). Some examples of the proportion in which the place of origination and destination were the same are western New York cities, 22%, Mohawk Valley noncities, 9.3%; downstate cities, 20.7%. These low proportions are additional evidence that tramps were circulating throughout the state. Many, though, had not wandered very far because a substantial share received aid in the countryside surrounding the cities where they had started: for example, in the Finger Lakes, 25.6%; the Catskills (the highest), 46.2%; and the Hudson Valley, 8.9%.

About 15% of the total were going to downstate cities, although this proportion was higher among tramps originating in certain places: 22% of those from western New York, 23.7% from downstate noncities, and 36% of New Englanders. Western New York was the destination for about 6.6% of all tramps; between 9% and 10% were headed for the Finger Lakes region, Mohawk Valley cities, and the noncity areas of the Adirondacks. Slightly more, about 10.5%, were going to Hudson Valley cities, though the area drew a disproportionately large number from the Catskills and downstate cities. Thus, aside from New York City, most of the disproportionately large population flows are explained simply by contiguity. No area exerted a very great pull on the tramps. Some, as I will point out, attracted people with specific trades, but most tramps were just circulating, looking for work near where they last had lived. It is not surprising that they had been on the tramp only for a short time.

Among tramps who were laborers, no geographical patterns of move-

---

[103]I have used the grouping of counties into regions of the state developed by Laurence Glasco for his study of the 1855 census of Buffalo.

[104]See Part II of this chapter, Note 36.

ments existed. They began tramping everywhere in roughly proportional numbers. A somewhat disproportionately high number of people in building, food, and white-collar work began tramping in downstate cities. A relatively high number in transportation originated in the Mohawk Valley; in maritime occupations, in western New York and the Hudson Valley; and in domestic work, in western New York cities, the Finger Lakes, and the Southern Tier. Textile and apparel workers had started in disproportionate numbers in New England, the Middle Atlantic region, and the South. Metal workers (a notable 20%) had come from the Middle Atlantic states and a sizable share from outside the United States as well. Cabinet and furniture workers slightly more often began in cities in the Southern Tier, Mohawk Valley, and Hudson Valley and outside of cities in the Catskills.

Especially interesting is the general similarity in the occupations of people leaving and going to the same place. Again the image is one of population circulation, as people with similar characteristics moved in and out of the same places. On the basis of their stated destinations, a few general observations are possible: Western New York cities attracted people in a wide variety of trades; this may have been because they were relatively less hard hit by the depression than were other areas of the state. Women employed as domestics, who sought upward mobility, may have thought it necessary to make a long-distance move, because many were headed either to New York City or to the West. New York City, in fact, has always always remained a magnet for all sorts of people. Finally, laborers and metal workers may have been particularly hard hit by the depression, because their movement showed no geographical pattern within the state.

Why, then, were these people on the tramp? Most, it would seem, were poor, out of work, and looking for a job (see Table A.52). Certainly this is the image they wished to convey when asked why they were on the tramp. Here, if anywhere, tramps were unlikely to be truthful. They would not, after all, tell a potential benefactor that they were on the tramp because they did not like to work. Nonetheless, it is instructive to observe what they did say. Three major reasons were given: destitution, unemployment, and sickness. The proportion in each category varied somewhat by sex. Among men 57.3% reported unemployment as the reason; 37.2% destitution; 5.2% sickness; and the rest, 12.9%, did not give a reason. Among women more (54.7%) claimed destitution; fewer (37.2%) unemployment; and more (26.3%) did not answer the question. Black males, probably truthfully, reported the highest unemployment, 73.1%. Of those whose occupations were known, 69.2% of the laborers claimed to be unemployed, and only 19.2% destitute. By contrast, 66.3% of the domestics claimed destitution, and only 26.1%, unemployment. Over the age of 20 there were no significant age-related differences among either men or women.

These figures are sensible and consistent with the other patterns in the data, but they do not match contemporary images of tramps. However, their lack of fit with late nineteenth-century social imagery should not cast doubt on their authenticity because, as I have shown, the imagery itself was badly deficient. Of course any interpretation that ignored unemployment during a period of depression should be treated skeptically. Tramps, it is true, were largely single, young, or middle-aged men. They also were often foreign born, but they were not recent immigrants, and most of them had started tramping within New York State. Nor, by and large, were they either drunks or illiterates. Nor did they constitute a permanent class. All but a fraction had been on the tramp less than 1 month. Most had a trade. They were circulating between cities, stopping most often in country towns, looking for work. Given these characteristics, it is hard to imagine that most tramps were dangerous, a threat to the honor of women, the security of property, and the relations between labor and capital.

Tramps did have one special handicap: They lacked families. Here there is a rough parallel with older almshouse inmates who had very few children. Among the elderly poor it probably was their children who kept many men and women out of almshouses. Among younger men it may have been working wives. Perhaps unmarried men were not so much rootless as unable to fall back upon a second family income during periods of unemployment. New York's tramps were a classic reserve army of the unemployed, mobile wage laborers, unbuffered by wives and children, free to bargain or to suffer.

## THE PROBLEM OF CAUSAL ATTRIBUTION

The demography of New York's tramps, as captured in the State Board of Charities' survey, differed sharply from prevailing social imagery. Respectable New Yorkers managed to ignore the relation of the depression of the 1870s to the increase in young men wandering from place to place in search of work. Instead they unleashed a collective hysteria that contributed to neither the analysis nor the alleviation of the problem. The question is, Why?

First, it is very likely that social imagery had some connection with social fact. A small minority of tramps had been on the road a relatively long time.

For them tramping had become a way of life. As the most visible and colorful tramps, they became the subject of amateur ethnographers and aspiring novelists. It was these relatively permanent tramps who behaved most boldly, rode the rails, acted belligerently when not aided, and attracted most public attention. Very likely the social imagery of tramps relflected a crude extension of the characteristics of the permanent minority to the entire group.

But the mass of tramps were quiet, desperate men and women, hungry, on the road in search of work or, simply, sustenance. Although most of these less visible tramps were traveling from one city to another, a disproportionate share were aided in country towns and villages. Most social commentary on tramps, however, originated in cities. Within cities some of them may have found work relatively soon after arrival and blended into the rest of the working class.

However, we should not let the respectable classes escape from their misperceptions quite so easily. After all, even without modern social science, it would not have been too difficult to acquire a better grasp of what was happening. Or would it? Perhaps, as Thomas Haskell would argue, the question about the gap between perception and reality is inappropriate if asked about the period prior to 1890.

Haskell dismisses as naive moralism any attempt to question the failure of pre-1890 social commentators to move beyond individualistic explanations of pauperism. The reason, he argues, is that social observers remained trapped within a paradigm that attributed cause to direct surface phenomena and that failed either to probe deeply into the source of social problems or to link human agency with social conditions. Only when a paradigm shift occurred, when what Haskell terms interdependence emerged as a new mode of causal attribution, did social commentators begin to connect pauperism with forces outside the control of individuals.[105]

Haskell ascribes the older mode of causal attribution to long-standing mental habits rooted in both philosophy and social structure. The "presumption of individual autonomy," he writes, was, first, "rooted in the basic possessive individualist assumptions of liberal thought going all the way back to the seventeenth century." and, second, "sustained not only by class interest but, more important, by the habits of proximate causal attribution appropriate to simple societies." [106]

---

[105]*Emergence of Professional Social Science.*

[106]*Ibid.,* p. 30; Morton White, *Social Thought in America: The Revolt against Formalism* (Boston: Beacon Press, 1957).

Because individualistic assumptions, whatever their origins, so shaped the conceptions with which people regarded the world, no amount of evidence could shake their view that pauperism, to take one example, reflected individual inadequacy. Citing Thomas Kuhn, Haskell contends that we must:

> never . . . underestimate the ability of a basic assumption to survive untouched in the face of evidence that seems, in the light of the historian's own assumptions, to be plainly disconfirmatory . . . . The abandonment of the idea that pauperism resulted from a failure of character for which the impoverished individual himself was primarily at fault cannot be explained merely by pointing to the 'brute facts' of proliferating poverty and unemployment in an industrializing society. The overarching assumption of individual potency that made the pauper seem a sufficient cause of his own poverty was supple enough to accommodate almost any increase in numbers. The poor probably were most visible and perhaps proportionally more numerous in pre-industrial society, when the ethic of self-reliance was strongest, than later when it collapsed. [107]

Thus Haskell would argue that my entire line of inquiry is misguided. He would look not to the cause of distortion but to the delineation of the moral system of the time and its boundaries. Much of the work on poverty and social work in the late nineteenth century, he writes,

> is flawed . . . by a parochial moralism that underestimates the magnitude of the gulf between the moral world of Frank Sanborn's generation and that of the Progressives and ourselves. Historians can be forthright moral critics without merely carping at rival moral systems. All systems of morality set finite limits to moral responsibility: just where the limits are set is to a considerable extent an arbitrary and conventional matter. To criticize one system from the vantage point of another is a very difficult task. [108]

Haskell's argument is powerful. How can one expect historical actors to have answered a question that was never posed, to step outside of the paradigm that ruled their mental habits? Let us grant Haskell two points: First, most social commentators in the 1870s did offer proximate causal arguments. Few of the major American commentators reflected an

---

[107] Haskell, *Emergence of Professional Social Science*, p. 31. Copyright © 1977 by the University of Illinois Press.

[108] *Ibid.*, p. 32. See also Furner, *From Advocacy to Objectivity*.

interdependent understanding of the social world. Second, it may be inappropriate to judge the past by a moral system other than its own. I am unwilling to accept this proposition without argument or refinement, but for the sake of the discussion let us at least not contest it here. Even with these concessions, Haskell's argument, which is the strongest sort of attack on the underlying problem in this part, is vulnerable.

First, Haskell's thesis assumes the dominance of one mode of causal attribution relatively unchanged between the seventeenth century and 1890. It implies that no change occurred in explanations of poverty, crime, mental illness, or other social phenomena. It does not allow for the existence of serious or fundamental debate about the nature of these problems.

Even without an extended exploration of earlier modes of causal attribution, Haskell's thesis fails badly. Consider, for example, the shift away from the concept of innate depravity and original sin in religious thought to the more optimistic and Arminian notions of the nineteenth century. Here was a shift of major proportions in causal attribution.[109]

During the late eighteenth and early nineteenth centuries ideas about crime, poverty, ignorance, and mental illness shifted toward a more complex and environmental basis. Until the 1860s Progressive theorists, reformers, and administrators argued that deviance and dependence were connected to the development of modern civilization, intertwined inexorably with industrial and urban life. True, they developed no very satisfactory theories about the interconnections, but they did translate their assumptions into reform schools, penitentiaries, mental hospitals, and public school systems, all of which were premised in their early years upon environmental and optimistic beliefs. Thus a sense of the complexity of social problems lay at the very heart of antebellum mainstream social policy. Indeed, for all their limitations, insights about the interdependence of social behavior and social context flash through the reports of men like Horace Mann and Charles Loring Brace.

Only in the 1870s, when environmentally based policy seemed to have failed, did hereditarian theory begin to dominate explanations of deviance and dependence. Coupled with a reassertion of the individualist strand already present in social thought, individualist assumptions were woven into a new and harsher configuration of beliefs about deviance and

---

[109]Bernard Wishy, *The Child and the Republic: The Dawn of Modern American Child Nurture* (Philadelphia: University of Pennsylvania Press, 1968), pp. 11–23.

dependence. One has the sense that active and intelligent people, such as Josephine Shaw Lowell, constructed and deployed a qualitatively distinct social philosophy rather than remaining stuck, unable to pull themselves out of an old mental rut. [110]

The reformers of the 1870s were not stolid, unreflective people. Rather —and this is the second point—they actively shaped social policy. They saw themselves as unsentimental realists who rejected the wishful thinking inherent in protoliberalism and believed that not only drink but also misguided humanitarianism and soft social policy had created a crisis of dependence that threatened to escalate into a fiscal and social crisis of major dimensions. Even genteel reformers such as Carroll Wright, Josephine Shaw Lowell, or Frank Sanborn knew very well what sort of social and economic changes were underway in late nineteenth-century America. They were perfectly capable of making the intellectual connection between those changes and social dependence. But, in most cases, they did not.

In an odd way, it is Haskell who denigrates the older generation of reformers, for he portrays them as stolid, incapable of linking together the aspects of social reality. As evidence he derides the organization of the American Social Science Association into units that reflected social problems and the organization of professional life rather than academic disciplines. But an approach to poverty or crime not based upon academic disciplines is not inherently unsophisticated or superficial. Indeed, it can be argued that the reduction of social problems to narrow discipline-bounded fragments represented a retreat from the possibility of a comprehensive and useful analysis. [111]

Third, Haskell does not consider the implications of alternative social theories, although he does mention their existence. If no one could escape the limits of proximate causal attribution, if only the occasional unread, unknown visionary transcended the prevailing paradigm, then, perhaps, we would be forced to concede Haskell his point. But the evidence of alternative beliefs is abundant. One has only to think of Karl Marx, Henry George, or the emergent labor movement to realize that clear, intelligent alternatives had been formulated and widely disseminated. To retain an

---

[110]On the shift to heredity, see Michael B. Katz, *The Irony of Early School Reform: Educational Innovation in Mid-Nineteenth-Century Massachusetts* (Cambridge, Mass.: Harvard University Press, 1968), pt. 3; Gerald N. Grob, *The State and the Mentally Ill: A History of Worcester State Hospital in Massachusetts, 1829–1920* (Chapel Hill, N.C.: University of North Carolina Press, 1966), pp. 229–262.

[111]Furner, *From Advocacy to Objectivity.*

individualist interpretation of dependence in this context implied not merely a failure to transcend an ancient paradigm but a deliberate rejection of alternatives as well. [112]

Where, then, do these three criticisms—inattention to change over time, neglect of the relation of ideas to policy, and the presence of alternative theories—leave Haskell's argument? As a rejection of the need to explain the failure of reformers to connect pauperism or tramping with economic conditions, Haskell's thesis lies in shreds. Yet, clearly, as he writes, a revolution of sorts occurred in late nineteenth-century intellectual life, whether it is called interdependence or, in the terms of Morton White, the "revolt against formalism." [113] Clearly, too, this change in the structure of intellectual discourse was connected to the reorganization of intellectual life into disciplines housed in reconstructed or new universities. Nor can one deny the strongly individualist assumptions, the readiness to make individuals the agents of their own destiny, that permeated—and indeed still permeates—much American thought. The problem, however, is to account for the different manifestations of individualist thought, its role and character over time, and to see its relative dominance or subordination within social commentary.

A concentration on academic social thought, however, can deflect attention away from the trenches. Even as the economists battled over the fate of classical economics, social reformers and administrators worked with less consistent, less completely articulated assumptions. Within the realm of social policy and social administration, I suspect, the break in the mode of causal attribution was less sharp, more nuanced, and less complete. In his discussions of social thought Haskell moves from practical administrator–social scientists to academics, from Frank Sanborn to Richard Ely. But as the role of social scientist–social reformer–administrator split apart, academics represented only part of the legacy. To grasp the nature of the ideas and policies that affected dependence, it is necessary to turn, as well, to the secretaries of state boards of charities, the superintendents of insane asylums, the superintendents and overseers of the poor, the agents of Charity Organization Societies, and others who grappled with social problems daily and created their own literature of dependence. [114] It is about the latter group that I want to pose the question

---

[112]For one coment on the influence of Henry George, see Chester McArthur Destler, *American Radicalism, 1865–1901* (Chicago: Quadrangle, 1966), pp. 12–13.

[113]Morton White, *The Revolt Against Formalism.*

[114]A good place to start to read the views of the administrators is in the Proceedings of the Annual Conventions of the County Superintendents of the Poor in New York, starting in 1870.

of the relation of ideas and social reality, for between the 1870s and 1890s it was these able and energetic people who managed to overlook the structural origins of social problems.

Nor, finally, can we accept Haskell's essentially functional account of the shift to interdependence among any group, for he presents interdependence as the only appropriate and inevitable paradigm for late nineteenth-century America. Spurred by their own concern with authority, social theorists finally caught up with social change and exchanged paradigms of causal attribution. But, at the danger of repetition, interdependence was not the only appropriate paradigm. Radical social thought, for instance, offered other possibilities. Interdependence, however, was especially useful because it denied the existence of any central driving force within social development. Hence it deemphasized the role of conflict and of class. It stressed interconnectedness, the mutual adjustment of interests, and obscured the asymmetrical power relations that sustained political and social inequality. At the very moment when American life erupted in class violence, social scientists deployed a new paradigm in which conflict was pathological and class an overly simple and reductionist category. [115]

In contrast to Haskell, my hypothesis is that interdependence was a class-related choice among intellectual options. Is there any reason to believe that the individualist theory of dependence in the 1870s did not have a similar origin? What is important about the heritage of proximate causal attribution and individualism is its respectability and availability. Long present, often used, intuitively appealing for many reasons, it provided a ready alternative, a clear and easy option on which to base a repressive social policy aimed at disciplining labor, dividing the working class, defusing radicalism, and cutting taxes.

I am arguing, thus, that the response to tramps and paupers reflected a collective hysteria, a fear that swept through the respectable classes in the 1870s. The Paris Commune, the railroad strike of 1877, the emergence of the labor movement—these were developments that threatened property and raised the specter of violence and social conflict. Not the tramps, paupers, or even tax bills, I suspect, touched off the collective hysteria that gave the emotional edge to social policy. Rather, the source was the spectacle of the working class organizing, gathering itself for massive protest and what many feared would be a massive assault upon American social institutions. Antitramp legislation, the abolition of outdoor relief,

---

[115]On sociologists and class, see Charles Hunt Page, *Class and American Sociology* (New York: Dial Press, 1940), p. 250.

and related policies, especially the concentration on breaking up the families of the poor by separating parents and children—all were forms of repression, attempts to weaken collective action, to reassert class control, and to bring as many of the dangerous classes as possible under the immediate authority of social agencies and institutions. In this way social policy was the counterpart of sending in the troops to abort a strike.

If repression was the aim of social policy, how explicitly and by whom was it recognized? How is one to account for the relative absence of such explicit chains of reasoning in public social commentary? How is one to handle the question of intentionality—for that, after all, is the issue— without falling into a crude reductionism or cynicism? It is possible that more extensive and directed research will make the necessary connections more explicitly. At the same time, we must not feel too constrained about questioning the overt content of discourse, for, after all, I have shown that in important ways it cannot be believed.

# CHAPTER 3

# AMERICAN HISTORIANS
# AND DEPENDENCE

Two great themes stand out from the mass of detail in the case studies that make up the first two chapters of this book. They are, first, that dependence was a structural, almost normal, aspect of working-class life. Many paupers were old working-class people who lacked families to care for them; many others were young men temporarily out of work; most tramps were men on the road in search of a job. The Sullivans became destitute when Mr. Sullivan, a teamster, had no work in the winter; they stayed destitute when spring came, and he took sick and died. People lacked jobs because of the nature of work: its unsteady, irregular, seasonal quality. They took sick often because they lacked the money for a healthful diet, adequate housing, and effective sanitation. When they were sick, they found it hard to purchase adequate medical care. When people grew too old to work, they had no pensions or Social Security, and when working-class men died, they left no savings or insurance for their families.

The other great theme is the discrepancy between the structural roots of dependence and the perception of it in social thought. Despite the fundamental insecurity of working-class life—which, after all, any moderately perceptive person could recognize—most people who spoke and wrote about welfare continued to blame the very poor for their dependence. Over and over again the case studies in this book have shown the distortions in those contemporary descriptions. I have made some suggestions about the source and role of those distortions, but much about them—indeed, much more about the lives of the poor and the history of welfare—remains to be learned.

Unfortunately, not nearly enough can be discovered by reading the existing historical literature. Contemporary American historical writing about dependent populations follows three major streams. One is the historiography of philanthropic reform: evangelical philanthropy in the Jacksonian period; the Charity Organization Societies of the Gilded Age; the settlement house movement and the origins of social work in the Progressive era, to name its most well-known topics. Second is the historiography of institutions: mental hospitals and general hospitals, reformatories, prisons, and, to some extent, public schools. Third, and least prominent now in contrast to the 1930s, is the historiography of public welfare, which focuses on the emergence of Social Security and related legislation. A fourth group, the study of the poor and of poverty within specific cities, may be emerging. No contemporary historian, however, has made the politics and administration of public welfare his or her central concern.[1]

Against the background of the case studies, this chapter explores each of the three major kinds of writing about dependent populations in contemporary historiography, stressing the limitations of each. It argues that they are limited, first, by their isolation from one another; second, by their failure to relate public and private responses; third, by their inattention to the characteristics and activities of the dependent populations themselves; and fourth, by the neglect of fine-grained analyses of the politics and administration of public welfare on the state and local level.

## HISTORIANS AND PHILANTHROPY:
### *URBAN MASSES AND MORAL ORDER IN AMERICA*
### AS THE CULMINATION OF A
### HISTORIOGRAPHICAL TRADITION

In *Urban Masses and Moral Order in America* Paul Boyer has shaped the familiar elements of urban philanthropy between the Jacksonian era and

---

[1]Raymond Mohl, *Poverty in New York, 1783–1825* (New York, Oxford University Press, 1971); John F. Alexander, *Render Them Submissive: Responses to Poverty in Philadelphia, 1760–1800* (Amherst: University of Massachusetts Press, 1980). For an excellent bibliography of social welfare history, see James Leiby, *A History of Social Welfare and Social Work in the United States* (New York: Columbia University Press, 1978), pp. 389–416.

the 1920s into an arresting new synthesis. The major elements in this stream of historical writing are evangelical Protestant philanthropy and the attempt to rescue city children in the antebellum period; the scientific charity movement of the Gilded Age; and the settlements and other voluntary reform movements of the Progressive period.

Boyer argues that an urban moral or social control tradition dominated social reform for a century. Using "social control" and "moral control" almost "interchangeably," he focuses on "individuals and groups who sought through consciously planned and organized (but voluntarist and extra-legal) effort to influence that range of social behavior usually considered outside the purview of criminal law, yet not entirely private and personal."[2]

The impetus to moral and social control, contends Boyer, reflected a fear of the city, emerging first in the Jacksonian era and gathering strength throughout the century. Stated succinctly, his thesis is that throughout the century between roughly 1820 and 1920,

> the process of urbanization functioned as a potent catalyst for social speculation and social action. Fears about industrialization, immigration, family disruption, religious change, and deepening class divisions all focused on the growing cities. Social thinkers, reformers, philanthropists, and others whose assumptions and activities seemed otherwise very different were often linked by a shared preoccupation with the city, and, more specifically, by a common interest in controlling the behavior of an increasingly urbanized populace.[3]

Thus Boyer has written about the perceptions and activities of reformers—generally white, affluent, and Protestant—working outside the public sector. As a consequence, he bypasses public responses to the same problems and in only a few instances considers the clients of reform attention.

The urban moral–social control tradition started with the tract societies and Sunday schools of the Jacksonian era, efforts tied closely to evangelical Protestantism and directed not only at cities but also at the threat to civilization posed by the western frontier. Especially valuable is Boyer's

---

[2]Paul Boyer, *Urban Masses and Moral Order in America, 1820–1920* (Cambridge, Mass.: Harvard University Press, 1978), p. viii. Another example of this historiographical tradition is Carroll Smith-Rosenberg, *Religion and the Rise of the American City: The New York City Mission Movement, 1812–1870* (Ithaca, N.Y.: Cornell University Press, 1971).

[3]Boyer, *Urban Masses*, p. viii.

description of the efforts of Sunday schools to teach deference and reinforce social hierarchy as well as to inculcate Christianity.[4]

In the middle decades of the century rapid urban growth and the immigration of the famine Irish heightened anxieties. As a consequence, reformers, themselves often migrants to the city from farms and villages, focused their efforts more directly on the alleviation of specific urban problems and severed their direct connections with religious denominations, although their efforts remained diffused with evangelical Protestantism. The most important innovations of this era were the friendly visiting of the Association for Improving the Condition of the Poor, the shipment of city children to the West by the Children's Aid Society, and the Young Men's Christian Association's (YMCA) attempt to protect young men migrating from the country to the city. The highlight of Boyer's account of these innovations is his interpretation of Charles Loring Brace, founder of the Children's Aid Society, as a maverick, an opponent not only of institutions but also of families.[5]

In the Gilded Age reform assumed even greater urgency, according to Boyer, as fears of class violence, the "ragged edge of anarchy," provided the "emotional context of urban social control." Aware of their growing irrelevance to social problems, Protestant churches renewed their efforts to reach the poor, especially through the creation of missions in slum districts. However, the leading innovation of the period was scientific charity, embodied in Charity Organization Societies, which attempted to systematize and coordinate American urban philanthropy. The emphasis of Charity Organization Societies on identifying and counseling the urban poor represented less an innovation than an updating of friendly visiting and the attempt to reestablish personal contact between social classes that had been advocated at least since the inception of the Association for Improving the Condition of the Poor in the 1840s. In the supercharged context of late nineteenth-century America these ideas, buttressed increasingly by data from social investigations, finally dominated private philanthropy, albeit for the relatively brief period before the emergence of the settlement house movement and the innovations of the Progressives.[6]

In the 1890s, Boyer contends, the urban moral–social control movement bifurcated into what he terms negative and positive environmentalism. Environmentalism shifted attention from the reformation of individuals to

---

[4]*Ibid.*, pp. 34–53.

[5]*Ibid.*, pp. 85–107.

[6]*Ibid.*, pp. 143–161.

changes in the social order that produced deviant or immoral behavior. The negative version consisted of coercive attempts to mold behavior, especially through two great crusades: the battles against the brothel and the saloon. The former culminated in the Mann Act, the latter in the Eighteenth Amendment. By contrast, positive environmentalism, which was more often advocated by settlement workers and wealthy reformers (who did not often support coercive measures), urged changes in the physical structure of the city. Drawing increasingly on experts and hard data, positive environmentalists advocated housing reform, parks, and playgrounds. Within a couple of decades their campaigns merged into an attempt to increase social order through a heightened civic loyalty engendered by beautifying cities. Out of the city beautiful movement, asserts Boyer, emerged city planning.[7]

Boyer believes that in the 1920s the urban moral–social control tradition began to fade. Champions of urbanism, critics of small town life, and advocates of cultural pluralism all rejected the vision that had united reformers throughout the century. That vision had been rooted firmly in nostalgia for an older, simpler way of life.

> Common to almost all the reformers considered in this book was the conviction—explicit or implicit—that the city, although obviously different from the village in its external, physical aspects, should nevertheless replicate the moral order of the village. City dwellers, they believed, must somehow be brought to perceive themselves as members of cohesive communities knit together by shared moral and social values.[8]

This nostalgia, according to Boyer, took a century to die. One should ask, though, whether the moral–social control tradition has faded entirely, as Boyer contends. Certainly much urban reform rhetoric in the 1960s echoed the moral–social control tradition. Perhaps it is more accurate to say that other competing traditions have emerged and that the balance between them now shifts from time to time. Indeed, the political rhetoric of the early 1980s—the opposition to the Equal Rights Amendment, the Right to Life movement, and the Moral Majority—reflects the coercive strains in negative environmentalism quite as much as the War on Poverty appears, in retrospect, a revival of the positive environmental tradition.

Despite some strain between the characters he pushes onto the same stage, Boyer has defined a strand in American social reform. Although

---

[7] *Ibid.*, pp. 233–274.

[8] *Ibid.*, p. viii.

most elements of the tradition have been written about by other historians, although his synthesis will not provoke major surprise, Boyer's achievement should be recognized. He has provided a rich, definitive account of the main line of private Protestant reform in America. Historians now should build upon his achievement, overcoming its limitations, broadening its scope, and enriching its theoretical base.

One limitation is the emphasis on private relief. In the early nineteenth century the line between public and private remained fuzzy throughout American social and even economic life. Reformers undoubtedly felt they were performing public duties, and institutions and agencies that later became entirely public, such as the New York Public School Society, began as private corporations serving the public at large. Indeed, one major theme in nineteenth-century history is the emergence of the distinction between public and private.[9]

Therefore, any distinction between public and private cast back early in the century misrepresents the character of reform efforts; even cast forward it still constricts the history of responses to social problems. By the late nineteenth century urban poverty, to take a major issue, dominated the agendas of public agencies and officials as well as those of private ones, such as the Charity Organization Societies or settlements. Indeed, three points must be emphasized.

One is that even late in the century public and private agencies cooperated, sharing personnel and functions. An example is the relation between the New York Board of State Charities and the private Charities Aid Association of New York. The latter inspected almshouses on behalf of the board, and individuals such as Josephine Shaw Lowell served on both. Within a year after an almshouse superintendent objected to the visits of Charity Aid Association members, the association managed to persuade the state legislature to mandate its authority. In Indiana the establishment of a Charity Organization Society preceded the formation of a state board of charities, and its leading members managed to write the principles of charity organization into the operating procedures of the new state agency.[10] When the depression of the 1890s finally jolted some politicians,

---

[9]Oscar Handlin and Mary Flug Handlin, *Commonwealth: A Study of the Role of Government in the American Economy: Massachusetts, 1774–1861* (New York: New York University Press, 1947); Morton J. Horwitz, *The Transformation of American Law, 1780–1860* (Cambridge, Mass.: Harvard University Press, 1977); John S. Whitehead, *The Separation of College and State: Columbia, Dartmouth, Harvard, and Yale, 1776–1876* (New Haven, Conn.: Yale University Press, 1973); William O. Bourne, *History of the Public School Society of the City of New York* (New York, 1870).

[10]*First Annual Report of the State Charities Aid Association to the State Commissioners of Public Charities of the State of New York, March 1873* (New York: Cushing, Barua, 1873), pp. 15–19;

**Plate 11.** *Kings County Alms House, exterior photo showing the rear of the Women's Building. (Photograph by Byron, The Byron Collection, Museum of the City of New York.)*

businessmen, and charity workers into the recognition that unemployment was a social as much as an individual problem, many cities began experiments with public works and employment bureaus. In a number of cities private sources contributed the funds for public work projects. In Philadelphia it was the private sector that sponsored and shaped the creation of the city's first welfare department in the years following World War I.[11]

---

*Third Annual Report of the State Charities Aid Association to the State Board of Charities of New York, March 1875* (New York, 1875), p. 14.

[11]Susan E. Davis, "The Underdevelopment of Public Welfare in Philadelphia 1913–1931," in Michael B. Katz and Associates, Appendix to Final Report NIMH Grant No. R01MH32520, November 1981; L. A. Halbert, "Boards of Public Welfare and Good City Government," *Proceedings, National Council of Charities and Corrections* 40(1913): 212–221, and "Boards of Public Welfare: A System of Government Social Work," *Proceedings, National Council of Social Workers* 45(1918): 220–229; Stanley H. Howe, "The Development of Municipal Charities in the United States," *National Conference of Charities and Corrections* 40(1913): 208–212.

Second, throughout the century public officials undoubtedly touched more lives than did private reformers. Consider only the massive numbers affected by local poormasters, superintendents of poorhouses or insane asylums, and wardens of jails, reformatories, and penitentiaries. Private reformers provided the most eloquent rhetoric, but public officials supplied the day-to-day administration of relief and custody. In New York State in 1900 the state institutions supported 8494 people, and the almshouses, 73,117. Private societies aided 30,560 people with outdoor relief, compared with 209,092 given temporary, or outdoor, relief by almshouses.[12]

The institution that touched the very poor most directly, the poorhouse, has received only cursory treatment. Only a few historians in recent years have examined a poorhouse with any care. Nonetheless, dreary and despised though they were, poorhouses probably cared for more prople than any of the other residential institutions about which historians have written at length. Important as the poorhouse was, most people receiving public assistance during the nineteenth century were given outdoor relief. For instance, in 1860 of 8324 people "supported or relieved" in Erie County, New York, 6283 were "relieved temporarily," that is, given public outdoor relief. In Kings County, New York, in the same year, 19,938 people received temporary assistance out of a total of 25,508 recipients of relief.[13]

Third, it is wrong to assume that public officials always accepted and acted upon the viewpoints of theorists of social problems. Their daily activities often heightened their sense of the complex, ambiguous nature of poverty or mental illness; and they had to respond to the constituencies from which their clients came. Poormasters and superintendents of the poor, for instance, often were elected, dependent on the votes of the poor for the maintenance of their office. In these circumstances, reformers and administrators often clashed.[14]

Poor relief policy provides an example. At the same time that Jacksonian reformers were starting tract societies and Sunday schools, state legislatures organized commissions to recommend new poor relief policy.

---

[12]Michael B. Katz, "The Configuration and Social Structure of Erie County Institutions in 1900," in Katz and Associates, Appendix.

[13]*Annual Report of the Secretary of State in Relation to the Statistics of the Poor*," New York State Assembly Document No. 17, February 11, 1890, p. 9.

[14]Examples of the relatively greater sensitivity and responsiveness of the county superintendents may be found in *Proceedings of the Annual Convention of the County Superintendents of the Poor of the State of New York*, which began in 1870: for instance, 14(1884): 61; 17(1887): 41; 18(1888): 20, 28; 20(1890): 23, 93; 22(1892): 23; 24(1894): 29, 34, 38–39.

While evangelicals distributed Bibles and tracts, public officials debated the merits of indoor and outdoor relief, trying to stem what they perceived as an upsurge of pauperism. The result was the network of poorhouses strung out across—to take the three best-known instances—New York, Massachusetts, and Pennsylvania. However, the new poorhouses did not eliminate outdoor relief, which continued to grow and vastly to exceed indoor relief.[15]

Alarmed especially by the appearance of great numbers of tramps after the depression of 1873, private and public officials mounted a new attack on outdoor relief. Led by the Charity Organization Societies, the campaign succeeded in abolishing it in 10 of the country's 40 largest cities by 1900 and reducing it in others.[16] Two points about the campaign against outdoor relief should be stressed. First, the charity organization movement and the acceptance of its approach to poverty, which, recall, had been advocated for 30 or 40 years, can be understood only as part of the concern about outdoor relief. It must be seen as one strategy for dealing with a serious social problem, not isolated as a manifestation of a private tradition.

Second, the campaign against outdoor relief was contested. Although it was difficult to find supporters of outdoor relief in influential journals or in national and statewide organizations, opposition to its abolition remained strong. For instance, in New York State county superintendents of the poor refused to vote for its total abolition. Even though most of them, at least for the record, deplored outdoor relief, they argued that its abolition would create unjust hardships for the worthy poor and foment social discontent, which they would be unable to stem. Indeed, running throughout the comments of superintendents on outdoor relief was the theme of popular demand. The "community" or the friends of the poor would not permit public officials to remove the worthy poor from the rolls or to separate widows from their children.[17]

Public and private officials disagreed about another aspect of the question, too: the relative merits of public relief versus private charity. The

---

[15]Reports from Massachusetts, New York, and Pennsylvania leading to the founding of poorhouses are collected in *The Almshouse Experience: Collected Reports, 1821–1827*, a volume in the Poverty, USA, The Historical Record series (New York: Arno Press and New York Times, 1971).

[16]Frederick Almy, "The Relation between Private and Public Outdoor Relief," *The Charities Review* 9(1899–1900): pt. 1, pp. 22–30, pt. 2, pp. 65–71.

[17]References by the superintendents of the poor to community pressure are found in *Proceedings of the Annual Convention of the County Superintendents of the Poor of the State of New York:* for example, 12(1882): 17; 17(1887): 41, 73; 22(1892): 23; 23(1893): 55.

return of almsgiving to private organizations, argued the advocates of abolition, would restore to it the aura of charity essential to the avoidance of degradation and would recreate bonds between classes. At the same time, it would remove one source of graft from the venal politicians who used relief to line their own pockets and solidify their power. Superintendents of the poor, by contrast, not surprisingly often had difficulty seeing the distinction between public and private relief.[18] The important point here about the debate is not so much its details as its illustration of the way in which private philanthropy, as embodied in the moral–social control tradition, developed as an explicit counterpoint to public activities.

By the early twentieth century the charity organization movement had foundered, partly, as Boyer mentions, because it no longer represented the cutting edge of reform but also (a point he does not discuss) because of its opposition to an important public issue: mothers' pensions. Forced on the defensive by opponents of outdoor relief, superintendents of the poor and other advocates of the continuation of public assistance relied on the image of the virtuous widow with small children who, if deprived of temporary aid, would be forced into the poorhouse and separated from her family. This concentration on the plight of women escalated into a movement for mothers' pensions, which their advocates distinguished sharply from poor relief. By the 1920s the campaign had succeeded in several states over the unceasing opposition to mothers' pensions of the charity organization movement, whose hostility earned it increasing public scorn. (In fairness, it should be noted that not all Charity Organization Societies officials opposed mothers' pensions.)[19]

The complex relation between public and private was reflected, too, in the child saving movement, not discussed by Boyer. Although Boyer briefly notes the attention to children so prominent in the late nineteenth and early twentieth centuries, he does not use the term *child saving*, which became ubiquitous in both public and private reform literature. Reformers

---

[18]For a strong propublic statement, see *ibid.* 17(1887): 73–78; for a defense of the role of the private sector, see the remarks at the convention made by Josephine Shaw Lowell, *ibid.* 20(1890): 10; for a defense of the superintendents and a discussion of the difficulties of their role, see the comments by J. A. Page, *ibid.* 30(1900): 23–28.

[19]There is a discussion of mothers' pensions in Hace Sorel Tishler, *Self-Reliance and Social Security, 1870–1917* (Port Washington, N.Y.: Kennikat Press, 1971), pp. 141–158, and in Roy Lubove, *The Struggle for Social Security, 1900–1935* (Cambridge, Mass.: Harvard University Pres, 1968), pp. 91–112. The attitudes of the charity organization movement toward mothers' pensions are also discussed in Frank Dekker Watson, *The Charity Organization Movement in the United States* (New York: Macmillan, 1902), pp. 393–399, 511, 512.

and public officials who otherwise differed on various issues united in the belief that the ineffectual results of attempts to change adult behavior pointed unmistakably to the need to concentrate energy on children who should be rescued from faulty homes, inadequate legal protection, and unhealthful surroundings. Child saving explicitly considered a movement by contemporaries, does not fit easily into either of Boyer's positive or negative environmental categories since it had elements of both. Nor, of course, can it be understood solely by reference to either public or private efforts.[20]

Child saving highlights the contradictions of nineteenth-century reform, for it posed a very complicated question: When is it permissible to separate children from their parents? And who has the authority? The question was asked frequently by the critics of Charles Loring Brace and the New York Children's Aid Society. It also was one question posed, but not discussed, by the removal of children from the poorhouses of New York State, as required by the Children's Act of 1875. Surely poorhouses were awful places for children, but sending them to special institutions often meant separating them from their parents. So did refusing outdoor relief to families, thereby forcing parents and children into different institutions. Reformers in the 1870s often argued that it was better to break up a poor family than to risk accustoming children to life on the dole, which was so inherently demoralizing that it would transform them into lifelong paupers. At the same time, reformers argued that the number of children in orphanages was rising fast because greedy and selfish poor parents were less reluctant to send their children to a special institution than to an almshouse. They remained unable or unwilling to connect the increase in the number of children in orphanages to either the cutback in outdoor relief or the hardships of the 1870s.[21]

As a response to the abuses within the family life of the poor reformers created societies for the protection of children from cruelty. It is

---

[20]For some examples of child saving discussions, see A. A. Fuller, "Child Saving Work," *Proceedings of the Annual Convention of the County Superintendents of the Poor of the State of New York* 21(1891): 28; 22(1892): 11; 23(1893): 7. See also Homer Folks, *The Care of Destitute, Neglected and Delinquent Children* (New York: Macmillan, 1902). Also of interest is Neil Sutherland, *Children in English-Canadian Society: Framing the Twentieth-Century Consensus* (Toronto: University of Toronto Press, 1976).

[21]*Report of the Committee of homes and asylums of the Board of Supervisors of Kings County in the matter of Providing for the Support of Pauper and Destitute Children, presented to the Board of Supervisors, October 26, 1877* (New York; Charles M. Cornwell, 1877). For the conventional interpretation of the Children's Act of 1875, see David M. Schneider and Albert Deutsch, *The History of Public Welfare in New York State, 1867–1940* (Chicago: University of Chicago Press, 1941), pp. 60–71.

undeniable that many children suffered terrible abuse. Yet the new societies showed little appreciation of the difficulties faced by poor families and little hesitation about separating parents from children. They encouraged neighbors to report abuses, and poor families often lived in dread of "the Cruelty," as it was called at least in Philadelphia, and its agents. Sometimes the Society for the Prevention of Cruelty to Children (SPCC) prosecuted parents when other agencies, including the courts, saw no grounds for breaking up families. In Philadelphia not only did the SPCC try to persuade judges to take children away from their parents, but it also had parents convicted of abuse sent to jail for 3 months not so much as punishment but as a way of giving the SPCC a chance to move their children elsewhere. In Indianapolis, members of the Board of Children's Guardians, a private agency, acted as truant officers for the public schools and threatened to take children away from parents who did not make sure they attended school. By the 1890s the emphasis on child saving had softened. Reformers who wanted to remove children from families increasingly were on the defensive, and more and more it was argued that only the most awful circumstances justified the breaking apart of families. This shift also was part of the background of the mothers' pension movement.[22]

Aside from its concentration on private activity, Boyer's story is limited by its Protestant focus. Like most American historians of reform, philanthropy, or institutions, Boyer neglects the activities of the Catholic church. Yet, especially when its finances improved after the 1860s, the Catholic church made heroic efforts to alleviate suffering, dependence, and sickness within cities. The Saint Vincent de Paul Society and the New York Catholic Protectory are two well-known examples that could be multiplied hundreds of times across the country. In Buffalo late in the nineteenth century Catholics probably provided at least one-half of the money for children's institutions in the city. Given their limited access to public funds and their relative poverty, Catholic communities may have spent more of their income on charity than did Protestant ones.[23]

---

[22]Examples of varying positions on the breakup of families may be found in the *Proceedings of the Annual Convention of the County Superintendents of the Poor of the State of New York*. Some comments opposing the separation of children from their parents are in: 16(1886): 81–89, 96; 17(1887): 14; 12(1882): 35; 18(1888): 18; 25(1895): 44–45. Comments less hostile to breaking up families are in: 12(1882): 17, 81; 17(1887): 41; 21(1891): 10, 59; 31(1901): 47. An interesting observation on the origins of day nurseries as a compromise between opponents and supporters of breaking up families is in: 25(1895): 44–45.

[23]Jay P. Dolan, *The Immigrant Church: New York's Irish and German Catholics, 1815–1865* (Baltimore: Johns Hopkins University Press, 1975), is useful on Catholic charity in this period.

Catholic spokesmen distrusted the moral–social control tradition because of its Protestant, often militantly anti-Catholic bias. They viewed the Children's Aid Society, for instance, as an agency designed to place Catholic children in Protestant homes. Certainly this must have happened thousands of times. Catholic clergy also complained about their lack of access to Catholic inmates in institutions because in the mid-nineteenth century they were excluded from many asylums and reformatories. The unwillingness of Protestant reformers and officials to honor Catholic sensibilities cannot be missed. Even late in the century, Protestant public officials and reformers in New York repeatedly opposed a law that required children removed from almshouses to be placed either in institutions or in families of the same religion as their parents. Clearly, by "nondenominational" the representatives of the moral–social control tradition meant Protestant, and most American historians have continued to see reform and philanthropy through their eyes. As a consequence, a major component of social history—Catholic charity and institution building—remains relatively unknown.[24]

Boyer underemphasizes the importance of both public and Catholic responses to poverty because he views the past through the eyes of the moral–social control reformers. For the same reason, he accepts too uncritically Protestant reform images of preindustrial communities and of the urban poor. Boyer argues that a sentimental view of farm and village life as cohesive, warm, and stable formed the model that reformers tried to replicate within cities. Although he criticizes it as inappropriate, he accepts the model as grounded in reality. Reformers wanted to recapture a simple and more cohesive America that they remembered, not that they imagined.[25] Of course Boyer is much too perceptive to miss the reformers' ambivalence. The proponents of the moral–social control tradition remained attracted to as well as repelled by the new urban and industrial order that they and their friends were energetically creating. Indeed, it must be remembered that reformers had chosen to leave the countryside or to remain within cities. They had not been forced to lead urban lives. Rural America surrounded them, easily accessible if they decided to retreat. But they did not. They chose cities and helped to build them.

What the reformers wanted was to control their creations, to stave off the consequences of urbanization and industrialization as they appeared

---

[24]For three examples of hostility to the law requiring children to be placed in an institution or with a family of the same religion as their parents, see *Proceedings of the Annual Convention of the County Superintendents of the Poor of the State of New York* 15(1885): 41; 17(1887): 50; 21(1891): 25.

[25]Boyer, *Urban Masses*, p. viii.

elsewhere, especially in English cities. Thus Boyer becomes most convincing when he stresses fear of immigrants, disorder, violence, and working-class political power. Fear differs from sentimental nostalgia. Reformers represented social groups with concrete interests, with stakes they thought threatened, and their reactions reflected not only a humanitarian impulse to relieve distress or a wistful longing to import rural styles into the city but also, even more, self-protection.

In the reform language quoted by Boyer the missing ingredient is not so much warmth and neighborliness as it is deference. Deference is less a property of village and farm life than of the kind of social order that dissolved quickly in early nineteenth-century northern towns and cities. It lingered longer in the South and probably never was so strong in the West. Where deference governed social relations, political ties reflected a social hierarchy tinged with mutual obligation, and bonds between employers and employees remained personal as well as economic. Deference was the mode of social control with which reformers were most familiar, either through personal experience or through literature. It was the model to which they instinctively turned as they attempted to order the confusing and frightening new world that they had helped to create.[26]

Stripped of rhetoric, the goals of much nineteenth-century reform can be reduced to a desire to lower property taxes and keep the streets safe. Although some reform advocates claimed lofty social goals, by and large prosaic fears of crime and rising expenses for poor relief fueled the moral–social control tradition for most of a century. These limited goals are important to remember. Despite a century of concern, inheritors of the moral–social control tradition did not confront poverty frontally. Reform strategies never were structural or redistributive. Rather, reformers sought to rub the rough edges off urban society, to preserve social order, contain taxes, and promote deference through friendly visiting and by diffusing evangelical religion, public education, temperance, and urban playgrounds.

Reform efforts to contain sexuality form another motif that runs through the moral–social control literature for a century, though one that remains by and large implicit in Boyer's account. (In many ways the classic discussion of sexual fear remains Oscar Handlin's essay, "The Horror.") After all, these were the years of the great campaign against masturbation. Although historians such as Carroll Smith-Rosenberg, Carl Degler, and Steven Marcus have shown that Victorian sexual ideology is at best a crude

---

[26]The best discussion of deference in this era is in Gareth Stedman Jones, *Outcast London* (London: Oxford University Press, 1971), especially his chapter, "The Deformation of the Gift," pp. 241–261.

guide to actual behavior, the rhetoric of the times did reflect a profound uneasiness about sexuality. Within reform literature "sensuousness" was a moral weakness, a quality to be erased, whereas "restraint" remained a key virtue. In fact, the attempt to exercise sexual restraint may have been a major tension within bourgeois life as clerks, entrepreneurs, and professionals began to limit the size of their families during a period when birth control was considered illegitimate. They may have resented what they saw as the indulgence of the poor in the sensual pleasures that they denied themselves, especially because the consequences, they believed, translated into rising taxes and crime. This tinge of envy, one can speculate, gave to the campaigns against drink and sexuality their hard and nasty edge.[27]

Superimposed upon the fear of sexual indulgence was anxiety over sex roles, a theme brilliantly discussed by Daniel Calhoun. The definition of roles within the home, the relative influence of fathers and mothers in child rearing, remained a source of unease, never resolved fully by bourgeois families. Even female sexuality, as the writing and activity of early gynecologists show, remained a source of male fear. The point of these examples is not to detour into the history of sexuality. Rather, it is to point to another emotional current in nineteenth-century reform, a counterpoint to the fear of disorder, lurking everywhere, irrepressible if illicit, providing much of the brittle, often hysterical edge to the moral–social control tradition.[28]

However, one can become too preoccupied with the wellsprings of reform and ignore its objects, as most historians have done. In only two places, for instance, does Boyer probe behind reformers' images of their clients. He points out that Charles Loring Brace was one of the few reformers who liked the people with whom he worked. By emphasizing Brace's admiration for the independent, quick street urchin, Boyer implicitly highlights the stereotypical quality of most reform observations about the poor and their children. The other instance is his discussion of prostitution. Commenting on the wealth of descriptive detail in the

---

[27] Oscar Handlin, "The Horror," in *Race and Nationality in American Life* by Oscar Handlin (Garden City, N.Y.: Doubleday, Anchor Books, 1957), pp. 111–132; Carroll Smith-Rosenberg and Charles Rosenberg, "The Female Animal: Medical and Biological Views of Women in Nineteenth-Century America," *Journal of American History* 60(1973): 332–356; Carl Degler, *At Odds: Women and the Family in America from the Revolution to the Present* (New York: Oxford University Press, 1980), pp. 249–278; Steven Marcus, *The Other Victorians* (New York: Basic Books, 1966).

[28] Daniel Calhoun, *The Intelligence of a People* (Princeton, N.J.: Princeton University Press, 1973), pp. 188, 195, 204.

antiprostitution reports compiled in many cities, Boyer observes that prostitutes did not conform at all nicely to the images with which they were depicted in reform literature. By and large they seemed neither depressed nor unhappy, trapped in their work not so much by artful and wicked white slavers as by a labor market that otherwise would have confined them to dull, demeaning, and poor-paying jobs. (As an aside, the image of smug crusaders interviewing prostitutes, drawing out the details of their lives and activities, dutifully recording the going rate for oral sex, underscores the complex sexual motif in the moral–social control tradition.)[29]

The characteristics of the poor never match what is said about them in respectable sources. Nineteenth-century discussions of pauperism either omitted or rejected the impact of depressions, economic cycles, seasonal unemployment, and technological change on the ability of men to find work. They wrongly described paupers as mainly intemperate, the degenerate offspring of defective parents. They incorrectly ascribed an increase in pauperism to recent immigrants. They refused to acknowledge that most tramps were men on the road only a short time seeking work, not a permanent and dangerous class. They missed the single most important characteristic of the dependent poor: their lack of spouses or children to whom they could turn for support. Sometimes, too, they confounded all the "dependent, defective, and delinquent" into one great class and failed to see the important distinctions between them.[30]

Wherever historians look closely, the behavior of the poor, criminals, or delinquents—the objects of reform—appears complex, defying stereotypes of passive degradation. Both public and private agencies sought to achieve reform through imposition, through the creation of institutions, the passage of legislation, and the active diffusion of morality and religion. Although they had the power and resources to create asylums, reformatories, public schools, and philanthropic societies, even to reach many of their legislative goals, they could not control the use to which their achievements were put, for the clients of reform retained the ability to manipulate the institutions and agencies designed to train or constrain them.

Magistrate's courts often turned into forums for the resolution of working-class domestic difficulties; reform schools became havens for the children of the poor during family crises; poorhouses served as temporary refuges for ablebodied men during economic downturns. In some cities the poor successfully resisted the abolition of outdoor relief and learned

---

[29]Boyer, *Urban Masses*, pp. 202–204.

[30]See the case studies in Chapter 2.

*Plate 12.* *Kings County Alms House, exterior photo showing line of men. (Photograph by Byron, The Byron Collection, Museum of the City of New York.)*

how to exploit various relief agencies. Tramps knew exactly which cities to avoid, developed a secret code with which they marked houses whose occupants were generous, and fought a low-key guerrilla war with railway officials. Even city jails became refuges, deliberately sought in the winter. No history of philanthropy, reform, or institutional life, it should be clear, can rely on the descriptions of clients in official sources. The image of passive degradation, so energetically promoted by the urban moral–social control tradition, no longer can be accepted seriously as anything other than an ideology.[31]

---

[31]Michael B. Katz, Michael J. Doucet, and Mark J. Stern, *The Social Organization of Early Industrial Capitalism* (Cambridge, Mass.: Harvard University Press, 1982), pp. 349–391; Barbara M. Brenzel, "The Girls at Lancaster: A Social Portrait of the First Reform School for Girls in North America, 1856–1965" (Ph.D. diss., Harvard University, 1978): Josiah Flynt (Josiah Flynt Willard), *Tramping with Tramps: Studies and Sketches of Vagabond Life* (New York, Century, 1899); *Proceedings of the Annual Convention of the County Superintendents of the Poor of the State of New York* 26(1896): 127.

Part of the ideology is its emphasis on the city as a powerful moral (or, more accurately, immoral) force. By not probing beyond the statistics of urban growth, immigration, and industrial development obvious even to reformers in the nineteenth century, historians have remained trapped in the same surface explanations as their subjects. Like nineteenth-century reformers, contemporary historians cannot account very well for the connections between urban growth, the quality of family life, the crime rate, and the incidence of poverty, to take one chain of phenomena. Exactly what about cities caused the damage? Was the damage even real? Champions of the urban moral–social control tradition had no very good answer. Neither do most historians.

One reason for the inadequate explanations is that an emphasis on urbanization and industrialization (and Boyer provides an example) neglects to factor out the history of capitalism as an independent influence. Although industrialization, urbanization, and capitalism are related, they remain, it must be remembered, conceptually distinct. The emergence and spread of capitalism preceded industrialization, and the two should not be confused. Capitalism, it should be emphasized, encompasses more than private property and profits. Rather, it is defined by a style of relations: wage labor.[32]

Prior to industrialization the class structure of American cities altered as the older, more personal and deferential social order began to disappear. By the early decades of the nineteenth century wage labor had become the template for social relations that crystallized into a class structure that remained intact in North American cities during both their commercial and early industrial phases. Reformers did not recognize that their attempt to revive social class relations based on deference and a sense of mutual obligation clashed with the diffusion of social agreements modeled on the basis of contractual relations between free parties. The working class received contradictory messages. It was told that it was free, unbound, an equal partner in a wage relation, hence no longer in need of paternalistic protection through law or custom. At the same moment, it was criticized as undeferential, assertive, and hostile. This contradiction between the message of social reform and the actual pattern of social relations undercut the urban moral–social control tradition from the start.[33]

---

[32] For an excellent discussion of the nature and importance of the distinction between capitalism and industrialization, see Raphael Samuels, "The Workshop of the World: Steam Power and Hand Technology in mid-Victorian Britain," *History Workshop Journal* 3 (Spring 1977): 6–72.

[33] One example of the contradictory messages given the working class can be found in the example of the company town established in Pullman and the subsequent strike as discussed

Thus reformers of the Progressive period departed from the moral–social control tradition more fully than Boyer recognizes, for he points out that they shifted their emphasis from the individual to the group, adopting an increasingly abstract analytic style. In the process, reformers at last discarded a precapitalist model of social order based on deference and adopted a model more congruent with the prevailing style of social and economic relations. However, even reformers committed to a more appropriate model of social relations could not meet their objectives because they remained reluctant to undertake structural or redistributive change.[34]

Ironically, the most humane and progressive reformers, the settlement house workers, became the advocates of social amelioration through personal contact. Early settlement workers often were ardent champions of social reform. More sympathetic to cultural diversity than other reformers, more critical of economic, social, and political relations, their forays into the slums combined a deferential model of reform with genuinely innovative attempts to help the urban poor. Within 2 or 3 decades, a process of professionalization, described by Roy Lubove, began to transform settlement workers into "professional altruists," namely, social workers. The model for the settlement worker shifted from the gifted, committed, college-educated amateur to the specially trained professional. As schools of social work, national professional associations, and an increasing body of literature emerged, social work began to exchange the passion for social reform for individual casework. Adopting a psychological rather than a social theory, social work concentrated on teaching individual people to better their lives by changing their behavior. As it became more modern and professional, social work thus assumed the mantle of the urban moral–social control tradition.[35]

## HISTORIANS AND INSTITUTIONS: DAVID ROTHMAN AND ASYLUMS

The creation of institutions played counterpoint to urban philanthropy throughout the nineteenth century. During the late eighteenth and early nineteenth centuries, the same period when the urban moral–social control tradition emerged, physicians and philanthropists created the first

---

by Jane Addams. Jane Addams, *Democracy and Social Ethics* (New York: Macmillan, 1907), pp. 137–177.

[34]Boyer, *Urban Masses*, p. 255.

[35]Roy Lubove, *The Professional Altruist: The Emergence of Social Work as a Career, 1880–1930* (Cambridge, Mass.: Harvard University Press, 1965).

urban general hospitals, and state legislatures established networks of poorhouses. In the Jacksonian period, as some evangelical Protestants organized tract societies, others created reform schools, mental hospitals, and new kinds of prisons. In cities experiments with mass education began under private auspices early in the nineteenth century, and by the middle decades of the century public educational systems had started to appear. As the threat of urban poverty increased in the middle decades of the century, some city children were shipped west; more were sent to enlarged reform schools; and most were sent to public schools, which in some states became compulsory by late in the century. Also in the middle decades, as private philanthropists created YMCAs for young rural migrants to cities, other reformers founded specialized institutions for the deaf and dumb, blind, feebleminded women, and idiots, to name the most prominent. Accompanying the intensification and redirection of reform in the Progressive period were campaigns to alter the treatment of criminals, delinquents, the mentally ill, and school children. Probation, the juvenile court, the outpatient clinic, and progressive education were as integral to the period as was the war on prostitution and the saloon or model tenements and playgrounds.[36]

Parallels between institutional creation and social reform extend beyond their timing. Both were responses to dependence that rested on similar assumptions. The concern with social order and the anxiety about the consequences of immigration, industrialization, and urban growth that fueled the moral–social control tradition also motivated institutional sponsors. Fear of crime, poverty, and class estrangement pervaded the rhetoric of both philanthropists and institution builders, and both viewed the causes of dependent or delinquent behavior in similar ways. With some notable exceptions, the solutions they proposed were complementary rather than competitive. Even when strategies differed, philanthropy

---

[36]On the origins of institutions in the nineteenth century, see Gerald Grob, *Mental Institutions in America: Social Policy to 1875* (New York: Free Press, 1975) and *The State and the Mentally Ill: A History of Worcester State Hospital in Massachusetts, 1830–1920* (Chapel Hill, N.C.: University of North Carolina, 1966); W. David Lewis, *From Newgate to Dannemora: The Rise of the Penitentiary in New York, 1796–1848* (Ithaca, N.Y.: Cornell University Press, 1965); David Rothman, *The Discovery of the Asylum: Social Order and Disorder in the New Republic* (Boston: Little, Brown, 1971); Robert M. Mennel, *Thorns and Thistles: Juvenile Delinquents in the United States, 1825–1940* (Hanover, N.H.: University of New Hampshire Press, 1973); Susan E. Houston, "The Impetus to Reform: Crime, Poverty, and Ignorance in Ontario, 1850–1875" (Ph.D. diss., University of Toronto, 1974); Morris Vogel, *The Invention of the Modern Hospital: Boston, 1870–1930* (Chicago: University of Chicago Press, 1980); Estelle B. Freedman, *Their Sisters' Keepers: Women's Prison Reform in America, 1830–1930* (Ann Arbor, Mich.: University of Michigan Press, 1981).

and institutions retained a close relation. In the best-known strategic difference, of course, Charles Loring Brace's criticism of institutions in general and of reform schools in particular led him to propose the shipment of city urchins to the West as an alternative to their incarceration.[37]

It was more common for membership to overlap, for the same people to sponsor both private philanthropy and institutional creation or reform. The New York State Charities Aid Association, founded in the 1870s, provides a good example. Members worked closely with the New York Board of State Charities, visited poorhouses, served in the Charity Organization Society, argued for the abolition of outdoor relief, led the campaign for the removal of the mentally ill from county asylums to state mental hospitals, and organized a model after-care program for discharged mental patients.[38]

Late in the century the moral–social control tradition in philanthropy shared much with institutional critics who attempted to reform the mechanical, punitive, and custodial monsters into which earlier rehabilitative visions had degenerated with amazing speed. Nonetheless, in both periods major philanthropic and institutional reform movements remained complementary, sharing assumptions, goals, and, often, personnel.

The nineteenth-century commitment to social institutions was a radical departure in social policy. Prior to the nineteenth century in North America there were few specialized institutions. The poor, sick, and insane all mingled together in almshouses. Jails held prisoners only for short periods as they awaited trial or sentencing. Punishment was by fine, whipping, or execution, not by lengthy sentences in prison. Much early education took place within homes; schools were small and informal, and children attended irregularly. Dependent or troublesome strangers generally were simply warned out of town. All of this changed within 50–75 years. The informal and customary ways with which families and communities handled distress or deviance gave way to a network of increasingly specialized formal institutions administered by a new class of experts.[39]

Most of the new institutions began in a burst of optimism about their

---

[37]Charles Loring Brace, *The Dangerous Classes of New York and Twenty Years' Work among Them* (New York: Wynkoof and Hallenbeck, 1872).

[38]Schneider and Deutsch, *Public Welfare in New York*, pp. 92–96, discusses the role of the State Charities Aid Association in the care of the insane.

[39]See Note 36.

ability to reduce social problems and remake human nature. Although in some cases the optimism of institutional promoters appeared justified for a few years, all of the institutions soon disappointed their supporters. Rates of recovery in mental hospitals declined; recidivism among prisoners was high; the diffusion of public schools did not reduce crime and poverty. As expectations about what institutions could accomplish altered, so did their goals. The purpose of most institutions shifted by the 1860s away from reform or rehabilitation and toward custody.[40]

Institutions, of course, existed before the nineteenth century. There were poorhouses in colonial New England, and the role of religion was pervasive and disciplinary. Michel Foucault, in fact, has called the seventeenth century the age of the great confinement. What was novel in the nineteenth century was the use of secular institutions as deliberate instruments of social policy, their specialization, and their emphasis upon the formation or reformation of character.[41]

Historians have documented the shift from reform to custody in reform schools, penitentiaries, and mental hospitals. They have shown the downward shift of expectations, too, in public schools. David Rothman, in *The Discovery of the Asylum*, shows the parallels in the origins and early history of reformatories, poorhouses, mental hospitals, and penitentiaries. In *Mental Institutions in America to 1870* Gerald Grob has written a richly detailed account of the process in mental hospitals. Although there is wide agreement about when institutions were founded, the rhetoric through which they were justified, and the shape of their early history, there is less consensus about why they appeared when they did. Historians generally agree that the creation of major social institutions was a dramatic shift in social policy, but they do not concur about why it took place. Grob emphasizes the humanitarian impulses arising from the Second Great Awakening and the impact of Enlightenment thought; Rothman stresses the fear of disorder. However, as noted earlier, both accounts share similar limitations.[42]

---

[40]On the shift from reform to custody, see the discussions in Grob, *Mental Institutions* and *State and the Mentally Ill*; Rothman, *Discovery of the Asylum*; and Michael B. Katz, *The Irony of Early School Reform: Educational Innovation in Mid-Nineteenth-Century Massachusetts* (Cambridge, Mass.: Harvard University Press, 1968), pt. 3.

[41]Michel Foucault, *Madness and Civilization: A History of Insanity in the Age of Reason* (New York: Random House, 1965), pp. 38–64. On the disciplinary role of the church even in nineteenth-century communities, see Mary P. Ryan, *Cradle of the Middle Class: The Family in Oneida County, New York, 1790–1865* (New York: Cambridge University Press, 1981), pp. 38–41.

[42]Rothman, *Discovery of the Asylum*, p. xviii, 58; Grob, *Mental Institutions*, pp. 48, 86–87.

Most accounts, first, do not link institutions for deviants with other institutional developments of the time such as public schools, academies, or the YMCA. However there are striking parallels between all of them. Second, the definitions of social disorder and of social processes usually remain loose. Interpretations rely for the most part on immigration, urbanization, and industrialization, without any very precise analysis of what these terms signify or of the connection between social developments and the history of institutions. There has been almost no attempt to sort out the distinction between capitalism and industrialism, which I discussed earlier, and to discover how each affected the history of institutions. (The most thoughtful comments about the relation between the history of capitalism and the development of social institutions are in Harry Braverman's chapter on "The Universal Marketplace," in *Labor and Monopoly Capital: The Degradation of Work in the Twentieth Century*.)[43]

Most accounts do not analyze the nature of institutional support and opposition with much more precision than the characteristics of social change. David Rothman implies consensus about the institutional impulse and writes, simply, of "Americans." But who, exactly, supported institutions and who opposed them, and why? How was institutional support and opposition—and opposition did exist—related to social structure? To give adequate answers to these questions, historians will have to deal with the question of class. But, like most North American historians, most of the men and women writing about the origins of social institutions either neglect class or treat it in an offhand and imprecise fashion. Often an emphasis on class is wrongly thought to deny the existence of deeply felt humanitarian convictions. Class is treated as a simple socioeconomic category rather than as a social relation; an emphasis on class is incorrectly believed to be simplistic and reductionist. To say that institutional promoters thought they were acting in the best interests of their clients, and to leave the argument there, is to finesse a class analysis, not to refute it. Finally, most histories view inmates through the eyes of institutional promoters and administrators, just as Boyer views the poor through the writing of reformers. The result is a failure to probe descriptions of crime, poverty, mental illness, or ignorance offered in official sources and a consequent perpetuation of the stereotypes of the time.

In his new book, *Conscience and Convenience: The Asylum and Its Alternatives in Progressive America*, David Rothman continues the story he began in *The Discovery of the Asylum*. The new book focuses on attempts to

---

[43]Harry Braverman, *Labor and Monopoly Capital: The Degradation of Work in the Twentieth Century* (New York: Monthly Review Press, 1974). 271–283.

reform the treatment of criminals, delinquents, and the mentally ill between about 1890 and 1930. In some respects it shares important themes with Rothman's earlier book. Both argue that institutions for criminals, delinquents, and the mentally ill rested on similar assumptions about the nature of deviance and dependence, shared strategies for treatment, faced similar internal problems, and followed parallel courses of development. However, the more recent book departs from the earlier one in certain ways: It is less concerned with the social context of institutions and more concerned with their internal history. Above all, it is directed as much to contemporaries concerned with policy issues as it is to historians.

The title, *Conscience and Convenience,* expresses the mixed motives among sponsors of institutional reform in the Progressive period. Appalled at the horrors of institutional life and the failure of rehabilitative treatment, one group of reformers, argues Rothman, developed a coherent critique and a series of reform proposals. These proposals were adopted surprisingly often because they promised to alleviate problems faced by institutional managers and public officials such as judges and public prosecutors. Although the marriage of conscience and convenience fostered innovation, in actual practice the two motives often conflicted, and in the implementation of reform, convenience always won.

As depicted by Rothman, Progressive theory had three essential elements. The first was individualization, the belief that each criminal, delinquent, or mentally ill person should be diagnosed and treated in a unique and appropriate way. Second was the assumption of harmony between the interests of institutional constituencies: clients and custodians, reformers and managers, the state and individuals. Because of their belief in the harmony of interests, reformers saw no inherent confict between rehabilitation and custody. Third, Progressive reformers did not hesitate to expand the power of the state. They foresaw no threat to civil liberties in innovations that intruded upon the relations between parents and children or dispensed with customary notions of due process.[44]

Reformers confronted officials with serious problems. Institutions obviously did not work very well: Jails did not rehabilitate; reform schools did not reform; mental hospitals did not cure; and they all were expensive. These failures placed institutional officials on the defensive. Indeed, during the late nineteenth century critics of all major institutions launched scathing attacks against the inhuman, custodial, ineffectual, and expensive character of institutional life. Therefore, institutional officials welcomed

---

[44]David J. Rothman, *Conscience and Convenience: The Asylum and Its Alternatives in Progressive America* (Boston: Little, Brown, 1980), pp. 5–10.

*Plate 13.* "*Christmas Eve on Henry Street*" *about 1900 (could be the King's Daughters or the Jacob A. Riis House). (Photograph by Jacob A. Riis, Jacob A. Riis Collection, Museum of the City of New York.)*

innovations that promised to improve their image without undercutting their power or increasing the difficulty of their jobs. At the same time, judges and district attorneys faced overcrowded court dockets and sought reforms that would reduce the number of cases coming to trial. Innovations such as the juvenile court introduced ways of handling cases informally. They offered alternatives to incarceration, which was widely acknowledged to be a failure, and increased judges' discretionary power. In a parallel way prosecuting attorneys could use the promise of probation to induce guilty pleas, thus easing their jobs and enhancing their rates of conviction. These examples could be multiplied. The point is that major reform proposals appealed in theory to both reformers and public officials.[45]

---

[45] *Ibid., passim.*

The major innovations in criminal justice were probation, parole, and the attempt to introduce methods of rehabilitation within prisons. In juvenile justice they were the juvenile court and the attempt to reform the reformatory. Within the treatment of mental illness they were the outpatient clinics and the psychopathic hospital for acute cases. In each instance Rothman exposes the horrors of institutional life, describes reform proposals, delineates the coalition supporting reform, and then traces the implementation of innovations, showing how and why they all failed. The book ends with a stunning account of a foundation-sponsored innovation drawn from a diary kept at Norfolk Prison in Massachusetts in the early 1930s.

Rothman repeatedly asks why support for innovations, such as probation or the juvenile court, continued when they did not work in a way remotely approaching their promise. The answers he gives all are similar. Reformers believed that their ideas had never been properly tried, that parsimony or ignorance had undercut perfectly good principles that needed only a proper environment to flourish. At the same time, officials continued to sponsor innovations, even though they were imperfect, because they enhanced their power and their image. Although Rothman agrees that Progressive reformers accurately diagnosed weaknesses in implementation, he believes that they missed the deeper causes of failure, for they did not examine the assumption that a harmony of interests existed between all parties or that custody and rehabilitation could occur together. The experience of Progressive reform, Rothman implies, shows that both of these beliefs were wrong. Herein lies the message for contemporary policymakers. It is this message that, despite Rothman's exuberance, makes this a profoundly depressing book.[46]

*Conscience and Convenience* has great strengths. First is its skillful narrative depiction of reform efforts and its convincing assertion of parallels in assumptions, methods, and reasons for failure. It is indisputable that reasons for the failure of reforms must be sought within the web of assumptions and the style of implementation common to the reform movement as a whole, not simply in problems specific to particular institutions or branches of institutional life.

Second, Rothman devastates reform theory. The failure to recognize that interests conflicted or that custody and rehabilitation could not be reconciled is a flaw for which reformers legitimately can be held accountable. Nonetheless, they are assumptions that extend beyond the institutional reform movement, for a denial that conflict is a fundamental

---

[46]*Ibid.*, pp. 10–12.

feature of social life became an enduring tenet of American liberalism during these years. Rothman would have made the reformers' constricted vision more understandable had he connected it with the intellectual history of the period.[47]

Third, the analysis of coalitions supporting reform is a fundamental contribution to institutional history. Often it is unclear why one innovation is adopted and another rejected. The reason, as Rothman shows, rests in the scope of its appeal. By identifying the key institutional coalitions, Rothman has set forth a model for systematic analysis, and his book marks an important step toward a historical politics of social institutions. However, it would have been useful for Rothman to have made the analytic framework of his book more explicit and to have drawn together its theoretical implications.

Fourth, Rothman's concentration on implementation shows the importance of administrative history. It is not too difficult to write about the ideas of reformers or to locate and describe innovations. It is another matter to show how they actually worked in the day-to-day life of institutions. And it is, after all, what actually happened and why that really matters.

Fifth, nowhere have the tensions between reform and custody or the limits of institutions been made more clear. In his introduction Rothman offers a message of hope. As the story of alternatives, not inevitability, history shows that choices exist; it is a tale of possibilities. But Rothman's book belies its upbeat beginning. The best and the brightest failed for the better part of a century. Their options had been limited by both theoretical weaknesses and the interests they confronted. Today the forces opposing reformers have not weakened; theory has not improved dramatically— how much have we learned about how to rehabilitate criminals?—and the alternatives chosen are not working very well, as tales about the horrors of unplanned, fast decarceration show only too painfully. The answers seem no more at hand, innovations no more promising. It is not Rothman's function to provide answers, and he scrupulously avoids simple solutions. What he has done is to pose the questions in a way that cannot be evaded by anyone seriously concerned with the quality and outcome of institutional life.

Despite its contributions, *Conscience and Convenience* has limits that should not be overlooked. First, the book overstates the novelty of Progressive reform thought. Faith in the state was characteristic of

---

[47]Some understanding of why American social thought has downplayed conflict can be gained from Thomas L. Haskell, *The Emergence of Professional Social Science: The American Social Science Association and the Nineteenth-Century Crisis of Authority* (Urbana, Ill.: University of Illinois Press, 1977).

institutional sponsors from the 1840s onward. Promoters of public education and reformatories, for instance, referred over and over again to the state as a parent. Precisely because the state was the parent-at-large, they thought, it had responsibilities for all children that could override the prerogatives of natural parents. Also, serious criticism of institutions first emerged earlier than Rothman implies. In the 1850s not only Charles Loring Brace but also other reformers, including Samuel Gridley Howe and his supporters on the Massachusetts Board of State Charities, launched a searching criticism of institutions, especially reformatories, and proposed innovations such as the cottage system. Nor was the urge for classification in the Progressive period simply, as Rothman would have it, an expression of the eagerness to individualize treatment. It also reflected the bureaucratic impulse at work elsewhere much earlier, as in the introduction of grading in the public schools in the 1840s or of moral grading in reformatories in the same period. To use classification as an example of individualism is to obscure its significance, for it should be viewed, as well, as part of the history of bureaucracy.[48]

Rothman's history is primarily internal; he traces the process of innovation and deterioration within institutions. But why did reforms happen when they did? What political, social, and economic forces supported them? Institutions do not exist in a vacuum. They do not belong solely to reformers and public officials. They are, when public, part of the state, sustained, created, or modified by the interaction of social and economic factors with political processes. As his book on the early history of asylums shows, Rothman understands this point quite well, but he does not connect the story told in *Conscience and Convenience* with the great themes of the Progressive period in other than a cursory and superficial way.

Nor does Rothman probe beneath the surface of reform thought to locate its sources. He accepts reform proposals as disinterested and humanitarian and concerns himself only with their internal consistency, adequacy, and application. But why did a series of ideas implicitly denying the normality of conflict emerge during the decades of the most violent labor conflict in American history? Why did a peculiar ideology of institutional reform appear at this moment? Not only institutional reformers but also the most influential social scientists of the period—and they sometimes were the same people—worked to eliminate conflict from social theory. Reform proposals can be understood only as part of the emergent structure of liberal thought in these years. However, even though his story begs to be joined to broader analyses of the era, Rothman

---

[48]Katz, *Irony of Early School Reform*, pt. 3.

does not assess its relation to the work of Wiebe, Kolko, Weinstein, and others. As a consequence, his book floats in a vacuum as much historiographical as social and economic.[49]

Only by ignoring recent historical debates can Rothman use the label Progressive without definition or discrimination, even extending the Progressive period until the 1960s. Nowhere does he define Progressivism precisely or identify the Progressives. Nor does he recognize differences in ideas and strategies within the larger movement. Despite decades of historical writing on these questions, including the adequacy of the term *progressive* itself, Rothman's reformers of conscience appear over and over again simply as Progressives. Here the contrast to Boyer is striking, for Boyer, sensitive to the historiographical issues, cites the relevant literature and attempts to distinguish strands within the movement.[50]

One strand Rothman should have separated out was the child saving movement. Child savers did not share other Progressives' commitment to the possibilities of institutional reform. To the contrary, they attacked institutions, which, they said, harmed personality and moral development. Unless their rhetoric is to be entirely discounted, a stronger antiinstitutional strain than Rothman admits existed within Progressivism.[51]

Writing a survey limits Rothman to the surface of most events and controversies, which, as a consequence, he sometimes misinterprets. One example is the crisis at the Elmira (New York) Reformatory, founded in 1870 for male first offenders between the ages of 16 and 30. Intended as a model rehabilitative institution, the first American example of the so-called Irish system of prison organization, Elmira was run from its beginning until well into the 1890s by Zebulon Brockway, one of the country's best-known penal authorities and an advocate of the indeterminate sentence, one of the innovations Rothman classed as Progressive. Throughout the country reformers and penal authorities hailed Brockway's experience at Elmira as an example of what enlightened penology could accomplish; Brockway himself was an important figure in reform circles.[52]

---

[49]Gabriel Kolko, *The Triumph of Conservatism* (New York: Free Press, 1963); Robert Wiebe, *The Search for Order, 1877–1920* (New York: Hill and Wang, 1967).

[50]Boyer, *Urban Masses,* p. 196.

[51]Examples of attacks on institutions for children can be found in the *Proceedings of the Annual Convention of the County Superintendents of the Poor of the State of New York,* 12(1882): 42; 17(1887): 54; 18(1888): 49; 20(1890): 54.

[52]Zebulon Brockway, *Fifty Years of Prison Service; an Autobiography* (1912; reprint ed., Montclair, N.J.: Patterson and Smith, 1969); Paul Eisenhauer, "The Irish System of Convict Discipline and the Foundations of American Penology, 1820–1860," in Katz and Associates, Appendix.

In the 1890s charges of brutality at Elmira prompted the Board of State Charities to investigate Brockway's administration. Witness after witness recounted a pattern of brutalilty by the entire staff from Brockway down to his guards. Order in the model reformatory rested on official terror and physical violence. The board urged Brockway's immediate suspension. But Brockway had friends in high office. Within a year the legislature had stripped the board of its authority to monitor prisons, and its successor launched a new investigation that exonerated Brockway, who in his autobiography offered a self-serving account of the attempt of little men to hound him from office for partisan reasons.[53]

Rothman mentions the Brockway affair briefly and even admits that there probably was brutality at Elmira, but he ignores the detailed testimony given during the first investigation and does not mention the political struggle that Brockway won. Thus he misses, first, the entanglement of institutions with state politics. A clever superintendent such as Brockway built connections to powerful forces in the legislature. What happened at Elmira reflected not only, as Rothman would have it, an unsuccessful coalition of conscience and convenience but also a political process. Although the nature of the conflict—the reasons why an attempt to destroy Brockway happened when it did and the sources of the attack—remains unclear, the controversy does show the anchor of institutions in a social and political context.[54]

The dark, brutal side of institutional life should be probed more deeply than Rothman does. He admits that harsh physical punishment was common in late nineteenth- and early twentieth-century institutions. Punishment, he argues, inheres in institutional life because of the need, always, for one more sanction, whether it is another and harsher prison, solitary confinement, or beating. Thus he attributes corporal punishment mainly to the need to keep order and enforce obedience in potentially explosive situations. He does not condone it. Rather, he separates corporal punishment from personal motives and attributes it to the system itself.[55]

Rothman's point about the need for one more sanction is a good one. But there is more to the story. At Elmira, for instance, brutality extended beyond the requirements of institutional order. Nor was it measured,

---

[53]Edward H. Litchfield, chairman, "Report of the Special Committee to the State Board of Charities," in *Twenty-Eighth Annual Report of the State Board of Charities,* New York State Senate Document No. 36, March 25, 1895, pp. 346–386.

[54]Rothman, *Conscience and Convenience,* pp. 33–35.

[55]*Ibid.,* pp. 148–156.

executed carefully, limited by a concern with unnecessary suffering. If the testimony is to be believed at all, punishment at Elmira was sadistic. The blood running in bathtubs, the bodies covered with bruises, the super-intendent who crept up behind inmates so as to surprise them with blows—none of these, surely, were necessary for good order. They expressed the twisted behavior of men who enjoyed inflicting violence on others. The pervasive sadism within institutions, not simply corporal punishment, requires explanation. How did a climate that sanctioned brutality develop in one institution after another? Why were sadism and brutality condoned by supervisory groups, who surely were not fooled? Why—and this is the heart of the matter—has it been permissible to beat, maim, and terrorize the inmates of institutions? Convenience is not a satisfactory answer to these questions.[56]

Nor does the interplay between conscience and convenience capture the meaning of another key controversy of the time. Since the 1870s reformers had tried to remove chronically insane paupers from county poorhouses to state hospitals. The first state hospital for the chronically insane, the Willard Asylum, opened in 1870. However, it proved too small, and some counties were allowed to create their own asylums attached to poorhouses. Throughout the next 20 years counties fought for the right to retain their insane paupers instead of sending them to a state hospital. In the early 1890s they lost. The State Charities Aid Association sponsored investiga-tions of county asylums, which, they alleged, were filthy, poorly run holes inferior in every way to the well-administered, large state hospitals. The association's campaign not only convinced the legislature to order the chronically insane removed to state institutions but also has shaped historical accounts of the incident, including Rothman's, for he accepts the conclusions of the State Charities Aid Association and its allies without question.[57]

However, grounds for questions do exist. At their annual conventions the county superintendents of the poor vigorously and often bitterly opposed the removal of the insane and defended their own institutions. Of course, they had a stake in the issue. It was their management that was attacked and their control over state funds that was threatened. Nonethe-less, their counterarguments were as well documented as reformers' criticisms, which, the superintendents charged, rested on superficial observations and the distortion, even creation, of evidence. As a counter-

---

[56]See Note 53.

[57]Rothman, *Conscience and Convenience*, pp. 27–28; Schneider and Deutsch, *Public Welfare in New York*, pp. 91–97.

attack the superintendents developed an alternate point of view about the care of the insane, which included a devastating criticism of the state hospitals. Their arguments stressed the importance of keeping the insane in their own communities where they could be visited often by friends, where the staff treating them would be not strangers but neighbors, and where oversight by the community would prevent abuses from creeping into patient care. They contrasted the virtues of local institutions with the faults of those created by the state, which, they claimed, were too large to provide personal care, where staff treated patients coldly, and where patients were removed from those who loved them. Massive amounts of money, claimed the superintendents, were spent not on the welfare of inmates but on expensive, showy buildings and elaborate quarters for the superintendents. Even the rate of cure, they asserted, was higher in the county asylums than in the state hospitals.[58]

Despite their arguments, the county superintendents lost, and their side of the controversy never has been told by historians. But their case is significant. The resistance of the county superintendents points, first, to the danger in simply taking the accounts of victors at face value, as Rothman does. It also raises questions about the purposes of Progressive reform, in this instance embodied in the allegedly humanitarian attempt (an expression of conscience in Rothman's taxonomy) to move the chronic insane to state hospitals. Surely it was obvious that conditions at Willard were not ideal and that care there was inadequate. Surely, too, the point of view of the superintendents merited more attention than it received. The venom with which reformers attacked the administration of county superintendents gave their campaign more the air of a vendetta than of a crusade. The question, then, is Why? Exactly what were those people championing the cause of state hospitals trying to accomplish?

Advocates of state hospitals promoted a model of institutional reform that featured centralization, state supervision, classification, and expert administration, characteristics embodied adequately only in large institutions. County superintendents implicitly advocated an institutional model that stressed the drawbacks of size, the importance of community influence, the limits of centralization, the self-aggrandizement of administration, and the overconfidence of experts. In this way the contest between state reformers and county superintendents echoed a struggle between alternative models of social institutions going on since early in the nineteenth century.

Nonetheless, it must be remembered that the members of the State

---

[58]For opposition to the removal of the insane from the county poorhouses, see *Proceedings of the Annual Convention of the County Superintendents of the Poor of the State of New York,* 18(1888): 43–44, 45, 48; 19(1889): 14, 38, 40, 49–50; 20(1890): 5, 58–59; 21(1891): 17, 63.

*Plate 14.* *Police station lodgers, early 1890s, West 47th Street Station. (Photograph by Jacob A. Riis, Jacob A. Riis Collection, Museum of the City of New York.)*

Charities Aid Association, which spearheaded the drive for the removal of the insane from the poorhouses, had a long history of conflict with the county superintendents. For 2 decades they had visited county poorhouses and published reports critical of their administration. At the same time, Charities Aid Association members supported the abolition of outdoor relief, which, as a group, the county superintendents opposed. The removal of the insane poor offered members an issue with which to undercut the county superintendents by reducing their power and tarnishing their image. Thus the removal of the insane from county asylums was a more complex and interesting issue than Rothman recognizes, a reflection of political conflicts and competing models of social institutions as well as another demonstration of the inadequacy of conscience alone as a motivation for reform.[59]

[59]The county superintendents refused to support a motion advocating the abolition of outdoor relief. *Ibid.* 24(1894): 45.

Rothman also skims over the problems that institutions were supposed to alleviate. Were innovations in criminal justice, delinquency, and mental health a response to anything other than problems internal to institutions and their managers? Were the problems themselves, or perceptions about them, changing, too? Rothman, for instance, explains the large number of foreign-born inmates in insane asylums by suggesting that native Americans were better able to utilize expensive private asylums, leaving the state facilities to immigrants. But that is not very much of an answer. Observers at the time argued that the rate of mental illness was higher among immigrants than among natives and that the immigrants were responsible for a wave of insanity engulfing America. In fact, the foreign-born inmates of most institutions usually were not recent arrivals. Most had been in the United States at least 10 years. Thus the significance of the disproportionate admission of the foreign born to mental hospitals is not clear. Did it result from the accumulated strains of life in a new country? Were people who could not speak English unable to communicate their problems and incarcerated when quite sane? These are some of the questions that must be explored in order to move beyond institutional history as the interplay between conscience and convenience.[60]

There is a puzzle in the story Rothman tells. Progressive reforms were implemented in ways that were bound to make them fail. There never were nearly enough probation officers or psychiatrists in prisons and reformatories, for instance. Legislators, as reformers themselves often complained, never provided nearly enough money to test innovations properly. Rothman does not try to explain why innovations always were so badly undercut from the start. How is one to account for the disparity between the rhetoric of reform—the high expectations and bloated self-congratulations of those who introduced innovations—and the reality of change on the cheap?

Part of the answer lies in what Christopher Lasch has called the "single standard of honor." Inmates could be despised on account of their dependent status, for poverty or disability reflected not only misfortune but also moral failure, not bad luck but incapacity. Lacking productive ability, as Harry Braverman wrote, the poor and the helpless became a new stratum to be locked up, put away, out of sight. Neither conscience, nor convenience, nor their interaction captures this mean-spirited quality of response to the poor and dependent in American history.[61]

By almost ignoring the inmates of institutions, Rothman reinforces

---

[60]Rothman, *Conscience and Convenience,* pp. 24–25.

[61]Braverman, *Labor and Monopoly Capital,* pp. 279–280.

popular stereotypes of degradation. Inmates become objects to be reformed, incarcerated, classified, perhaps beaten, maybe paroled. They are passive clients or victims, not agents of institutional change. But the story, as I pointed out earlier, is much more complex. So-called dependent people manipulated agencies and institutions, often bending them toward purposes of their own. This happened even with the poorest, most despised institution—the poorhouse. In prevailing images paupers were the most degraded poor, not only without money but also without energy, lingering in a moral torpor, incapable of caring for themselves, a class of permanent dependents vegetating their lives away within poorhouses. In fact, the demography of poorhouses contradicts this image.[62]

The population of the Erie County (New York) Poorhouse is the only one reconstructed over a long time period. Between 1829 and 1886, as I showed earlier, the institution went through a sequence of stages. At first it was partly familial because in its early years it was used as a refuge in times of crises by entire families. The shift away from the family refuge took place as its ethnic composition changed during the Irish immigration of the 1840s and 1850s. Native-born people began to use it less, and fewer whole families entered. Second, the poorhouse was used especially heavily during depressions. When employment was scarce, the number of young men increased. Third, most inmates remained only for a short time. The poorhouse clearly was used by most people as a temporary haven during periods of distress. For only a minority was it a place of long-term residence. Fourth, a state law of 1875 completed the removal of children aged 2–16 from the poorhouse, which increasingly became an old age home, although it was used frequently by young poor women as a maternity hospital and shelter for single mothers with infants. By 1900 almost 85% of its inmates were elderly. Thus the poorhouse was a complex institution whose history reflected changing ethnic relations and the cyclical nature of the economy. Whatever the official purposes of the poorhouse, the poor themselves put it to their own uses. Although legislative acts created the poorhouse and sometimes shaped its development, its history also was made by the poor themselves.[63]

Nor did contemporaries accurately portray the people unfortunate enough to need outdoor relief. Few appear to have been willfully idle, living happily on the dole. They were not by and large drunk and degenerate, sunk into the torpor of permanent pauperism. In the very years when the protest against tramps intensified, most tramps in New

---

[62]On the demography of poorhouses, see Chapter 2, Part I.

[63]*Ibid.*

York State were young men on the road only a short time in search of work. During the years when the outcry against outdoor relief was reaching its peak, most people who received outdoor relief in Pennsylvania were women and children. In the entire state in the year ending September 30, 1875, 12.46% of the recipients of outdoor relief were men, 32.83% women, and 54.71% children under 16. In 45.12% of cases the reason they needed outdoor relief was "Destitution caused by death, absence, or desertion of husband or father." Another major reason for outdoor relief, 32.68%, was "Destitution caused by temporary sickness or want of work of male heads of families and single men." Of the adults relieved, almost three-quarters were 50 years old or over, 98.51% were residents of the "relief district," and only 7.58% were intemperate.

The initiatve exercised by the very poor belies the stereotype of degradation fostered by contemporaries and repeated by historians such as Rothman. At the same time, it bears upon an important question about the nature of class structure. In the image of degradation paupers appear as a lumpen proletariat, a demoralized group so apathetic that it existed outside the class structure. But suppose pauperism (as defined by residence in a poorhouse or receiving public welfare) was not usually permanent or a long-term condition. Then paupers emerge, as they rightly should, as members of the working class who had fallen temporarily on hard times. They were victims of the forces built into the structure of working-class life. Unemployment, illness, death of a spouse—all of these could devastate working-class people whose employment varied with the business cycle and the seasons and whose low wages made saving impossible. Working-class life lurched from crisis to crisis; for some people the crisis never broke. The dependent poor were not degraded; they were unlucky. It is important to expose the fallacy that paupers and other dependents were a lumpen proletariat, for by making them outcasts this idea has served to fragment the working class by encouraging the working poor to despise and resent the dependent poor, to object to social welfare, and, thereby, to oppose their own best interests.[64]

## THE HISTORY OF PUBLIC WELFARE:
## ROY LUBOVE ON SOCIAL INSURANCE

In theory, historians of public welfare avoid some of the limitations common to historians of philanthropy and institutions. They deal with

---

[64]For an example of the role of crisis in the lives of the poor, see the case of the Sullivan family, Chapter 1.

both public and private sectors, treat both institutional and noninstitutional strategies, and focus on responses to specific problems rather than on groups of reformers. Often, however, their work also is limited, sometimes by concentrating more on responses than on problems, sometimes by the same lack of attention to the clients of welfare that is in histories of reform and institutions, and often by a Whig interpretation in which high-minded reformers struggle against vested interests in order to expand the scope of state supervision and activity in the field of public welfare.

The preoccupation of early public welfare history with the transformation of private charity into public social insurance is understandable. Its authors, like Sophonsiba Breckenridge and Edith Abbott, were leaders in the field of social work, actively engaged in the struggle to protect children and deploy the power of the state in the cause of social improvement. Along with their colleagues and students, they wrote informative, documentary histories of welfare designed to inspire progressive social policy. Interest in the history of public welfare gathered strength in the early twentieth century. Historians affiliated with social work and public welfare even started a modest trend toward an American historiography of the poor law—represented, for example, by books on Massachusetts, New York, Pennsylvania, Indiana, and Louisiana—and others traced the history of public welfare in single states. Most notable of the latter approach is Schneider's and Deutsch's two-volume study of New York.[65]

Schneider and Deutsch tell a straightforward story of the expansion of the state's supervisory power and involvement. They begin in the colonial period and, in their first volume, end with the first Board of State Charities. The second volume starts with the Board of State Charities in 1867 and follows developments through the 1930s, emphasizing the accomplishments during the Great Depression decade. It is a comprehensive study, carefully researched, generally reliable, and full of useful detail. However, its Whig character colors its interpretation, for there is no ambiguity about the expansion of state power, no concern with the mixed consequences of juvenile courts for civil liberties, for instance, or with the complex motivation of those urging changes in welfare legislation. This interpretation is inadequate, to take one example, in their discussion of the legislation in the 1890s requiring the removal of the insane from county asylums to state hospitals. Like Rothman, the authors accept critics' views of county asylums, ignore rebuttals, and view the legislation as unambig-

---

[65]David M. Schneider, *The History of Public Welfare in New York, 1609–1866* (Chicago: University of Chicago Press, 1938); Schneider and Deutsch, *Public Welfare in New York*. See also the bibliography cited in Note 1.

uously progressive, missing the controversy over alternative models of treatment and the charges of distorted evidence, to which I already pointed.

Public welfare history remained more or less dormant from the early 1940s until the late 1960s and early 1970s. Only now is a modest revival apparent. Examples are James Leiby's history of public welfare in New Jersey and his survey of public welfare in American history, Walter Trattner's survey of welfare history and study of child labor reform, June Axinn's and Hal Levin's documentary history of welfare, Neal Sutherland's history of the child saving movement in Canada, Blanche Coll's work on antebellum welfare, Hace Sorel Tishler's account of the social insurance movement between 1870 and 1917, and Roy Lubove's monographs on the history of social work and on the origins of Social Security.[66]

Lubove's *The Struggle for Social Security, 1900–1935* narrates the history of the social insurance movement from its origins in the campaign for workmen's compensation, through the failure of health insurance, the partial success of mothers' pensions, the first step toward old age security, the controversies about unemployment insurance, and the Social Security Act of 1935. It is a story with two clear themes:

> This book focuses upon the clash between the social insurance goals and the ideology of institutions of voluntarism. As a rule, historians have not appreciated the significance of the social insurance movement, which launched a national debate over fundamental issues of liberty, the role of the state, and the dimensions of security in a wage-centered, competitive economy. My secondary theme concerns the influence of voluntarism upon the social insurance movement. Social insurance was introduced into an incongruous, inhospitable environment. The voluntary framework determined the limits of achievement, and even shaped social insurance programs.[67]

---

[66]James Leiby, *Charity and Correction in New Jersey: A History of State Welfare Institutions* (New Brunswick, N.J.: Rutgers University Press, 1967); Walter I. Trattner, *From Poor Law to Welfare State: A History of Social Welfare in America* (New York: Free Press, 1974) and *Crusade for the Children: A History of the National Child Labor Committee and Child Labor Reform in America* (Chicago: Quadrangle Books, 1970); June Axinn and Herman Levin, *Social Welfare: A History of the American Response to Need* (New York: Dodd, Mead, 1970); Sutherland, *Children in English-Canadian Society*; Tishler, *Self-Reliance and Social Security*; Lubove, *Struggle for Social Security* and *Professional Altruist*; Blanche Coll, *Perspectives in Public Welfare* (Washington, D.C.: U.S. Government Printing Office, 1969) and "Public Assistance in the United States: From Colonial Times to 1860," in *Comparative Development in Social Welfare*, ed. E. W. Martin (London: Allen and Unwin, 1972), pp. 128–158.

[67]Lubove, *Struggle for Social Security*, p. 2.

The American social insurance movement officially began in 1906 with the founding of the American Association for Labor Legislation. The new association marked a break with nineteenth-century traditions that had equated relief with charity and relied to a large extent on voluntary societies. Although voluntary associations had played a critical role, social insurance advocates argued that these groups no longer remained adequate to the task of relief. The growth, diversity, and complexity of American society had outstripped the capacity of private groups to organize effective responses to distress. Social insurance advocates also rejected the equation of relief or assistance with charity. Rather, the alleviation of the problems associated with accident, poverty, sickness, and old age were basic human rights to be guaranteed by the state, not left to either private charity or the benevolence of employers.[68]

The social insurance movement arrived late in the United States, which was the last major Western country to adopt measures such as workmen's compensation or unemployment insurance. Indeed, foreign models were influential, inspiring advocates, offering alternative policies, and serving as grist for jingoist opponents who identified social insurance with foreign and alien traditions.[69]

Within the American social insurance movement two strands coexisted uneasily from the start, breaking into open competition in the 1920s. The controversy was between advocates of prevention and supporters of economic maintenance. Identified with prevention were John L. Commons and John B. Andrews, secretary of the American Association for Labor Legislation; the most notable advocate of maintenance was I. M. Rubinow. Lubove writes:

> By the 1920's a distinctive conception of social insurance had emerged, stressing prevention as the primary goal. From the beginning, Commons and Andrews had viewed prevention as something more than an expedient or secondary objective.... The "American" approach to social insurance, compatible with individual economic incentive and responsibility, was to provide financial inducements for prevention.... Economic maintenance was the primary purpose of any social insurance or assurance program, according to Rubinow, not a trivial function which treated the symptoms rather than the causes of distress. No matter how efficient our social institutions, there would remain a residue of need, best handled by a social insurance machinery which responded predictably, promptly, and ade-

---

[68]*Ibid.*, pp. 29–31.

[69]*Ibid.*, p. 24.

quately. Any preventive role assigned to social insurance evolved from this primary responsibility to economic maintenance.[70]

Thus the history of social insurance is more than a story of a struggle between opponents and supporters. It is also a history of the competition between conceptions of insurance, overlayed, in Lubove's account, with bitter personal rivalries.

Rivalries within the movement, however, should not be allowed to overshadow the opposition met by proponents of every social insurance measure. Insurance companies opposed workmen's compensation; doctors and their associations campaigned against health insurance; social work agencies tried to defeat mothers' pensions; employers' groups argued against compulsory pensions. Given the strength of their opponents, advocates of social insurance managed only partial victories, and in some instances, such as health insurance, they met total defeat. In fact, victories occurred only when social insurance proposals won the support of business groups. Concerned with the growth of unions, strikes, high labor turnover, and the cost of litigation in industrial accidents, late nineteenth- and early twentieth-century employers began to introduce the managerial strategies of welfare capitalism. These included some measures advocated by social insurance promoters. Even when employers' groups agreed to social insurance measures, they bent them toward their own needs, often undercutting the original purpose. As a result, the social insurance measures put into practice were an uneasy compromise between the goals of social insurance advocates and those of employers.[71]

In their struggle against social insurance measures opponents deployed the old American ideology of voluntarism, condemning the interference of the state, praising the efforts of private philanthropy, and stressing the importance of individual achievement. In place of voluntarism they held out the menace of social and racial degeneration, the destruction of the moral basis of American society, and the victory of alien social systems, that is, socialism and Bolshevism. By emphasizing this tension between voluntarism and social insurance, Lubove not only clarifies the sources of American opposition to social insurance but also underlines the complex relation between the private and public spheres, which forms a central theme in the history of American responses to dependence. Although the ideology of voluntarism often merely masked naked self-interest, it was

---

[70]*Ibid.*, pp. 42–43.

[71]*Ibid.*, p. 57.

*Plate 15. "Making of an American": What (Theodore) Roosevelt got for it from the yellow press. (Photograph by Jacob A. Riis, Jacob A. Riis Collection, Museum of the City of New York.)*

deeply believed as well. By relying on voluntarism, opponents of social insurance erected a noneconomic defense of their position. They undercut arguments based on economic hardship, uncertain labor markets, or the destitution of widows with small children by appealing to the values that, they said, sustained the distinctively worthwhile qualities of American life.[72]

Like Rothman, Lubove does not explicitly make the links between his

---

[72] *Ibid.*, pp. 1–24.

interpretation and other historical writing about the period. Nonetheless, his thesis clearly supports recent scholarship on measures such as railroad or antitrust legislation. None of these were the result of victories of social reformers over vested interests. Rather, social insurance measures, railroad regulation, and antitrust measures were implemented only when favored by business groups for practical economic reasons. The partners in the coalition of reformers and businessmen were not equals (anymore than were those in Rothman's coalition of conscience and convenience), and the result always was the dilution of measures directed at economic or political change. Lubove's account also intersects another strand in recent historical writing about the late nineteenth and early twentieth centuries: the emergence of the social sciences and the academic expert. Lubove highlights the involvement of academics in the social insurance movement, especially the way they promoted the role of experts trained in the social sciences. As other historians have shown, in the late nineteenth century the first generation of university-based professional social scientists sought to win recognition and standing by emphasizing their technical expertise and its usefulness in the formulation and administration of public policy. Advocacy of social insurance was part of this campaign for the professionalization of social science.[73]

Lubove's account of the opposition to social insurance shows that resistance, like support, had a complex, shifting quality. By no means did it reflect only the self-interest of mean-spirited businessmen, any more than did support flow from disinterested benevolence. Opponents, too, organized themselves into coalitions. Organized labor, for instance, especially through Samuel Gompers, opposed workmen's compensation. Labor both feared the involvement of the state and wanted to retain as much control of welfare for itself as possible. Certainly, at times business groups opposed measures fiercely, but so did, as already noted, the medical profession and social work agencies. It is hard to find a more virulent campaign against a social insurance measure than the one waged by representatives of scientific charity against mothers' pensions.[74]

Supporters of scientific charity voiced widespread attitudes that legitimated harsh and inadequate responses to poverty and dependence. The American style of relief, as Lubove observes, has combined "inadequate assistance and harassment of the recipient." Because "the fact of dependency is . . . evidence of personal inadequacy if not pathology," policies

---

[73]Mary Furner, *From Advocacy to Objectivity: A Crisis in the Professionalization of American Social Science, 1865–1905* (Lexington, Ky.: University of Kentucky Press, 1975).

[74]Lubove, *Struggle for Social Security*, pp. 102–103.

have emphasized "behavioral considerations" as much as "economic need."[75]

In *Self-Reliance and Social Security, 1870–1917*, Hace Sorel Tishler disagrees with Lubove's emphasis on the failures of the social insurance movement. To Tishler, Lubove "begs what in America is the really critical question: How in such hostile territory did the social insurance movement achieve even the limited success that it had?" Lubove fails to answer this question, according to Tishler, because he emphasizes the reduction of objective economic need as the overriding goal of the movement. If income redistribution was the aim, then without question the movement failed. However, argues Tishler, "Far from being a scientific and technical answer to an objective condition, the social insurance movement was from its inception a broadly conceived response to the problems of the individual's security and responsibility and to the problem of society's security and responsibility." By uniting what previously had been competing concerns—the preservation of individualism and the welfare of society—social insurance advocates attempted to show that their proposals did not undermine the American tradition of voluntarism. Instead, they argued "their case in the name of old fashioned thrift, economic independence, and mobility." At the same time, they predicted that social insurance would be a "means of preserving the social order, enhancing national prestige, preventing class conflict, and assimilating the foreigner." As Tishler points out, "A number of those engaged in the crusade against pauperism and public outdoor relief to the able-bodied were also among the few who showed any interest in social insurance." In Philadelphia in the years after World War I charity reformers dropped their blanket condemnation of outdoor relief and supported the creation of a public welfare department, which they justified with familiar arguments about the goals of socialism, now overlaid with an almost hysterical fear of socialism, and a weary confession of the inability of private philanthropy to match public need.[76]

In the late 1870s charity workers and reformers nearly universally condemned public relief. By about 1915 many supported its inevitability and argued for a division of labor between public and private agencies: The former should give out money; the latter should restrict themselves to casework. This shift in position was the result of at least two factors. First, the difficulty of raising money and the enormous size of the problems they

---

[75]*Ibid.*, p. 111.

[76]Tishler, *Self-Reliance and Social Security*, pp. x–xi; Davis, "Underdevelopment of Public Welfare."

encountered convinced many voluntary workers that private agencies could not alleviate dependence by themselves. Second, this shift from volunteer to professional, so well described by Lubove in *The Professional Altruist*, made the source of funds appear less important than their management. As professionals, social work officials supported what in effect was a compromise between supporters and opponents of public outdoor relief. The problem, they said, was not so much one of principle as one of administration. Outdoor relief should be administered by experts, and the poor should be classified into subcategories with a special program designed for each. Public agencies by and large should give out the money, whereas private agencies should develop appropriate forms of casework. Through their emphasis on classification, social workers transmuted the distinction between the worthy and the unworthy poor, at the core of scientific charity, into a typology of distinctions between dependent groups. In this way they shared in the emphasis on individualizing treatment that, according to Rothman, characterized approaches to crime, delinquency, and mental illness in the same period. They also championed innovations that were convenient: The arrangements they proposed heightened their roles as experts with technical skills and relieved them of the day-to-day burden of raising money and dispensing relief.

By softening their hostility toward public relief, social workers were able to develop coalitions with public welfare officials, who themselves were developing a professional identity, symbolized in New York by the transformation of the Convention of County Superintendents of the Poor into the Association of Public Welfare Officials in 1913. Although no one has studied either the superintendents of the poor or the process by which they became professionals, it is clear that by the First World War they, too, began to see themselves as experts, interested in expanding their status and responsibilities by promoting the scientific basis of their work, improving their administrative methods, and enhancing the role of public agencies. For these reasons, many private social workers and public officials supported the creation of municipal departments of public welfare.[77]

Lubove, it should be stressed, does not argue for a simple conflict between voluntarism and collectivism. Rather, he observes that two different kinds of collectivism competed: that of voluntary organizations or

---

[77]Davis, "Underdevelopment of Public Welfare"; Halbert, "Boards of Public Welfare and Good City Government" and "Boards of Public Welfare: A System of Government Social Work"; Howe, "Development of Municipal Charities."

groups of employers and that of the state. According to Lubove, the nature of collectivism, not its existence, was the central issue. Still, Tishler's point remains important because it conveys how social insurance advocates supplemented arguments based on economic need with appeals to widespread American values and goals.

Whether, as Tishler contends, Lubove begs the essential question remains more debatable. After all, all other Western countries, even though capitalist, introduced social insurance before the United States, and their coverage still remains more extensive. The important question may well be why the American experience has differed, why, that is, social insurance has so often failed. Lubove leaves no mystery about why social insurance was implemented in a watered-down fashion, doomed to fail from the start. Social insurance was shaped by the interests that created the problems it was supposed to regulate. Powerful forces ensured that social insurance in America would not meet its goals. In Philadelphia, for example, the business interests, which long had dominated the charity reform movement, advocated the establishment of a municipal department of public welfare as part of their campaign for municipal reform in the second decade of the twentieth century. They tried to ensure that welfare practice would defuse political agitation, bypass political machines, and operate in as economic and efficient a manner as possible. They had no interest in income redistribution or, even, in the alleviation of poverty.[78]

If it is obvious why social insurance measures failed to meet their goals, it is less easy to say why the forces opposing social insurance were so much stronger and why business interests in America were able to exert a greater influence on legislation than they were elsewhere. Lubove's answer relies on the American tradition of voluntarism. But, although voluntarism is a proximate cause, it is not a sufficient explanation, for it is the source and tenacity of the voluntary tradition that needs explanation. This question merges with larger issues about the weakness of the Left in American history. These, of course, are not Lubove's concern, but, as with Boyer and Rothman, it is important to see how the history of responses to dependency connect with major themes in American history.

Three themes emerge from any account of the history of dependency in America. The first is the rippling upward of supervisory authority and financial responsibility from the local (town or county) to the state to the federal level of government. Of the three, the local level has been explored least systematically. For instance, although Lubove reports innovations in specific cities, he does not analyze the nature and meaning of local

---

[78]Davis, "Underdevelopment of Public Welfare."

variation in practice. Thus he and Tishler recount the attempt to abolish outdoor relief in the late nineteenth century, noting its success in some cities. But they do not explore the varied ways in which urban policy reacted to the tenets of scientific charity. Why did Brooklyn abolish outdoor relief when Buffalo did not? Why did different counties in the same state give quite different amounts of relief to each applicant? Were variations random, a result of the meanness or generosity of local officials, or were there systematic relations between labor markets, local politics, location, and relief, to name some possible influences?

The second theme is the relationship between public and private roles and responsibilities. The definition of public and the bounds of public authority remained problematic throughout the century. They were at issue in the Dartmouth College case in 1819; they remained blurred even in the 1890s when the New York State Supreme Court ruled unconstitutional legislation requiring agencies wholly supported by private funds to submit to the supervision of the Board of State Charities. Although its increasing scope and authority remain the overwhelming motif, the state, of course, did not entirely supersede the private sector, which, in America, retains an exceptionally wide range of social responsibilities. Even so, voluntarism in America retains little of its nineteenth-century flavor. As a response to the competition of the state and the complexity of its tasks, voluntarism has become more centralized and professional, as in the Community Chest movement described by Lubove in *The Professional Altruist*, and, of course, many voluntary agencies rely more on public funds than on private donations.[79]

The third theme is the expansion of coverage. The incorporation of successive groups under the welfare umbrella has eroded the conception of welfare as charity. Despite the stigma still attached to poverty and the behavioral criteria attached to relief, measures considered controversial earlier in the century—such as workmen's compensation, unemployment insurance, or Social Security—no longer are questioned seriously and have passed from the category of philanthropy to entitlement in the minds of most people. This, surely, is one moral of the current outcry against attempts to reduce Social Security benefits.

Indeed, the dramatic expansion of welfare in the period between the mid-1960s and mid-1970s is one major theme of James Patterson's important book. In his chapter "The Unsung Revolution," he points out:

> The growth in all social welfare programs was staggering. Expenditures rose between 1965 and 1976 at an annual rate of 7.2 percent in constant

[79]Lubove, *Professional Altruist*, pp. 180–182.

dollars, compared to 4.6 percent annually between 1950 and 1965. In 1960 such spending was 7.7 percent of the GNP; in 1965, 10.5 percent; in 1974, 16 percent. By far the largest sums went for non-means-tested programs like Social Security, unemployment compensation, and Medicare. But public aid also rose during these years.... These figures reveal that the war in Vietnam, however draining, did not prevent vast increases in domestic spending. On the contrary, social welfare expanded to dimensions that would have been unimaginable in 1960.

The result, Patterson contends, was dramatic. "This growth of social welfare expenditures, broadly defined, was effective in reducing poverty in the United States."[80]

A second moral, however, is that the expansion of coverage will not continue automatically. Those categories of welfare not yet accepted as entitlements will be cut back or eliminated, and few, if any, extensions of coverage will be made in the next several years. No unseen hand guides the progress of social welfare in an upward direction. Welfare policy is always the result of a political process whose outcome is uncertain. Public welfare was drastically curtailed in American cities during the last quarter of the nineteenth century; it is about to be cut back again.

If the expansion of coverage (no matter how inadequate), if the transference of some categories of assistance from charity to entitlement are worthwhile, then the story is at least partly one of progress. Indeed, it is impossible to deny the inadequacy of charity and relief in past times and the hardship and suffering of the poor, sick, and elderly. Equally unmistakable are the administrative chaos, confusion, and corruption of welfare practices in the nineteenth century.

Nonetheless, other considerations undercut any simple story of progress. The social insurance movement did not unfold in a linear process. Its history cannot be captured by any simple notions of progress or of the triumph of benevolence over self-interest. Social insurance, as already observed, emerged from a complex political process. At every stage alternative proposals existed, and the ones chosen by no means embodied the most comprehensive or progressive solutions. In practice, moreover, social insurance has been blunted, undercut in its implementation by the forces it threatened. Nor has the association of degradation with dependency been erased. Poverty still denotes moral failure, and through the linkage of aid to behavior, the welfare system reinforces the social stigma

---

[80]James T. Patterson, *America's Struggle against Poverty, 1900–1980* (Cambridge, Mass.: Harvard University Press, 1981), pp. 164–165.

attached to public relief. This is one of the ways in which the welfare system aggravates the problems it was designed to reduce.[81]

Nor have centralization and the increase in state power always been the best alternative. Centralization has promoted the power of state officials by investing them with the authority to administer increasingly arcane regulations and to control the behavior of their clients. An alternative such as the negative income tax would undercut that power, and, as much as employers, state officials are reluctant to relinquish authority. A more historical example is the controversy over county care of the insane, already discussed. It is not clear that the insane profited from their removal from county to state hospitals. But the state bureaucracy did profit. Thus it is misleading automatically to equate increases in state power with social progress, as was common in Progressive historical writing from about the end of World War II until the mid-1960s.

Public welfare's role in labor discipline (not discussed by Lubove) also conflicts with a Whig version of its history. In *Regulating the Poor* Frances Fox Piven and Richard Cloward argue that poor relief has been an instrument of social and labor discipline, extended to pacify the poor in times of acute distress or potential violence and withdrawn during periods of labor scarcity when the poor are anxious for work. According to them, welfare remains inadequate because its purpose is to discourage workers from idleness. The stigma attached to poverty is not the obverse of a faith in independence or a corollary of voluntarism. Like the inadequacy of relief or the dread of the poorhouse, it is a mechanism for labor control, a way of maintaining the will to do hard, dull work for low wages.[82]

Piven and Cloward believe that the poor have gained more from their own direct action than from coalitions of reformers and businessmen. In *Poor People's Movements* they document their argument with case studies of gains won through the self-activity of the poor during the twentieth century. Had they concerned themselves with the nineteenth century, they could have found other examples. The militancy of the poor, as the New York county superintendents said, was one of the factors that prevented the complete abolition of outdoor relief in some towns and cities. In fact, one source of the variation in relief practice in late nineteenth-century cities could have been the activity of the poor. Political machines, after all, depended partly on the mobilization of the poor. Perhaps in some cities a

---

[81]On welfare since the 1930s, see Gilbert Y. Steiner, *Social Insecurity: The Politics of Welfare* (Chicago: Rand McNally, 1966).

[82]Frances Fox Piven and Richard Cloward, *Regulating the Poor: The Functions of Public Welfare* (New York: Random House, 1971), p. 149.

coalition of local politicians attracted by the graft and patronage supplied by the administration of relief and poor people with an immediate stake in public welfare blocked the abolition of outdoor relief. This remains only speculation for the present, but it does point research in a direction not pursued by Lubove, or indeed by most historians of welfare, who more or less ignore the activity of the poor on their own behalf.[83]

James Patterson is an exception. With Piven's and Cloward's work very much in mind, he tries to assess the role of the poor themselves and of conflict in promoting the expansion of welfare in the 1930s and the 1960s. His conclusion is that neither the actions of the poor themselves nor social conflict had very much to do with progress in social welfare. During the 1930s, he argues, the poor and unemployed remained by and large apathetic and exerted little pressure on political leaders. In the 1960s, he admits, the civil rights movement did influence welfare, but the National Welfare Rights Organization (NWRO), a major example used by Piven and Cloward, had little effect:

> Applications for AFDC [Aid to Families with Dependent Children] and rates of acceptance began to grow dramatically well before 1967, when the NWRO became visible. The NWRO, indeed, never had more than 22,000 members— or around 2 percent of the adult recipients of public assistance. It is equally doubtful that urban disorders, including riots in the mid- and late 1960s, did much to liberalize welfare. Some evidence suggests that welfare rolls and expenditures did rise more rapidly in cities hit by disturbances than elsewhere, but the need tended to be greatest there, especially in areas literally burned to the ground by rioters. And did the riots, as well as the militant rhetoric of the NWRO, create a backlash that did more harm than good? One careful study concluded, "The import of the rioting was probably to stimulate 'law and order,' not welfare benevolence."

Patterson's evidence raises serious questions about aspects of Piven's and Cloward's thesis. But Patterson does not anchor his argument in any analysis of the political economy of capitalism, particularly changing labor market structures and problems of labor discipline. Nor does he examine the politics of welfare at the state and county or city level, where the actors in conflicts about the style and role of welfare often stood out with special clarity. Patterson focuses on national politics, demographic trends, and the growth of the welfare bureaucracy. These are, of course, crucial factors in welfare history, but they do not provide the evidence with which to refute Piven's and Cloward's claim that welfare has served to regulate labor.[84]

---

[83] Frances Fox Piven and Richard A. Cloward, *Poor People's Movements: Why They Succeed and How They Fail* (New York: Pantheon, 1977).

[84] Patterson, *America's Struggle*, pp. 180–181.

In *Regulating the Poor* Piven and Cloward make an essentially functional argument. They infer the intention of welfare practice primarily from its role. In *Poor People's Movements* they add a sense of process by documenting cases of conflict. However, they ignore the gains in non-cash-, non-means-related welfare that Patterson documents and that, on the surface, did not emerge from the kind of conflict they describe. What they have not done yet is to connect satisfactorily their larger argument about the role of welfare with a sense of historical process, an account of the way in which a welfare system actually emerges and changes over time. The two issues at stake between them and Patterson—the role of the welfare system and the roles of the poor and of social conflict in its development— remain unresolved. What makes Piven and Cloward compelling at the moment is their ability to connect their thesis with the current attack on welfare. Although Patterson expects few expansions in welfare in the 1980s, his book offers very little help in understanding the sources, nature, or timing of the current attempt to role back the welfare state. Only a broader analysis of American political economy and American society will explain the power of current attempts to reverse the history of the welfare state, and only a different sort of history, a series of detailed case studies, will show under what conditions relief has been reduced in American cities and how politics and poor people actually interacted.

Consider, for example, the case of Brooklyn, New York, in the 1870s. The absence of an effective coalition between the machine and the poor may have enabled Brooklyn to abolish public outdoor relief in 1878—an action hailed by charity reformers and critics of poor law administration around the country. Poor relief in Brooklyn, closely tied to partisan politics, was riddled with graft, more so, some observers claimed, than in any other city in the country. Its abolition was part of a municipal reform movement, led by wealthy and influential citizens like Seth Low, which promised to clean up city government and reduce taxes. Low claimed that Brooklyn abolished outdoor relief without hardship to the poor and without very much opposition, and his version was repeated by supporters throughout the country. It has not been challenged by historians.[85] Nonetheless, Low did meet opposition. His supporters controlled the city's Board of Supervisors, which appropriated money, but not the elected overseers of the poor, who distributed it. The latter—more closely tied to the Democratic machine and closer, as well, to the poor—protested, pointing to the threatening crowds who demanded relief and to the unprecedented suffering that, they claimed, the new policy had caused.

---

[85]Davis, "Uses of Outdoor Relief" in Katz and Associates, Appendix.

But the Brooklyn poor, relying on the support of a discredited political machine, could not force a change in policy.[86] Whether the same factors, working in a different fashion, prevented the abolition of outdoor relief in other cities remains an open question; so do the consequences of the abolition of outdoor relief for the poor. What happened to people when their relief was cut off? Did they find work, as Low implied, or did they leave the city, turn to hospitals and orphanages for assistance, draw on relatives, or starve? No one, right now, knows the answer.

The Brooklyn experience shows the importance of local case studies to the historical and theoretical interpretation of public welfare. In fact, two hypotheses about the rhythm, nature, and extent of public welfare can be tested only through detailed local studies. One begins with Piven's and Cloward's claim that welfare has varied with the political activity and power of the poor, the business cycle, and the attempt to secure labor discipline. According to Piven and Cloward:

> Relief arrangements are ancillary to economic arrangements. Their chief function is to regulate labor, and they do that in two general ways. First, when mass unemployment leads to outbreaks of turmoil, relief programs are ordinarily initiated or expanded to absorb and control enough of the unemployed to restore order; then as turbulence subsides the relief system contracts, expelling those who are needed to populate the labor market. Relief also performs a labor-regulating function in this shrunken state, however. Some of the aged, disabled, the insane and others who are of no use as workers are left on the relief rolls, and their treatment is so degrading and punitive as to instill in the laboring masses a fear of the fate that awaits them should they relax into beggary and pauperism.[87]

Piven's and Cloward's argument has little sense of process or of agency. Relief appears governed, almost, by a hidden hand that moves automatically in the interests of the capitalist state. But, as I have said, relief policy varied even from county to county within the same state, and explanations need to be sensitive to the reasons for local differences and the political processes through which different policies were developed. Nor does Piven's and Cloward's thesis quite fit the facts. The ablebodied never were wholly expelled from relief rolls, as they imply. Nor did the rhythm of relief match economic cycles and popular protest quite so closely. Outdoor relief was sharply cut back in the late nineteenth century during the decades of the most intense labor conflict and violence in American

---

[86]*Ibid.*

[87]Piven and Cloward, *Regulating the Poor*, p. 3.

*Plate 16.* Matron Webb of the Lost Children's Department at Police Headquarters with one of her charges, circa 1890. (Photograph by Jacob A. Riis, Jacob A. Riis Collection, Museum of the City of New York.)

history. The plan to abolish outdoor relief in Brooklyn and the election of Seth Low and his associates preceded the recovery from the depression that began in 1873, even though the improved economic situation in 1878 and 1879 helped reformers implement the new policy.

Nonetheless, it is clear that Piven and Cloward are right that poor relief has been kept deliberately inadequate and degrading in order to discourage the ablebodied from leaving hard and poorly paid work. They are also right that poor relief has been used as an instrument of social discipline. My modification of their thesis, in fact, stresses the use of relief policy as one weapon in each generation's arsenal of social discipline. I start from the connection of periods of welfare reform with periods of social disorder or violence, which frightened the respectable classes. The late 1870s, the mid-1890s, the years following World War I, the Great Depression, and the 1960s—these were the major periods of welfare reform and, as well, periods of turmoil. In each of them public and private authorities deployed strategies of social discipline with a consistent style. During the first labor protests, in the 1870s, the characteristic style was repression: Send in the troops; end Reconstruction; abolish outdoor relief. By the 1920s welfare capitalism had replaced repression, and social discipline featured attempts to reduce labor mobility, promote working-class home ownership, and expand facilities for secondary education, workmen's compensation, industrial psychology, and mothers' pensions. The 1890s, in this view, were not so much a new as a transitional era when the responses of authorities vacillated between repression and concilia-tion. Thus there was more argument about outdoor relief and the breaking up of families than in either the 1870s or 1920s, when choices appeared much clearer. Welfare policy is an especially good guide to the broader strategies of social discipline in any era, for assumptions about class, work, and social authority usually are stated more clearly and less guardedly than in discussions of other areas, such as education, housing policy, or, even, labor management. Even today, politicians use fewer euphemisms when they talk about welfare than when they discuss almost anything else.[88]

Relief policy, however, has its own internal dialectic. By stressing the need for a scientific approach to dependence, revealing the scope of the problem, and heightening public sensibility, charity workers and private welfare officials helped ensure the dominance of public authority in the repertoire of responses to social crisis. Through their annual conventions, shared problems, and attempts to defend their reputation and authority, county superintendents of the poor developed a professional identity as public welfare officials and began to advance their interests through supporting administrative reform. Relief policies changed the relation between dependence and authority. Charity workers attempted to rede-fine poverty from a declaration to a certification of need. Attempts to distinguish between the worthy and unworthy poor were overlaid with increasingly fine distinctions between the categories of dependence, each treated appropriately and individually by specialists. These professional aspirations, administrative interests, and new definitions set a context for reform, channeling and limiting successive attempts to alter the scope of relief or to connect welfare policies more tightly with other strategies of social discipline.[89]

---

[88]Davis, "Uses of Outdoor Relief."

[89]J. Kenneth Benson, "Organizations: A Dialectical View," *Administrative Science Quarterly* 22(1977): 1–21, is a formal discussion of the way a dialectical approach may be applied to institutions.

One major source of the variation in relief policy may be the labor market. Dual-labor-market theorists have pointed out that today employers who draw on the secondary labor market are more sympathetic to public welfare than are large industrialists who use labor in the primary market. Michael Piore, for example, asserts that "a principal function of the public-assistance system," particularly Aid to Families with Dependent Children, is to create "a stable base of income for the clients, who are then able and willing to take low-status, insecure, dead-end jobs." In the nineteenth century where the secondary labor market was large, relief may have stayed relatively extensive, as in the cities along internal waterways that froze during the winter. Indeed, none of the cites along the Great Lakes or the Erie Canal abolished outdoor relief. Where women and children made up a large proportion of the work force, however, it may have been easier to abolish outdoor relief because families had more than one wage earner. The economies of Brooklyn and Philadelphia, which abolished outdoor relief, offered relatively abundant work to women. Buffalo, which did not abolish outdoor relief, had unusually few jobs for women. Moreover, employers of secondary labor may have been politically stronger in certain cities. Perhaps in large, old cities, such as Brooklyn and Philadelphia, affluent professionals, committed more to civic economy, the reestablishment of deference, and moral uplift than to the regulation of the labor market, wielded enough political power to override the interests of the small and medium-size businesses that depended on the secondary labor market.[90]

These three types of interpretations—the relation of welfare policy to social discipline, the dialectic of relief policy, and the role of the labor market—are complementary, not competitive. None has been tested with detailed local case studies. But it is important to know whether they are right, because the interpretation of welfare history has tangible consequences. If the Whig version is accepted, progress can be expected through electoral politics and enlightened administration. Although slow, the system works. Unfortunately, this Whig interpretation is wrong. Social insurance is extended only through the fragile coalitions of self-interest and commitment that arise from time to time; even then progressive measures are undermined from the start by powerful interests, and gains, we are relearning today, are reversible. In the 1930s and 1960s Democratic administrations wanting to stay in office were forced to appeal to a

---

[90]Michael J. Piore, *Birds of Passage: Migrant Labor and Industrial Societies* (Cambridge: Cambridge University Press, 1979), pp. 89–90; Jones, *Outcast London*, pp. 268–269.

coalition of workers, blacks, and liberals, but that coalition, which supported the extension of welfare and civil rights, has disintegrated. We are left by default with the militant activity of the poor on their own behalf. The moral may be no more complex than this: When affluent America stops being afraid of "social dynamite" in the slums, it will stop caring about them as well.[91]

---

[91] The metaphor of "social dynamite" is from James Bryant Conant, *Slums and Suburbs* (New York: McGraw-Hill, 1961), p. 2.

# EPILOGUE:
# THE SIGNIFICANCE OF
# WELFARE HISTORY

Public policy often is made on self-interest and sold on myth. This is one reason why history is important. Without historical analysis it is hard to see the recurrent connections between welfare policy and strategies of social discipline or to appreciate the stale, repetitive, and self-serving quality of myths about the poor. Without history, it is hard to understand why a welfare system that nobody likes or trusts is so resilient to change. History serves, too, to undercut any lingering notions of the inevitability of progress or improvement in the lives of the poor. A few benefits may have passed from the category of charity to entitlement, but most are still fragile. They have been rolled back before, and they will be rolled back again.

Welfare in America is a historical product, the accretion of layers over time. There is, in fact, an identifiable style of welfare policy and practice in America with 12 major characteristics:

1.   The individual and degraded image of the poor. It is the fault of individuals that they are poor. America is a land that offers work and at least modest rewards to all who try. The poor lack the moral fiber of respectable, hard-working citizens.

2.   The division of the working class into two groups. These have been called the worthy and the unworthy poor, the working and the non-

working poor, or the working class and the lumpen proletariat. The result is the same, whatever the terms: to set off people who receive welfare as outside the working class, as, in fact, in drain upon those who work, and, hence, to divert working-class sympathy away from welfare measures.

3. The gap between images of poverty or dependence and demography. Wherever contemporaries, historians, or social scientists have examined the demography of dependence with care, the characteristics of the poor have not matched their image. The causes of poverty have had little to do with individual moral weakness and much to do with the organization of economic and political life. Periodic dependence has been a predictable, structural feature of working-class life throughout most of American history.

4. The punitive character of policy. Welfare policy has penalized the poor even more than it has helped them. One explicit purpose of early poorhouses was to discourage the working poor from seeking welfare. The degrading, punitive features of contemporary welfare policy have been documented over and over again.

5. The reversibility of progress. There is nothing inevitable about the welfare state. Welfare has been decreased or restricted at various points in the past, and there is every reason to believe that it will be cut back again.

6. Welfare policy as part of a strategy of social discipline. Every generation has had its characteristic style of social discipline. In the 1870s it was repression; by the early decades of the twentieth century, it was welfare capitalism. Welfare policy is one key component of the strategy, and one whose study shows the assumptions and styles of an era with special force and clarity.

7. Welfare policy is dialectical. Policy emerges not only from a series of political, social, and economic forces but also from an internal process. Policies create administrative structures and officials whose aspirations and interests help shape or resist innovation. Social scientists and other academics have acquired a stake in policies that depend on experts and technical advice.

8. The early and pervasive role of the state. There has never been a golden age of voluntarism in America. Some level of government always has been active, usually providing most of the money. Voluntarism never has proven adequate to the problems of urban welfare.

9. The intermixture of public and private. Despite the attempt to differentiate public and private spheres in the nineteenth century, the two never became distinct. Groups with power and resources have used the state to advance their own interests in welfare policy as well as in other

areas of public life. The irony of welfare reform is that it usually has meant lowering taxes by taking away benefits from poor people.

10.   The achievement of progress through conflict and coalition. The poor have gained very little through the disinterested benevolence of individuals or the state. Gains have come through the formation of coalitions based on various interests, the attempt to win votes, and the fear of radicalism and violence.

11.   The activity of the poor on their own behalf. The poor have bent institutions and policies to their own purposes. There has always been a difference between the purposes for which policies were adopted and the uses to which they were put. In every era the poor have created strategies of survival whose resourcefulness belies the images of passive degradation with which poor people so often are portrayed.

12.   Welfare policy is not inevitable. There is no set of arrangements that magically fit any state of industrialization or modernization. At every point in its history, welfare policy has been the result of compromise and choice. And at every stage those choices have been controversial. Sane, reasonable people have seen the self-serving myths that have undergirded descriptions of the poor, the punitive nature of policy, and the interests really served by welfare. The existence of this alternative vision and its message that another way is possible is the only truly hopeful aspect of welfare in American history.

# APPENDIX

**TABLE A.1**
**Entrants to Erie County, New York, Poorhouse, 1829–1879: Number and Rate per 1000 Population**

| Year | Number | Per 1000 population | Year | Number | Per 1000 population |
|------|--------|---------------------|------|--------|---------------------|
| 1829 | 303  | 8.49  | 1857 | 1051 | 8.20 |
| 1830 | 212  | 5.94  | 1858 | 1044 | 7.87 |
| 1831 | 278  | 7.37  | 1859 | 1082 | 7.89 |
| 1832 | 320  | 8.02  | 1860 | 876  | 6.17 |
| 1833 | 226  | 5.37  | 1861 | 609  | 4.19 |
| 1834 | 420  | 9.44  | 1862 | 873  | 5.87 |
| 1835 | 349  | 7.41  | 1863 | 749  | 4.92 |
| 1836 | 480  | 9.66  | 1864 | 854  | 5.48 |
| 1837 | 383  | 7.30  | 1865 | 900  | 5.65 |
| 1838 | 344  | 6.20  | 1866 | 1037 | 6.35 |
| 1839 | 313  | 5.33  | 1867 | NA   | NA   |
| 1840 | 377  | 6.08  | 1868 | NA   | NA   |
| 1841 | 386  | 6.18  | 1869 | NA   | NA   |
| 1842 | 423  | 6.62  | 1870 | NA   | NA   |
| 1843 | 475  | 7.29  | 1971 | NA   | NA   |
| 1844 | 550  | 7.29  | 1872 | 1285 | 6.89 |
| 1850 | 1466 | 14.51 | 1873 | 1677 | 8.81 |
| 1851 | 1685 | 16.12 | 1874 | 1727 | 8.88 |
| 1852 | 2199 | 20.34 | 1875 | 1291 | 6.51 |
| 1853 | 1403 | 12.54 | 1876 | 1488 | 7.34 |
| 1854 | NA   | NA    | 1877 | 1517 | 7.34 |
| 1855 | 1095 | 9.14  | 1878 | 1490 | 7.06 |
| 1856 | 877  | 7.08  | 1879 | 1317 | 6.11 |

**TABLE A.2**
**Indoor and Outdoor Relief, Erie County, New York, 1870–1896: Number Aided, Expense, and Rate of Relief**

| Year | Number of recipients | | Dollars spent (hundreds) | | Recipients per 1000 population | | Dollars per recipient, outdoor |
|------|--------|---------|--------|---------|--------|----------|----------|
|      | Indoor | Outdoor | Indoor | Outdoor | Indoor | Outdoor  |          |
| 1870 | 500    | 7,870   | 47     | 80      | 2.79   | 44.0     | 10.17    |
| 1871 | 521    | 5,638   | 44     | 80      | 2.78   | 30.9     | 14.19    |
| 1872 | 563    | 7,420   | 56     | 84      | 3.02   | 39.8     | 11.3     |
| 1873 | 789    | 6,917   | 92     | 77      | 4.14   | 36.3     | 11.1     |
| 1874 | 650    | 4,015   | 61     | 87      | 3.34   | 20.7     | 21.7     |
| 1875 | 605    | 10,000  | 99     | 128     | 3.05   | 50.4     | 12.8     |
| 1876 | 633    | 13,142  | 69     | 151     | 3.12   | 64.9     | 11.4     |
| 1877 | 715    | 11,284  | 60     | 133     | 3.46   | 54.6     | 11.7     |
| 1878 | 653    | 9,950   | 55     | 95      | 3.09   | 47.1     | 9.5      |
| 1879 | 665    | 5,844   | 67     | 78      | 3.09   | 27.1     | 13.3     |
| 1880 | 679    | 4,828   | 62     | 90      | 3.09   | 21.9     | 18.6     |
| 1881 | 673    | 5,182   | 62     | 66      | 2.96   | 22.8     | 12.7     |
| 1882 | 684    | 4,985   | 83     | 60      | 2.91   | 21.2     | 12.0     |
| 1883 | 605    | 4,151   | 73     | 59      | 2.49   | 17.1     | 14.2     |
| 1884 | 695    | 6,684   | 112    | 81      | 2.77   | 26.7     | 12.1     |
| 1885 | 706    | 3,596   | 97     | 51      | 2.73   | 13.9     | 14.1     |
| 1886 | 683    | 5,096   | 80     | 79      | 2.55   | 19.0     | 15.5     |
| 1887 | 664    | 4,194   | 69     | 36      | 2.40   | 15.7     | 8.5      |
| 1888 | 721    | 5,590   | 80     | 49      | 2.52   | 19.6     | 8.7      |
| 1889 | 721    | 6,324   | 94     | 49      | 2.44   | 21.4     | 7.8      |
| 1890 | 750    | 6,952   | 93     | 51      | 2.46   | 22.8     | 7.3      |
| 1891 | 706    | 7,144   | 114    | 57      | 2.25   | 22.8     | 7.9      |
| 1892 | 737    | 5,691   | 113    | 55      | 2.28   | 17.6     | 9.6      |
| 1893 |        |         |        |         |        |          |          |
| 1894 | 483    | 14,310  | 115    | 89      | 1.41   | 41.9     | 6.2      |
| 1895 | 696    | 11,316  | 124    | 98      | 1.98   | 32.2     | 8.6      |
| 1896 | 618    | 17,537  | 128    | 147     | 1.71   | 48.5     | 8.3      |

**TABLE A.3**
**Index of Entrants per Month, Erie County, New York, Poorhouse, 1829–1871**

|           | J   | F  | M  | A   | M   | J  | J  | A  | S  | O  | N   | D   |
|-----------|-----|----|----|-----|-----|----|----|----|----|----|-----|-----|
| 1829–1871 | 120 | 77 | 80 | 112 | 104 | 88 | 89 | 99 | 98 | 97 | 107 | 129 |
|           |     | 92 |    |     | 101 |    |    | 95 |    |    | 111 |     |

**TABLE A.4**
**Age Structure of Inmate Population, Erie County, New York, Poorhouse, 1829–1886**

| Year | Percentage in age groups | | | | | |
|------|------|-------|-------|-------|-------|------|
| | 0–14 | 15–19 | 20–29 | 30–39 | 40–49 | 50+ |
| 1829 | 28.0 | 3.1 | 26.5 | 24.4 | 9.4 | 8.7 |
| 1830–1834 | 32.7 | 4.1 | 24.5 | 20.4 | 10.2 | 8.2 |
| 1835–1839 | 35.7 | 6.5 | 19.1 | 17.3 | 10.4 | 11.1 |
| 1840–1844 | 30.6 | 4.4 | 24.4 | 18.4 | 9.8 | 12.3 |
| 1853–1854 | 34.2 | 5.2 | 17.0 | 19.9 | 10.8 | 12.8 |
| 1855–1859 | 30.3 | 4.9 | 21.5 | 16.8 | 12.5 | 14.7 |
| 1860–1864 | 28.3 | 6.6 | 18.4 | 14.3 | 12.1 | 20.2 |
| 1865–1869 | 32.2 | 6.5 | 18.3 | 15.1 | 7.5 | 20.4 |
| 1870–1874 | 12.7 | 5.7 | 19.4 | 17.5 | 16.2 | 29.4 |
| 1875–1879 | 3.0 | 5.4 | 33.5 | 19.6 | 14.1 | 24.3 |
| 1880–1886 | 6.0 | 5.4 | 22.3 | 16.1 | 12.1 | 37.3 |

**TABLE A.5**
**Proportion of Female Inmates by Age, Erie County, New York, Poorhouse, 1829–1886**

| Year | Percentage in age categories | | | | | | Total percentage |
|------|------|-------|-------|-------|-------|------|------|
| | 0–14 | 15–19 | 20–29 | 30–39 | 40–49 | 50+ | |
| 1829 | 40.5 | 55.6 | 56.3 | 17.4 | 3.5 | 28.0 | 29.9 |
| 1830–1834 | 37.5 | 50.0 | 25.0 | 30.0 | 40.0 | 25.0 | 32.7 |
| 1835–1839 | 38.9 | 50.0 | 59.2 | 27.7 | 35.7 | 10.0 | 37.8 |
| 1840–1844 | 45.9 | 58.3 | 52.9 | 31.4 | 29.6 | 21.9 | 41.1 |
| 1853–1854 | 39.6 | 54.1 | 49.3 | 50.0 | 36.7 | 22.4 | 44.2 |
| 1855–1859 | 44.6 | 60.0 | 52.3 | 40.4 | 28.9 | 22.2 | 40.1 |
| 1860–1864 | 45.4 | 71.1 | 66.0 | 53.7 | 44.3 | 21.6 | 47.1 |
| 1865–1869 | 40.0 | 50.0 | 52.9 | 50.0 | 14.3 | 10.5 | 36.6 |
| 1870–1874 | 36.7 | 45.2 | 26.5 | 21.3 | 19.4 | 14.7 | 22.6 |
| 1875–1879 | 25.0 | 20.4 | 9.7 | 13.7 | 12.6 | 11.0 | 12.2 |
| 1880–1886 | 37.8 | 33.3 | 35.0 | 30.3 | 13.9 | 24.0 | 27.5 |

**TABLE A.6**
Nativity of Inmates, Erie County, New York, Poorhouse, 1829–1886 (in Percentages)

| Year | Ireland | Germany | Britain | Canada | New York | New England | U.S. Other[a] | Other | All foreign |
|------|---------|---------|---------|--------|----------|-------------|----------------|-------|-------------|
| 1829 | 13.6 | 4.9 | 8.7 | 13.6 | 0.7 | 17.8 | 37.6 | 3.1 | 43.9 |
| 1830–1834 |  |  | 14.3 | 22.4 | 0.0 | 22.4 | 34.7 | 6.1 | 42.9 |
| 1835–1839 | 16.2 | 2.2 | 10.8 | 16.9 | 3.6 | 23.4 | 20.5 | 6.5 | 56.1 |
| 1840–1844 | 29.6 | 6.1 | 11.2 | 8.2 | 6.1 | 14.6 | 19.7 | 4.4 | 59.6 |
| 1853–1854 | 39.3 | 35.3 | 4.4 | 0.7 |  |  | 10.4 | 9.9 | 89.6 |
| 1855–1859 | 40.4 | 22.1 | 5.0 | 2.9 |  |  | 21.8 | 7.8 | 78.2 |
| 1860–1864 | 38.9 | 16.7 | 5.9 | 4.6 |  | 0.7 | 28.7 | 4.5 | 70.6 |
| 1865–1869 | 31.2 | 10.8 | 4.3 | 2.2 |  |  | 47.3 | 4.3 | 52.7 |
| 1870–1874 | 31.0 | 19.4 | 7.8 | 4.1 | 0.3 | 0.1 | 29.1 | 8.2 | 60.7 |
| 1875–1879 | 27.9 | 13.2 | 10.0 | 3.7 | 0.1 | 0.4 | 41.0 | 3.6 | 58.6 |
| 1880–1886 | 27.4 | 19.3 | 6.1 | 4.3 | 0.4 | 0.0 | 29.6 | 12.7 | 60.4 |

[a]This includes New York and New England born in 1853–1886.

**TABLE A.7**
Proportion of Inmates by Age and Nativity, Erie County, New York, Poorhouse, 1829–1886.

| Birthplace and year | N | Proportion by age | | | | | | | | |
|---------------------|---|-----|-----|-------|-------|-------|-------|-------|-------|-----|
|  |  | 0–4 | 5–9 | 10–14 | 15–19 | 20–29 | 30–39 | 40–49 | 50–59 | 60+ |
| **Ireland** |  |  |  |  |  |  |  |  |  |  |
| 1829–1844 | 171 | 3.5 | 1.8 | 4.7 | 2.3 | 33.4 | 28.1 | 16.4 | 7.0 | 2.9 |
| 1853–1869 | 682 | 10.3 | 7.8 | 10.9 | 4.5 | 19.9 | 19.1 | 12.9 | 6.2 | 8.5 |
| 1870–1886 | 953 | .5 | .0 | 1.2 | 2.0 | 18.2 | 20.0 | 19.3 | 14.9 | 23.9 |
| **Germany** |  |  |  |  |  |  |  |  |  |  |
| 1829–1844 | 38 | 13.2 | 7.9 | 5.3 | .0 | 15.8 | 18.4 | 15.8 | 7.9 | 15.8 |
| 1853–1869 | 403 | 7.4 | 6.9 | 8.4 | 4.7 | 17.9 | 18.4 | 14.4 | 10.7 | 11.2 |
| 1870–1886 | 535 | 1.1 | .2 | 2.4 | 3.9 | 15.5 | 18.7 | 15.9 | 17.6 | 24.7 |
| **Britain** |  |  |  |  |  |  |  |  |  |  |
| 1829–1844 | 95 | 5.3 | 3.2 | 4.2 | 3.2 | 21.1 | 28.4 | 17.9 | 8.4 | 8.4 |
| 1853–1869 | 89 | 2.2 | 3.4 | 3.4 | 3.4 | 21.3 | 24.7 | 21.3 | 13.5 | 6.7 |
| 1870–1886 | 288 | .3 | .3 | .3 | 3.8 | 30.2 | 24.0 | 14.2 | 12.5 | 14.2 |
| **Canada** |  |  |  |  |  |  |  |  |  |  |
| 1829–1844 | 121 | 24 | 19.8 | 12.4 | 8.3 | 14.9 | 14.0 | 4.9 | .8 | .8 |
| 1853–1869 | 50 | 10.0 | 8.0 | 10.0 | 10.0 | 28 | 14.0 | 2.0 | 14.0 | 4.0 |
| 1870–1886 | 131 | 3.8 | .8 | 3.8 | 10.7 | 38.9 | 15.3 | 8.4 | 9.2 | 9.2 |

*(continued)*

**TABLE A.7** *(continued)*

| Birthplace and year | N | Proportion by age | | | | | | | | |
|---|---|---|---|---|---|---|---|---|---|---|
| | | 0–4 | 5–9 | 10–14 | 15–19 | 20–29 | 30–39 | 40–49 | 50–59 | 60+ |
| New York | | | | | | | | | | |
| 1829–1844 | 30 | 16.7 | 3.3 | 16.7 | 6.7 | 30.0 | 16.3 | .0 | 3.3 | 6.7 |
| 1853–1869[a] | 0 | | | | | | | | | |
| 1870–1886[a] | 8 | | | | | | | | | |
| New England | | | | | | | | | | |
| 1829–1844 | 170 | 18.2 | 9.4 | 7.1 | 6.5 | 21.8 | 13.0 | 9.4 | 7.1 | 7.6 |
| 1853–1869[a] | 4 | | | | | | | | | |
| 1870–1886[a] | 9 | | | | | | | | | |
| Other U.S.[b] | | | | | | | | | | |
| 1829–1844 | 242 | 18.2 | 11.2 | 6.2 | 4.5 | 25.2 | 30.6 | 6.3 | 4.9 | 2.9 |
| 1853–1869 | 392 | 15.3 | 15.3 | 15.1 | 8.4 | 18.4 | 8.4 | 6.1 | 3.8 | 9.2 |
| 1870–1886 | 1185 | 1.8 | 9.3 | 4.9 | 9.3 | 40.4 | 17.0 | 10.6 | 5.1 | 10.0 |
| Other | | | | | | | | | | |
| 1829–1844 | 45 | 24.4 | 22.2 | 6.7 | 4.4 | 13.3 | 13.3 | 4.4 | 4.4 | 6.7 |
| 1853–1869 | 123 | 15.4 | 8.1 | 15.4 | 5.7 | 15.4 | 15.4 | 10.6 | 4.9 | 8.9 |
| 1870–1886 | 220 | 4.5 | 3.6 | 15.4 | 3.2 | 20.4 | 14.1 | 13.2 | 10.9 | 14.5 |

[a]Insufficient cases.
[b]This includes New York and New England born in 1853–1886.

**TABLE A.8**
**Proportion of Inmates Entering with Relatives, Erie County, New York, Poorhouse, 1829–1886**

| Year | Percentage with relatives |
|---|---|
| 1829 | 37.3 |
| 1830–1834 | 38.3 |
| 1835–1839 | 39.1 |
| 1840–1844 | 26.2 |
| 1853–1859 | 10.6 |
| 1860–1864 | 17.7 |
| 1865–1869 | 6.5 |
| 1870–1874 | 3.5 |
| 1875–1879 | 3.2 |
| 1880–1886 | 4.6 |

TABLE A.9
Inmates Entering with Relatives by Sex, Erie County, New York, Poorhouse, 1829–1844

| | Numbers | | | |
| | Males | | Females | |
| Year | With relatives | Without relatives | With relatives | Without relatives |
|---|---|---|---|---|
| 1829 | 140 | 59 | 38 | 47 |
| 1830 | 22 | 10 | 7 | 6 |
| 1831 | NA | NA | NA | NA |
| 1832 | NA | NA | NA | NA |
| 1833 | NA | NA | NA | NA |
| 1834 | NA | NA | NA | NA |
| 1835 | 26 | 14 | 8 | 14 |
| 1836 | 32 | 11 | 10 | 11 |
| 1837 | 31 | 13 | 15 | 16 |
| 1838 | 12 | 3 | 2 | 5 |
| 1839 | 16 | 8 | 10 | 10 |
| 1840 | 36 | 10 | 18 | 20 |
| 1841 | NA | NA | NA | NA |
| 1842 | 37 | 13 | 20 | 15 |
| 1843 | 38 | 7 | 31 | 6 |
| 1844 | 18 | 3 | 2 | 1 |

| | Proportions with relatives | |
| Year | Male | Female |
|---|---|---|
| 1820 | 29.6 | 55.3 |
| 1829–1834 | 33.3 | 50.0 |
| 1835–1839 | 29.5 | 55.4 |
| 1840–1844 | 20.4 | 37.2 |

TABLE A.10
Inmates Entering with Relatives by Age and Sex, Erie County, New York, Poorhouse, 1853–1886

| Sex | 0–4 | 5–9 | 10–14 | 15–19 | 20–29 | 30–39 | 40–49 | 50–59 | 60+ |
|---|---|---|---|---|---|---|---|---|---|
| Male | 25.2 | 19.2 | 9.5 | 3.0 | .8 | 1.8 | 1.3 | 1.0 | 3.4 |
| Female | 29.7 | 22.4 | 15.7 | 10.3 | 17.4 | 16.7 | 9.2 | 3.9 | 14.5 |

**TABLE A.11**
**Proportion of Female Inmates and Proportion of Inmates Entering with Relatives by Nativity, Erie County, New York, Poorhouse, 1829–1886**

| Year | Ireland | Germany | Britain | Canada | New York | New England | Other U.S. | Other |
|------|---------|---------|---------|--------|----------|-------------|------------|-------|
| | | | Proportion female by birthplace | | | | | |
| 1829 | 15.3 | 21.4 | 20.0 | 48.7 | 50.0 | 28.0 | 33.0 | 22.2 |
| 1830–1834 | .0 | | 42.9 | 27.2 | | 36.4 | 29.4 | 33.3 |
| 1835–1839 | 29.5 | 33.3 | 30.0 | 51.1 | 50.0 | 31.1 | 42.6 | 41.2 |
| 1840–1844 | 41.7 | 28.6 | 31.0 | 56.5 | 23.5 | 43.2 | 49.1 | 33.3 |
| 1853–1854 | 48.8 | 39.1 | 30.0 | 33.3 | | | 44.7 | 46.7 |
| 1855–1859 | 51.4 | 25.7 | 19.4 | 33.3 | | | 45.5 | 31.3 |
| 1860–1864 | 54.0 | 34.0 | 38.2 | 70.4 | | 100.0 | 44.0 | 36.0 |
| 1865–1869 | 44.4 | 20.0 | 50.0 | .0 | | | 36.4 | 50.0 |
| 1870–1874 | 24.2 | 13.2 | 13.4 | 51.4 | 33.0 | .0 | 28.0 | 14.3 |
| 1875–1879 | 12.5 | 8.0 | 5.6 | 23.9 | | 14.3 | 14.4 | 6.5 |
| 1880–1886 | 32.9 | 16.5 | 21.0 | 39.3 | .0 | .0 | 34.4 | 16.3 |
| | | | Proportion entering with relatives | | | | | |
| 1829 | 12.8 | 71.4 | 24.0 | 69.2 | 50.0 | 29.4 | 39.8 | .0 |
| 1830–1834 | .0 | .0 | 42.9 | 81.8 | .0 | 45.5 | 11.8 | .0 |
| 1835–1839 | 24.4 | .0 | 36.7 | 51.1 | 70.0 | 38.5 | 40.4 | 44.7 |
| 1840–1844 | 19.5 | 11.1 | 18.7 | 37.5 | 11.1 | 25.6 | 38.2 | 30.8 |
| 1850–1854 | 10.6 | 5.6 | .0 | 33.3 | | | 36.2 | 4.4 |
| 1855–1859 | 14.9 | 8.2 | .0 | .0 | | | 4.4 | 6.3 |
| 1860–1864 | 20.3 | 9.2 | 11.8 | 33.3 | 100.0 | .0 | 18.0 | 8.3 |
| 1865–1869 | 3.4 | .0 | .0 | .0 | .0 | | 9.1 | 25.0 |
| 1870–1874 | 3.7 | 2.4 | .0 | 14.3 | .0 | .0 | 3.1 | 4.2 |
| 1875–1879 | 2.4 | 1.7 | 1.7 | 7.5 | 33.3 | .0 | 3.9 | 4.7 |
| 1880–1886 | .5 | 1.6 | 2.4 | .0 | .0 | .0 | 8.6 | 13.3 |

**TABLE A.12**

**Probability $(p)$[a] of Entering Erie County, New York, Poorhouse with a Relative, 1829–1844 and 1853–1886: Results of Multiple Classification Analysis**

| | | | | | 1829–1844 | | | Month | |
| Age and sex | | $p$ | Birthplace | $p$ | Year | $p$ | entered | $p$ |
|---|---|---|---|---|---|---|---|---|
| 0–4 | M | .66 | New England | .32 | 1829 | .37 | January | .52 |
| | F | .76 | Mid-Atlantic | .36 | 1830–1834 | .42 | February | .26 |
| | | | Other U.S. | .36 | 1835–1839 | .39 | March | .31 |
| 5–9 | M | .78 | Canada | .43 | 1840–1844 | .28 | April | .32 |
| | F | .74 | Britain | .39 | | | May | .41 |
| | | | Ireland | .32 | | | | |
| 10–14 | M | .53 | Germany | .39 | | | June | .31 |
| | F | .36 | Other | .19 | | | July | .34 |
| 15–19 | M | .20 | | | | | August | .33 |
| | F | .23 | | | | | September | .40 |
| 20–24 | M | .03 | | | | | October | .36 |
| | F | .41 | | | | | November | .29 |
| 25–29 | M | .11 | | | | | December | .40 |
| | F | .38 | | | | | | |
| 30–34 | M | .13 | | | | | | |
| | F | .70 | | | | | | |
| 35–39 | M | .12 | | | | | | |
| | F | .39 | | | | | | |
| 40–44 | M | .16 | | | | | | |
| | F | .46 | | | | | | |
| 45–49 | M | .16 | | | | | | |
| | F | .24 | | | | | | |
| 50–54 | M | .11 | | | | | | |
| | F | .34 | | | | | | |
| 55–59 | M | .08 | | | | | | |
| | F | .01 | | | | | | |
| 60+ | M | .15 | | | | | | |
| | F | .29 | | | | | | |

$$\text{Grand mean} = .35$$
$$R^2 = .33$$

**1853–1886**

| Cause | $p$ | Year entered | $p$ | Age and sex | | $p$ | Month entered | $p$ | Birthplace | $p$ |
|---|---|---|---|---|---|---|---|---|---|---|
| Destitute | .07 | 1853–1854 | .06 | 0–4 | M | .23 | January | .11 | United | |
| Specific | | 1855–1859 | .06 | | F | .28 | February | .08 | States | .07 |
| illness | .07 | 1860–1864 | .13 | 5–9 | M | .18 | March | .03 | Ireland | .08 |
| General or | | 1865–1869 | .00 | | F | .19 | April | .06 | Germany | 06 |
| chronic | | 1870–1874 | .06 | 10–14 | M | .08 | May | .07 | Britain | .05 |
| illness | .06 | 1875–1879 | .07 | | F | .14 | June | .13 | Other | .07 |
| | | | | | | | July | .06 | | |

*(continued)*

**TABLE A.12** *(continued)*

| Cause | p | Year entered | p | 1853–1886 Age and sex | | p | Month entered | p | Birthplace | p |
|---|---|---|---|---|---|---|---|---|---|---|
| Old age | .00 | 1880–1886 | .06 | 15–19 | M | .04 | August | .05 | | |
| Moral or | | | | | F | .10 | September | .10 | | |
| criminal | .05 | | | 20–29 | M | .02 | October | .05 | | |
| Family | | | | | F | .17 | November | .06 | | |
| disruption | .19 | | | 30–39 | M | .02 | December | .08 | | |
| Other | .07 | | | | F | .17 | | | | |
| | | | | 40–49 | M | .02 | | | | |
| | | | | | F | .09 | | | | |
| | | | | 50–59 | M | .02 | | | | |
| | | | | | F | .05 | | | | |
| | | | | 60+ | | .02 | | | | |
| | | | | | | .16 | | | | |
| | | | | Grand mean = .07 | | | | | | |
| | | | | $R^2 = .12$ | | | | | | |

[a]Probability = adjusted deviation and grand mean.

**TABLE A.13**
**Occupations of Nonrelatives among Inmates, Erie County, New York, Poorhouse, 1853–1886**

| | **All nonrelatives 1853–1886** | |
|---|---|---|
| Occupation | N | Percentage |
| Domestic | 140 | 3.0 |
| Laborer | 1963 | 41.4 |
| Other (not listed) | 2640 | 55.7 |

| | **Selected ages** | | | | | |
|---|---|---|---|---|---|---|
| | 20–29 | | 30–39 | | 40–49 | |
| Occupation | N | Percentage | N | Percentage | N | Percentage |
| Domestic | 42 | 3.4 | 26 | 2.9 | 14 | 2.1 |
| Laborer | 549 | 43.9 | 383 | 42.6 | 309 | 45.4 |
| Other | 660 | 52.8 | 491 | 54.6 | 357 | 52.5 |

| | **Sex** | | | |
|---|---|---|---|---|
| | Male | | Female | |
| Occupation | N | Percentage | N | Percentage |
| Domestic | 8 | 51.9 | 57 | 11.0 |
| Laborer | 1898 | 51.9 | 57 | 4.3 |
| Other | 1753 | 47.9 | 1133 | 84.7 |

TABLE A.14

Causes of Commitment to the Erie County, New York, Poorhouse, 1853–1886, by Selected Variables

| Cause | Male (%) | Female (%) | N | Total percentage | 0–4 | 20–29 | 60+ |
|---|---|---|---|---|---|---|---|
| | | Sex | | | Selected ages (%) | | |
| Destitute | 40.8 | 22.7 | 1795 | 35.9 | 19.2 | 41.7 | 39.3 |
| Specific illness | 20.0 | 10.7 | 876 | 17.5 | 2.1 | 21.5 | 11.7 |
| General or chronic illness | 6.4 | 6.7 | 324 | 6.5 | .8 | 5.6 | 12.1 |
| Old age | .8 | .7 | 39 | .8 | .0 | .0 | 5.1 |
| Moral or criminal | 2.1 | 10.4 | 216 | 4.3 | .0 | 7.0 | 2.8 |
| Family disruption | 1.1 | 2.2 | 70 | 1.4 | 10.4 | .2 | .4 |
| Other or missing | 28.7 | 46.7 | 1676 | 33.5 | 67.5 | 24.0 | 28.6 |

| Cause | 1870–1874 | 1875–1879 | 1880–1886 | Entrants with relatives (%) |
|---|---|---|---|---|
| | Year of commitment (%) | | | |
| Destitute | 44.4 | 64.2 | 29.9 | 20.1 |
| Specific illness | 34.4 | 25.3 | 2.1 | 9.1 |
| General or chronic illness | 1.7 | .6 | 38.8 | 4.5 |
| Old age | 1.4 | .5 | 1.0 | .0 |
| Moral or criminal | 1.7 | .8 | 1.0 | 6.6 |
| Family disruption | .0 | .0 | .6 | 6.9 |
| Other or missing | 16.7 | 8.6 | 26.5 | 52.9 |

**TABLE A.15**
Length of Residence in Erie County, New York, Poorhouse, 1829–1844 and 1853–1886, by Age of Inmate (Percentage)

| Age | Less than 1 week | 1–3 weeks | 3–6 weeks | 3 weeks to 3 months | 3–6 months | 6–12 months | 1 year + | Unstated | N |
|---|---|---|---|---|---|---|---|---|---|
| | | | | **1829–1844** | | | | | |
| 0–4 | 17.2 | 17.2 | 19.5 | 12.5 | 7.8 | 3.1 | 22.7 | .0 | 128 |
| 5–9 | 19.7 | 13.2 | 21.1 | 10.5 | 13.2 | 2.6 | 19.7 | .0 | 76 |
| 10–14 | 28.6 | 21.4 | 12.5 | 16.1 | 5.4 | .0 | 12.5 | 3.6 | 56 |
| 15–19 | 19.5 | 17.1 | 19.5 | 17.1 | 12.2 | .0 | 14.6 | .0 | 41 |
| 20–24 | 11.9 | 17.9 | 19.0 | 28.6 | 3.6 | 4.8 | 11.9 | 2.4 | 84 |
| 25–29 | 20.8 | 15.8 | 22.5 | 20.0 | 6.7 | 3.3 | 10.8 | .0 | 120 |
| 30–34 | 19.3 | 29.5 | 22.7 | 10.2 | 3.4 | 1.1 | 10.8 | .0 | 88 |
| 35–39 | 16.3 | 27.9 | 16.3 | 14.0 | 7.0 | 3.5 | 15.1 | .0 | 86 |
| 40–44 | 26.5 | 16.3 | 18.4 | 18.4 | 2.0 | 8.2 | 10.2 | .0 | 49 |
| 45–49 | 17.9 | 17.9 | 23.1 | 12.8 | 10.3 | 2.6 | 15.4 | .0 | 39 |
| 50–54 | | | | | | | | | |
| 55–59 | 33.3 | 33.3 | 8.3 | 8.3 | 8.3 | .0 | 8.3 | .0 | 12 |
| 60+ | 23.3 | 20.9 | 18.6 | 7.0 | .0 | 2.3 | 25.6 | 5.4 | 43 |
| | | | | **1853–1886** | | | | | |
| 0–4 | 15.2 | 14.0 | 14.6 | 13.5 | 10.1 | 5.6 | 0.6 | 26.4 | 178 |
| 5–9 | 14.6 | 10.4 | 13.5 | 15.6 | 15.6 | .0 | 2.4 | 29.2 | 96 |
| 10–14 | 10.6 | 20.5 | 10.6 | 13.4 | 5.9 | 3.9 | 2.4 | 32.7 | 254 |
| 15–19 | 33.5 | 20.9 | 11.0 | 8.7 | 8.7 | 2.7 | .8 | 13.7 | 263 |
| 20–29 | 44.5 | 13.4 | 10.1 | 7.2 | 7.1 | 3.0 | .5 | 14.3 | 1210 |
| 30–39 | 32.4 | 16.5 | 10.4 | 11.4 | 8.0 | 3.9 | .7 | 16.7 | 863 |
| 40–49 | 24.9 | 15.8 | 11.4 | 8.2 | 10.5 | 5.0 | .8 | 23.5 | 659 |
| 50–59 | 20.2 | 15.2 | 11.3 | 10.2 | 10.0 | 5.2 | 1.9 | 26.0 | 480 |
| 60+ | 14.7 | 14.0 | 11.5 | 12.7 | 10.0 | 3.6 | 1.0 | 32.5 | 693 |

TABLE A.16
Length of Residence in Erie County, New York, Poorhouse, 1829–1844 and 1853–1886, by Birthplace of Inmates (Percentage)

| Length of residence | Period | Birthplace | | | | | | | | |
|---|---|---|---|---|---|---|---|---|---|---|
| | | Ireland | Germany | Britain | Canada | New York | New England | Other U.S. | Other | All |
| Less than 1 week | 1829–1844 | 15.7 | 13.5 | 27.2 | 20.9 | 32.1 | 16.8 | 25.9 | 28.6 | 19.8 |
| | 1853–1886 | 25.2 | 21.2 | 39.0 | 28.1 | .0 | 27.3 | 34.6 | 23.3 | 28.5 |
| 1–3 weeks | 1829–1844 | 23.3 | 18.9 | 23.9 | 13.6 | 3.6 | 19.3 | 20.0 | 21.1 | 19.6 |
| | 1853–1886 | 13.5 | 15.2 | 16.8 | 22.8 | 33.3 | 9.1 | 15.5 | 18.1 | 15.3 |
| 3–6 weeks | 1829–1844 | 17.6 | 37.8 | 12.0 | 20.0 | 32.1 | 18.6 | 21.3 | 11.9 | 19.6 |
| | 1853–1886 | 11.1 | 12.6 | 7.4 | 12.6 | 33.3 | 27.3 | 10.6 | 10.7 | 11.0 |
| 3 weeks to 3 months | 1829–1844 | 17.6 | 8.1 | 13.0 | 15.5 | 14.3 | 16.8 | 15.2 | 9.5 | 15.1 |
| | 1853–1886 | 10.3 | 9.6 | 9.3 | 13.2 | 33.3 | 9.1 | 10.2 | 8.1 | 10.1 |
| 3–6 months | 1829–1844 | 5.0 | .0 | 5.4 | 12.7 | 3.6 | 5.0 | 8.7 | 2.4 | 6.6 |
| | 1853–1886 | 10.6 | 10.6 | 8.0 | 2.4 | .0 | .0 | 6.9 | 6.6 | 8.8 |
| 6–12 months | 1829–1844 | 3.1 | 5.4 | 3.3 | 2.7 | .0 | 1.2 | 4.3 | 2.4 | 3.0 |
| | 1853–1886 | 5.0 | 3.8 | 4.9 | .0 | .0 | .0 | 2.8 | 4.2 | 3.8 |
| 1 year | 1829–1844 | 17.0 | 16.2 | 14.1 | 13.6 | 14.3 | 21.1 | 10.4 | 23.8 | 15.5 |
| | 1853–1886 | .7 | 1.2 | .5 | 1.2 | .0 | .0 | 2.8 | 4.2 | .9 |
| Unknown | 1829–1844 | .6 | .0 | 1.1 | .9 | .0 | 1.2 | .9 | .0 | .8 |
| | 1853–1886 | 23.6 | 25.8 | 14.0 | 19.8 | .0 | 27.3 | 18.7 | 24.6 | 21.6 |
| N | 1829–1844 | 159 | 37 | 92 | 110 | 28 | 161 | 230 | 42 | 859 |
| | 1853–1866 | 1514 | 841 | 364 | 167 | 3 | 11 | 1487 | 309 | 4696 |

**TABLE A.17**
**Length of Residence in Erie County, New York, Poorhouse, by Sex of Inmates and Presence of Relatives, 1829–1844 and 1853–1886 (Percentage)**

| Length of residence | Period | Male | Female | Without relatives | With relatives |
|---|---|---|---|---|---|
| Less than 1 week | 1829–1844 | 21.7 | 16.8 | 19.2 | 20.9 |
| | 1853–1886 | 34.3 | 12.2 | 29.3 | 16.8 |
| 1–3 weeks | 1829–1844 | 20.2 | 19.2 | 19.9 | 18.8 |
| | 1853–1886 | 14.6 | 17.3 | 15.1 | 18.8 |
| 3–6 weeks | 1829–1844 | 18.9 | 20.5 | 18.0 | 22.6 |
| | 1853–1886 | 9.8 | 14.3 | 10.9 | 12.8 |
| 6 weeks to 3 months | 1829–1844 | 14.2 | 17.5 | 16.6 | 12.3 |
| | 1853–1886 | 8.9 | 13.8 | 9.8 | 13.5 |
| 3–6 months | 1829–1844 | 7.4 | 5.1 | 7.4 | 5.1 |
| | 1853–1886 | 7.4 | 13.1 | 8.4 | 13.5 |
| 6–12 months | 1829–1844 | 2.8 | 3.4 | 3.2 | 2.7 |
| | 1853–1886 | 3.9 | 3.6 | 4.0 | 2.0 |
| 1 year + | 1829–1844 | 14.3 | 16.2 | 14.8 | 16.8 |
| | 1853–1886 | .8 | .8 | .8 | 2.0 |
| Indeterminate | 1829–1844 | .6 | 1.3 | 11.4 | 28.6 |
| | 1853–1886 | 20.3 | 24.9 | 21.7 | 20.7 |
| N | 1829–1844 | 530 | 297 | 567 | 292 |
| | 1853–1886 | 3425 | 1202 | 4392 | 304 |

**TABLE A.18**
**Length of Residence in Erie County, New York, Poorhouse, by Time Period, 1829–1886 (Percentage)**

| Period | 1 week | 1–3 weeks | 3–6 weeks | 3 weeks to 6 months | 3–6 months | 6–12 months | 1 year + | Indeterminate |
|---|---|---|---|---|---|---|---|---|
| 1829 | 18.5 | 15.9 | 25.9 | 10.7 | 13.0 | 5.6 | 9.3 | 1.1 |
| 1830–1834 | 10.2 | 24.5 | 12.2 | 18.4 | 2.0 | .0 | 30.6 | 2.0 |
| 1835–1839 | 26.5 | 26.1 | 20.5 | 14.4 | 3.4 | 1.9 | 6.4 | .8 |
| 1840–1844 | 16.5 | 16.1 | 13.9 | 19.8 | 4.4 | 2.2 | 26.7 | .4 |
| 1853–1854 | 17.3 | 19.9 | 14.1 | 13.8 | 20.5 | 7.3 | .3 | 6.7 |
| 1855–1859 | 11.8 | 15.4 | 15.4 | 14.9 | 17.6 | 5.8 | .0 | 19.1 |
| 1860–1864 | 10.6 | 16.3 | 11.8 | 18.5 | 13.8 | 2.7 | .4 | 26.0 |
| 1865–1869 | 15.6 | 21.1 | 18.9 | 20.0 | 23.3 | .0 | 1.1 | .0 |
| 1870–1874 | 20.4 | 18.4 | 13.2 | 7.5 | 2.9 | 5.8 | .2 | 31.6 |
| 1875–1879 | 46.6 | 11.0 | 7.5 | 7.1 | 6.7 | 3.4 | .2 | 17.6 |
| 1880–1886 | 26.2 | 19.3 | 10.7 | 6.8 | 2.0 | .2 | 5.3 | 29.5 |

**TABLE A.19**

**Estimated Probability[a] of Selected Lengths of Residence in Erie County, New York, Poorhouse, 1829–1844 and 1853–1886, Other Factors Constant: Multiple Classification Analysis**

| Factor | Under 3 weeks | | 3 weeks to 6 months | | Over 6 months | |
|---|---|---|---|---|---|---|
| | 1829–1844 | 1853–1886 | 1829–1844 | 1856–1886 | 1829–1844 | 1853–1886 |
| Birthplace | | | | | | |
| Ireland | .35 | .40 | .41 | .27 | .17 | .16 |
| Germany | .37 | .37 | .43 | .27 | .18 | .13 |
| Britain | .47 | .47 | .32 | .26 | .17 | .14 |
| Canada | .32 | .47 | .46 | .26 | .16 | .10 |
| New York | .36 | .26 | .47 | .50 | .12 | .00 |
| New England | .34 | .36 | .36 | .35 | .23 | .14 |
| Other U.S. | .36 | .42 | .40 | .30 | .15 | .12 |
| Other | .51 | .40 | .27 | .29 | .14 | .17 |
| Age and Sex | | | | | | |
| 0–4   M | .29 | .26 | .45 | .17 | .24 | .20 |
|        F | .38 | .28 | .34 | .20 | .20 | .14 |
| 5–9   M | .30 | .27 | .36 | .07 | .22 | .11 |
|        F | .30 | .15 | .40 | .15 | .16 | .09 |
| 10–14 M | .45 | .31 | .32 | .23 | .16 | .14 |
|        F | .45 | .30 | .22 | .10 | .09 | .17 |
| 15–19 M | .18 | .61 | .54 | .17 | .17 | .11 |
|        F | .56 | .31 | .33 | .41 | .17 | .08 |
| 20–24 M | .43 | | .35 | | .12 | |
|        F | .23 | | .59 | | .14 | |
| 25–29 M | .36 | | .46 | | .12 | |
|        F | .29 | | .49 | | .14 | |
| 20–29 M | | .58 | | .21 | .19 | .10 |
|        F | | .32 | | .39 | | .15 |

256

| | | | | | | | |
|---|---|---|---|---|---|---|---|
| 30–34 | M | .59 | | .28 | | .10 | |
| | F | .20 | | .59 | | .17 | |
| 35–39 | M | .39 | | .40 | | .14 | |
| | F | .37 | | .38 | | .25 | |
| 30–39 | M | | .53 | | .25 | | .12 |
| | F | | .32 | | .40 | | .15 |
| 40–44 | M | .42 | | .44 | | .12 | |
| | F | .42 | | .30 | | .20 | |
| 45–49 | M | .38 | | .33 | | .21 | |
| | F | .30 | | .43 | | .13 | |
| 40–49 | M | | .43 | | .28 | | .16 |
| | F | | .36 | | .36 | | .17 |
| 50–54 | M | .42 | | .43 | | .14 | |
| | F | .50 | | .21 | | .29 | |
| 55–59 | M | .80 | | .18 | | .02 | |
| | F | .00 | | .59 | | .53 | |
| 50–59 | M | | .38 | | .33 | | .18 |
| | F | | .36 | | .32 | | .15 |
| 60+ | M | .43 | .29 | .19 | .37 | .32 | .17 |
| | F | .29 | .28 | .36 | .33 | .34 | .14 |
| Year of entrance | | | | | | | |
| 1829 | | .33 | | .47 | | .12 | |
| 1830–1834 | | .32 | | .31 | | .34 | |
| 1835–1839 | | .50 | | .38 | | .09 | |
| 1840–1844 | | .32 | | .34 | | .27 | |
| 1853–1854 | | | .49 | | .41 | | .00 |
| 1855–1859 | | | .33 | | .41 | | .02 |
| 1860–1864 | | | .36 | | .37 | | .12 |
| 1865–1869 | | | .34 | | .73 | | .00 |
| 1870–1874 | | | .38 | | .23 | | .23 |
| 1875–1879 | | | .48 | | .20 | | .20 |
| 1880–1886 | | | .39 | | .20 | | .12 |

**TABLE A.19** *(continued)*

| Factor | Under 3 weeks | | 3 weeks to 6 months | | Over 6 months | |
|---|---|---|---|---|---|---|
| | 1829–1844 | 1853–1886 | 1829–1844 | 1856–1886 | 1829–1844 | 1853–1886 |
| Month entered | | | | | | |
| January | .20 | .30 | .58 | | .26 | .11 |
| February | .30 | .29 | .51 | | .12 | .12 |
| March | .41 | .36 | .39 | | .14 | .27 |
| April | .42 | .66 | .53 | | .00 | .00 |
| May | .76 | .42 | .03 | | .21 | .01 |
| June | .34 | .48 | .50 | | .05 | .16 |
| July | .39 | .47 | .36 | | .12 | .00 |
| August | .44 | .55 | .30 | | .18 | .00 |
| September | .41 | .42 | .17 | | .35 | .02 |
| October | .41 | .33 | .30 | | .26 | .17 |
| November | .23 | .28 | .16 | | .41 | .34 |
| December | .38 | .24 | .32 | | .32 | .40 |
| Entered with relative | | | | | | |
| No | .36 | .40 | | | .17 | .14 |
| Yes | .40 | .49 | | | .17 | .11 |
| Grand mean | .38 | .41 | | .28 | .17 | .14 |
| $R^2$ | .13 | .21 | | .14 | .17 | .23 |

[a]Probability = adjusted deviation and grand mean.

TABLE A.20
A Comparison of the Sample with the Entire Group[a]

|  | Sample | Entire group |
|---|---|---|
| Birthplace |  |  |
| New York | 31.3 | 39.2 |
| Other U.S. | 2.7 | 6.3 |
| Ireland | 37.6 | 34.3 |
| Germany | 11.7 | 8.9 |
| Other Foreign | 10.3 | 17.8 |
| Unknown | 1.6 | 1.7 |
| Sex |  |  |
| Male | 35.3 | 50.6 |
| Female | 64.7 | 46.4 |
| Age |  |  |
| 0–4 | 5.9 | 6.2 |
| 5–19 | 6.6 | 13.8 |
| 20–29 | 13.1 | 11.9 |
| 30–39 | 20.1 | 16.4 |
| 40–49 | 18.0 | 14.5 |
| 50–59 | 13.4 | 13.0 |
| 60+ | 21.7 | 25.0 |
| Unknown | 1.6 | 0.0 |
| Number | 3,689 | 12,614 |

[a]Source: Manuscript of examinations; Charles S. Hoyt, "The Causes of Pauperism," Tenth (1877) Annual Report of the State Board of Charities (New York, 1878), 99–102.

**TABLE A.21**
Demographic Characteristics of Sample by Institution Type

| Code | Institution | Number of inmates | With any kin | With child | Percentage all female | Percentage 60+ female | Percentage 0–9 | 60+ | Percentage US born | Percentage father US born |
|---|---|---|---|---|---|---|---|---|---|---|
| | | | | | **I. Large poorhouses (150+ inmates)** | | | | | |
| 1 | Monroe County | 204 | 8.3 | 3.9 | 41.9 | 34.8 | 2.5 | 45.1 | 33.8 | 10.8 |
| 2 | Albany County | 260 | 11.2 | 4.2 | 46.8 | 43.1 | 14.2 | 22.3 | 38.5 | 9.2 |
| 3 | Oneida County | 185 | 8.1 | 5.4 | 40.5 | 22.5 | 9.2 | 38.4 | 51.9 | 25.4 |
| 4 | Erie County | 275 | 3.6 | 2.6 | 43.0 | 28.4 | 3.6 | 38.2 | 24.7 | 11.6 |
| | Total | 924 | | | | | | | | |
| | | | | | **II. Small/medium poorhouses** | | | | | |
| 4 | Kingston | 25 | 28.0 | 16.0 | 36.0 | 50.0 | 28.0 | 16.0 | 36.0 | 8.0 |
| 5 | Newburgh | 42 | 4.8 | 0.0 | 38.1 | 27.8 | 4.8 | 42.9 | 45.2 | 11.9 |
| 6 | Lewis | 53 | 11.3 | 1.9 | 45.3 | 47.4 | 5.7 | 35.9 | 58.5 | 34.0 |
| 7 | Patnow | 39 | 33.3 | 18.0 | 43.6 | 27.3 | 30.8 | 28.2 | 84.6 | 48.7 |
| 8 | Oswego | 44 | 15.9 | 2.3 | 45.5 | 35.0 | 11.4 | 45.5 | 29.6 | 6.8 |
| 9 | Poughkeepsie | 70 | 8.6 | 7.1 | 44.3 | 37.5 | 7.2 | 45.7 | 67.2 | 41.4 |
| 10 | Clinton | 51 | 11.8 | 9.8 | 31.3 | 26.3 | 2.0 | 37.3 | 45.1 | 19.6 |

| | | | | | | | | | | |
|---|---|---|---|---|---|---|---|---|---|---|
| 11 | Cayuga | 85 | 2.4 | 1.2 | 43.5 | 40.9 | 3.5 | 51.8 | 60.0 | 43.5 |
| 13 | Allegany | 62 | 12.9 | 8.1 | 51.6 | 25.9 | 4.8 | 43.6 | 80.6 | 51.6 |
| 15 | Schoharie | 49 | 20.4 | 8.2 | 51.0 | 45.5 | 12.2 | 44.9 | 85.7 | 73.5 |
| 17 | Tioga | 46 | 21.7 | 13.0 | 32.6 | 18.8 | 10.9 | 34.8 | 87.0 | 56.5 |
| 18 | Green | 104 | 18.3 | 15.4 | 47.1 | 26.8 | 18.3 | 39.4 | 81.7 | 52.9 |
| 19 | Essex | 86 | 23.3 | 16.3 | 61.6 | 55.6 | 16.3 | 20.9 | 69.8 | 54.7 |
| 20 | Wayne | 72 | 5.6 | 2.3 | 46.5 | 35.5 | 4.2 | 43.1 | 75.0 | 48.6 |
| 21 | St. Lawrence | 104 | 11.5 | 8.7 | 58.7 | 41.0 | 7.7 | 37.5 | 46.2 | 21.2 |
| | Total | 932 | | | | | | | | |

### III. Insane depts

| | | | | | | | | | | |
|---|---|---|---|---|---|---|---|---|---|---|
| 12 | Monroe | 124 | 0.8 | 0.8 | 62.9 | 72.2 | 0.0 | 14.5 | 29.0 | 25.8 |
| 14 | Oneida | 128 | 0.0 | 0.0 | 65.6 | 70.0 | 0.8 | 15.6 | 49.2 | 18.7 |
| 16 | New York City | 1165 | 0.0 | 0.0 | 97.7 | 89.7 | 0.0 | 5.8 | 14.7 | 2.8 |
| 22 | Erie County | 187 | 3.6 | 0.0 | 54.0 | 55.6 | 0.0 | 4.8 | 33.2 | 7.5 |
| | Total | 1604 | | | | | | | | |

### IV. Other

| | | | | | | | | | | |
|---|---|---|---|---|---|---|---|---|---|---|
| 23 | Randall's Island Infants Hospital | 229 | 38.9 | 34.5 | 65.5 | — | 59.0 | 0.0 | 70.3 | 9.2 |
| | Number | 3689 | | | | | | | | |

TABLE A.22

**Selected Family Characteristics among Inmates Aged 18 and Over in Large Poorhouses ($N = 1599$)**[a]

| Institution | Father[b] temperate | Moral or religious training in childhood | Father a pauper | Mother a pauper | |
|---|---|---|---|---|---|
| | | | | Male | Female |
| Monroe County | 49.6 | 74.2 | 1.1 | 1.3 | 0.0 |
| Albany County | 73.1 | 31.6 | 2.8 | 0.0 | 1.9 |
| Oneida County | 77.6 | 95.1 | 3.8 | 7.7 | 1.2 |
| Erie County | 79.8 | [c] | 1.2 | 3.3 | 1.5 |

[a]Source: Manuscripts of examinations.
[b]Father not a "constant drinker."
[c]Insufficient cases with answers to questions.

TABLE A.23

**Selected Occupational Characteristics of Inmates in Sample**[a]

**I. Selected occupations by poorhouse size and sex**

| | Men | | | |
|---|---|---|---|---|
| | Laborers | Agriculture | White collar | Unknown |
| Large poorhouses | 41.4 | 9.7 | 1.8 | 14.8 |
| Small/medium poorhouses | 27.2 | 18.6 | 2.3 | 25.4 |

| | Women | | |
|---|---|---|---|
| | Domestic | Textile/ apparel | Unknown |
| Large poorhouses | 35.4 | 21.6 | 40.5 |
| Small/medium poorhouses | 13.0 | 5.4 | 71.8 |

**II. Relation of occupation of inmate to occupation of father: all institutions**

| | Inmate occupation | | |
|---|---|---|---|
| Father's occupation | Laborer | Agriculture | Domestic |
| Laborer | 42.2 | 9.2 | 13.7 |
| Agriculture | 22.3 | 59.2 | 7.8 |
| Unknown | 22.5 | 19.7 | 68.9 |
| Other | 13.0 | 11.9 | 9.6 |

[a]Source: Manuscript of examinations.

TABLE A.24

A Comparison of Years Dependent, Total Time in Poorhouses, and Time in Poorhouses Where Examined by Sex[a]

| | Time in poorhouse (%) | | | | | | | | | | | |
|---|---|---|---|---|---|---|---|---|---|---|---|---|
| | Less than 1 year | | 1–2 years | | 3–5 years | | 6–9 years | | 10 or more years | | Unknown | |
| | M | F | M | F | M | F | M | F | M | F | M | F |
| Large poorhouses | | | | | | | | | | | | |
| Total time in poorhouse | 40.7 | 31.5 | 12.6 | 7.8 | 20.7 | 18.9 | 13.2 | 18.6 | 11.9 | 21.6 | Nil | Nil |
| Time in poorhouse where examined | 41.6 | 32.4 | 12.1 | 7.8 | 20.7 | 18.0 | 13.2 | 18.6 | 11.5 | 22.2 | Nil | Nil |
| Small/medium poorhouses | | | | | | | | | | | | |
| Years dependent | 21.3 | 14.9 | 9.5 | 5.7 | 23.2 | 21.7 | 17.1 | 16.0 | 28.9 | 41.7 | Nil | Nil |
| Total time in poorhouses | 24.4 | 16.3 | 9.3 | 6.8 | 22.2 | 19.2 | 19.4 | 23.7 | 18.9 | 27.6 | 6.8 | 6.5 |
| Time in poorhouse where examined | 27.2 | 20.1 | 9.1 | 6.8 | 23.9 | 20.9 | 19.9 | 23.1 | 19.4 | 19.4 | 0.5 | 1.1 |
| Insane asylums | | | | | | | | | | | | |
| Years dependent | 20.4 | 26.7 | 8.2 | 11.4 | 17.0 | 23.7 | 21.1 | 18.4 | 33.3 | 20.0 | 28.8 | 5.7 |
| Total time in poorhouses | 17.4 | NA | 12.3 | NA | 21.9 | NA | 21.9 | NA | 20.0 | NA | 19.7 | 2.7 |
| Time in poorhouse where examined | 21.2 | 25.9 | 9.8 | 12.2 | 19.7 | 24.3 | 19.7 | 20.1 | 26.4 | 26.4 | 3.6 | 1.2 |

[a]Source: Manuscript of examinations.

263

**TABLE A.25**

**Age of Entrance to Poorhouses and Insane Asylums by Sex**[a]

| | Age entered | | | | | | | | |
|---|---|---|---|---|---|---|---|---|---|
| | 0–4 | 5–9 | 10–19 | 20–29 | 30–39 | 40–49 | 50–59 | 60+ | Unknown | N |
| Males | | | | | | | | | | |
| Large poorhouses | 0.7 | 0.0 | 3.1 | 11.5 | 10.8 | 17.6 | 17.0 | 38.1 | 1.3 | 454 |
| Small/medium poorhouses | 1.8 | 0.3 | 5.8 | 11.6 | 9.3 | 14.4 | 13.6 | 39.0 | 4.3 | 397 |
| Insane asylums | 0.0 | 0.0 | 4.7 | 22.3 | 29.0 | 20.7 | 5.7 | 2.6 | 15.0 | 193 |
| Females | | | | | | | | | | |
| Large poorhouses | 0.3 | 0.3 | 7.5 | 21.3 | 24.0 | 13.5 | 15.0 | 16.8 | 1.2 | 333 |
| Small/medium poorhouses | 2.8 | 2.5 | 10.7 | 18.3 | 17.2 | 15.2 | 11.0 | 17.2 | 5.1 | 355 |
| Erie County Insane Asylum | 0.0 | 1.0 | 4.0 | 37.0 | 20.0 | 25.0 | 12.0 | 1.0 | 0.0 | 100 |

[a]Source: Manuscripts of examinations.

**TABLE A.26**
**Proportion of Inmates 18+ with 0–1 Living Children by Institution Type and Sex**[a]

| Marital status | Sex | 0–1 living child | N |
|---|---|---|---|
| Single | | | |
| Large poorhouses | M | 98.5 | 200 |
| | F | 100.0 | 141 |
| Small/medium poorhouses | M | 98.5 | 195 |
| | F | 93.9 | 163 |
| Insane asylums | M | 99.2 | 119 |
| Married | | | |
| Large poorhouses | M | 52.0 | 75 |
| | F | 57.9 | 69 |
| Small/medium poorhouses | M | 48.9 | 92 |
| | F | 60.8 | 79 |
| Insane asylums | M | 53.3 | 62 |
| Widowed or divorced | | | |
| Large poorhouses | M | 63.8 | 188 |
| | F | 64.7 | 122 |
| Small/medium poorhouses | M | 59.6 | 109 |
| | F | 59.8 | 107 |
| Insane asylums | M | 66.7 | 9 |
| All | | | |
| Large poorhouses | M | 76.6 | 453 |
| | F | 78.4 | 333 |
| Small poorhouses | M | 76.3 | 397 |
| | F | 86.3 | 354 |
| Insane asylums | M | 82.9 | 193 |

[a]Source: Manuscript of examinations.

**TABLE A.27**
**Age by Sex by Poorhouse Type (Percentage)**

| Age | Large poorhouses | | Small and medium-size poorhouses | |
|---|---|---|---|---|
| | Male | Female | Male | Female |
| 0–4 | 3.6 | 5.3 | 12.8 | 16.6 |
| 5–9 | .1 | .3 | 1.0 | .9 |
| 10–19 | 4.5 | 10.5 | 9.2 | 11.3 |
| 20–29 | 17.8 | 23.9 | 10.1 | 16.1 |
| 30–39 | 17.6 | 14.0 | 19.3 | 10.3 |
| 40–49 | 15.4 | 10.6 | 8.7 | 10.3 |
| 50–59 | 16.9 | 9.9 | 10.5 | 7.6 |
| 60+ | 23.8 | 24.5 | 34.8 | 23.6 |
| Unknown | .3 | 1.0 | 2.6 | 3.1 |
| N | 1732 | 791 | 721 | 542 |

**TABLE A.28**
**Inmate and Father Birthplaces by Institution Type (Percentage)**

| Birthplace | Large poorhouses | | | | Small and medium-size poorhouses | | | |
|---|---|---|---|---|---|---|---|---|
| | Male | | Female | | Male | | Female | |
| | Inmate | Father | Inmate | Father | Inmate | Father | Inmate | Father |
| New York | 31.7 | 8.1 | 36.4 | 9.4 | 54.2 | 15.9 | 60.9 | 18.8 |
| Other U.S. | 7.7 | 8.4 | 4.4 | 7.0 | 7.7 | 7.3 | 7.8 | 4.1 |
| Ireland | 24.4 | 32.4 | 30.0 | 35.7 | 16.6 | 18.7 | 15.6 | 19.3 |
| Germany | 16.8 | 17.5 | 11.8 | 14.8 | 7.0 | 6.3 | 4.6 | 4.3 |
| Other foreign | 19.2 | 20.3 | 16.2 | 17.2 | 11.3 | 13.1 | 6.9 | 10.8 |
| Unknown | .5 | 13.3 | 1.3 | 15.9 | 3.5 | 38.7 | 4.9 | 43.6 |
| N | 1717 | | 780 | | 716 | | 540 | |

**TABLE A.29**
**Time in United States by Sex**
**(Foreign Born Only, Percentage)**

| Years | Male | Female |
|-------|------|--------|
| 0–1 | 7.9 | 6.4 |
| 2–5 | 10.7 | 11.7 |
| 6–9 | 7.4 | 7.9 |
| 10–19 | 16.9 | 18.8 |
| 20+ | 56.3 | 54.0 |
| Unknown | .8 | 1.2 |
| All | 69.8 | 30.2 |
| N | 1341 | 580 |

**TABLE A.30**
**Marital Status by Age by Sex (Percentage)**

| Marital status | Age | | | | |
|----------------|-------|-------|-------|-------|------|
| | 20–29 | 30–39 | 40–49 | 50–59 | 60+ |
| **Males** | | | | | |
| Single | 91.3 | 68.8 | 46.4 | 35.2 | 21.5 |
| Married | 7.7 | 22.1 | 33.1 | 28.6 | 26.5 |
| Widowed or divorced | 1.0 | 9.0 | 20.5 | 36.2 | 52.1 |
| N | 414 | 420 | 347 | 420 | 699 |
| **Females** | | | | | |
| Single | 57.9 | 28.9 | 25.3 | 17.7 | 12.7 |
| Married | 36.8 | 45.3 | 40.4 | 30.8 | 17.5 |
| Widowed or divorced | 5.3 | 25.8 | 34.2 | 51.5 | 69.8 |
| N | 302 | 190 | 146 | 130 | 338 |

TABLE A.31
"If a Parent, How Many Children Living?" (Percentage)

| Age | 0 or blank | 1 | 2–3 | 4+ | N |
|---|---|---|---|---|---|
| | | **Male** | | | |
| 30–39 | 46.6 | 20.6 | 22.1 | 10.7 | 131 |
| 40–49 | 44.6 | 14.0 | 23.7 | 17.7 | 186 |
| 50–59 | 39.7 | 15.8 | 25.7 | 18.8 | 272 |
| 60+ | 43.5 | 13.3 | 23.9 | 19.3 | 549 |
| | | **Female** | | | |
| 30–39 | 40.7 | 16.3 | 28.9 | 14.1 | 135 |
| 40–49 | 45.0 | 16.5 | 19.3 | 19.3 | 109 |
| 50–59 | 54.2 | 14.0 | 20.6 | 11.2 | 107 |
| 60+ | 52.9 | 19.3 | 19.7 | 8.1 | 295 |

TABLE A.32
Outdoor Relief and Previously Poorhouse Inmate by Birthplace and Sex (Percentage)

| | Received outdoor relief | | Previously in a poorhouse | |
|---|---|---|---|---|
| Birthplace | Male | Female | Male | Female |
| New York | 14.6 | 29.2 | 7.9 | 11.0 |
| Other U.S. | 12.2 | 19.4 | 8.0 | 6.2 |
| Ireland | 11.3 | 26.4 | 18.9 | 21.1 |
| Germany | 6.9 | 3.9 | 10.9 | 8.3 |
| Foreign | 8.8 | 15.6 | 10.6 | 7.1 |

TABLE A.33
Previous Inmates Who Had Received Outdoor Relief (Percentage)

| | Previously inmate | | |
|---|---|---|---|
| Outdoor relief | Yes | No | Unknown |
| | | **Male** | |
| Yes | 30.2 | 7.0 | 55.3 |
| No | 69.8 | 93.0 | 44.7 |
| | | **Female** | |
| Yes | 44.5 | 16.5 | 71.6 |
| No | 55.5 | 83.5 | 28.4 |

**TABLE A.34**
**Occupations of Inmates and Fathers by Sex (Percentage)**

|                     | Males | | Females | |
|---------------------|--------|--------|--------|--------|
| Occupation          | Inmate | Father | Inmate | Father |
| Building trades     | 6.8    | 6.8    | 0      | 5.9    |
| Cabinets etc.       | 1.0    | .4     | .2     | .3     |
| Agriculture         | 6.9    | 20.1   | .4     | 20.4   |
| White collar        | 1.0    | 1.8    | .4     | 1.4    |
| Metal trades        | 4.2    | 3.2    | 0      | 2.4    |
| Food trades         | 1.7    | 2.2    | .1     | 1.5    |
| Maritime            | 2.3    | .7     | 0      | .6     |
| Domestic            | 5.1    | 2.7    | 61.1   | 1.7    |
| Textile and apparel | 2.0    | 2.2    | 2.1    | 1.5    |
| Labor               | 46.1   | 38.5   | 1.2    | 40.9   |
| Printing and books  | .4     | .1     | .1     | .2     |
| Transportation      | 2.3    | 1.1    | .1     | .7     |
| Other               | 4.6    | 2.8    | 2.9    | 3.7    |
| Unknown             | 15.7   | 17.4   | .1315  | 18.9   |
| N                   | 2645   | 2196   | 1441   | 1130   |

**TABLE A.35**
**Selected Occupations of Fathers by Inmate Occupations (Percentage)**

| Inmates' occupations | Fathers' occupations | | | |
|----------------------|-------------|-------|----------|----------------|
|                      | Agriculture | Labor | Domestic | White collar   |
| Agriculture          | 14.9        | 1.5   | 3.0      | 3.2            |
| Labor                | 28.2        | 42.4  | 31.5     | 17.4           |
| Domestic             | 27.7        | 27.6  | 3.7      | 20.6           |
| White collar         | 1.0         | .1    | 1.1      | 11.1           |

**TABLE A.36**
**Condition of Relatives**[a]

| Relative | Pauper | Self-supporting | Unknown |
|---|---|---|---|
| Paternal grandparents | 20 | 2187 | 1933 |
| Maternal grandparents | 16 | 2149 | 1975 |
| Brothers | 83 | 1961 | 2096 |
| Sisters | 71 | 1863 | 2206 |
| Father | 66 | 2671 | 1403 |
| Mother | 173 | 2609 | 1358 |
| Total | 429 | 13,440 | |

[a]The percentage of paupers among subjects' kin whose condition was known is 3.1.

**TABLE A.37**
**Habits of Inmates and Fathers (Percentage)**

| | Fathers' habits | | | |
|---|---|---|---|---|
| Inmates' habits | Temperate | Intemperate | Total | $N$ |
| Sons' habits | | | | |
| Temperate | 90.8 | 9.1 | 55.4 | 970 |
| Intemperate | 56.9 | 43.1 | 44.6 | 780 |
| All | 75.7 | 24.3 | 100.0 | 1750 |
| Daughters' habits | | | | |
| Temperate | 82.5 | 17.4 | 78.6 | 613 |
| Intemperate | 56.9 | 43.1 | 21.4 | 167 |
| All | 77.1 | 22.9 | 100.0 | 780 |

**TABLE A.38**
**Habits by Outdoor Relief by Sex (Percentage)**

| Outdoor relief | Temperate | Intemperate | $N$ |
|---|---|---|---|
| **Males** | | | |
| Yes | 52.4 | 47.6 | 227 |
| No | 53.1 | 46.9 | 1854 |
| **Females** | | | |
| Yes | 65.6 | 34.4 | 224 |
| No | 78.8 | 21.3 | 786 |

TABLE A.39
Age and Sex of "Dependent, Defective, and Delinquent" Classes in Selected New York Counties, 1880 (Percentage)

| Age | Prisoners | | Paupers | | Blind | | Idiots | | Homeless children | | Insane | | Deaf-mutes | |
|---|---|---|---|---|---|---|---|---|---|---|---|---|---|---|
| | Male | Female | Male | Female | Male | Female | Male | Female | Male | Female | Male | Female | Male | Female |
| 0–4 | .0 | .0 | 7.4 | 5.0 | 2.1 | 2.1 | 2.2 | 2.0 | 13.7 | 10.7 | .1 | .0 | 2.3 | 1.3 |
| 5–9 | .0 | .0 | 9.2 | 7.5 | 2.3 | 2.7 | 7.6 | 4.0 | 46.8 | 35.8 | .1 | .1 | 17.6 | 10.2 |
| 10–14 | .0 | .0 | 7.0 | 5.6 | 2.6 | 2.1 | 8.1 | 12.0 | 36.8 | 43.1 | .3 | .5 | 17.1 | 22.8 |
| 15–19 | 5.3 | 13.3 | 3.1 | 3.0 | 3.8 | 3.0 | 9.5 | 14.0 | 2.2 | 8.7 | 2.1 | 2.3 | 15.5 | 16.1 |
| 20–24 | 24.4 | 22.5 | 4.0 | 5.2 | 2.4 | 3.9 | 13.7 | 12.0 | .5 | 1.8 | 8.2 | 6.3 | 8.8 | 11.0 |
| 25–29 | 25.2 | 18.4 | 3.1 | 4.0 | .9 | 3.9 | 13.7 | 9.4 | .0 | .0 | 11.9 | 7.1 | 3.9 | 4.6 |
| 30–34 | 15.8 | 13.3 | 4.0 | 5.2 | 4.5 | 3.6 | 7.6 | 9.4 | .0 | .0 | 10.4 | 9.3 | 4.4 | 4.8 |
| 35–39 | 10.2 | 9.2 | 3.5 | 5.5 | 7.1 | 1.2 | 10.5 | 8.0 | .0 | .0 | 10.3 | 13.2 | 5.4 | 3.8 |
| 40–44 | 6.1 | 12.2 | 4.6 | 3.7 | 4.2 | 5.4 | 7.3 | 7.4 | .0 | .0 | 11.7 | 10.5 | 5.7 | 4.6 |
| 45–49 | 4.8 | 4.1 | 4.1 | 3.9 | 6.8 | 5.4 | 4.2 | 6.3 | .0 | .0 | 9.1 | 10.6 | 2.6 | 1.9 |
| 50–54 | 3.3 | 5.1 | 4.9 | 5.0 | 8.9 | 4.2 | 3.9 | 4.0 | .0 | .0 | 9.8 | 10.7 | 4.7 | 2.1 |
| 55+ | 5.1 | 2.0 | 46.4 | 47.8 | 54.4 | 62.6 | 12.0 | 11.7 | .0 | .0 | 26.3 | 29.4 | 14.3 | 18.2 |
| N | 1601 | 98 | 877 | 843 | 425 | 334 | 410 | 351 | 408 | 450 | 926 | 1045 | 386 | 373 |

**TABLE A.40**
**Birthplaces of Subjects and Fathers of "Dependent, Defective, and Delinquent" Classes in Selected New York Counties, 1880 (Percentage)**

| Inmate's status | Pauper | Deaf-mute | Prisoner | Blind | Idiot | Insane | Homeless children |
|---|---|---|---|---|---|---|---|
| Native with native parent | 43.3 | 46.2 | 47.5 | 53.7 | 59.6 | 36.6 | 20.3 |
| Native with foreign-born parent | 9.2 | 25.4 | 25.8 | 11.7 | 20.8 | 10.2 | 37.7 |
| Foreign born with foreign-born parent | 47.4 | 28.5 | 26.8 | 34.7 | 20.0 | 53.2 | 42.0 |
| Total N | 1720 | 773 | 1726 | 764 | 759 | 1968 | 876 |

**TABLE A.41**
**Marital Status by Age (Percentage)**

| Sex and status | Insane | Idiot | Deaf-mute | Blind | Prisoner | Pauper |
|---|---|---|---|---|---|---|
| **Age 15–29** | | | | | | |
| Male | | | | | | |
| Single | 85.80 | 98.6 | 94.10 | 100.00 | 76.00 | 87.90 |
| Married | 13.20 | 1.4 | 5.90 | .00 | 23.70 | 7.60 |
| Widowed | 1.00 | 0 | .00 | .00 | .80 | 4.50 |
| Total N | 197 | 141 | 68 | 32 | 840 | 66 |
| Female | | | | | | |
| Single | 74.80 | 97.5 | 88.60 | 93.50 | 55.60 | 70.70 |
| Married | 22.40 | 1.7 | 11.40 | 3.20 | 37.80 | 22.00 |
| Widowed | 2.70 | .8 | .00 | 3.20 | 6.70 | 7.30 |
| Total N | 147 | 120 | 88 | 31 | 45 | 82 |
| **Age 30–49** | | | | | | |
| Male | | | | | | |
| Single | 59.20 | 92.2 | 63.10 | 38.30 | 45.50 | 48.70 |
| Married | 36.40 | 7.8 | 32.30 | 58.50 | 49.0 | 45.40 |
| Widowed | 4.40 | 0 | 4.60 | 3.20 | 5.40 | 5.90 |
| Total N | 360 | 115 | 65 | 95 | 569 | 119 |
| Female | | | | | | |
| Single | 51.70 | 86 | 55.40 | 45.80 | 11.40 | 44.90 |
| Married | 38.50 | 11 | 35.70 | 50.00 | 65.70 | 33.10 |
| Widowed | 9.80 | 3 | 8.90 | 4.20 | 22.90 | 2.10 |
| Total N | 408 | 100 | 56 | 48 | 35 | 136 |

*(continued)*

**TABLE A.41** *(continued)*

| Sex and status | Insane | Idiot | Deaf-mute | Blind | Prisoner | Pauper |
|---|---|---|---|---|---|---|
| | | | **Age 50+** | | | |
| Male | | | | | | |
| Single | 37.20 | 81.50 | 35.80 | 17.90 | 26.60 | 28.20 |
| Married | 46.30 | 14.80 | 46.30 | 57.10 | 57.80 | 24.70 |
| Widowed | 16.50 | 3.70 | 17.90 | 25.00 | 15.60 | 47.20 |
| Total N | 309 | 54 | 67 | 252 | 128 | 369 |
| Female | | | | | | |
| Single | 34.50 | 64.20 | 32.40 | 17.90 | .00 | 25.30 |
| Married | 36.90 | 5.70 | 28.40 | 34.00 | 28.60 | 2.20 |
| Widowed | 28.60 | 30.20 | 39.20 | 48.10 | 71.40 | 62.50 |
| Total N | 388 | 53 | 74 | 212 | 7 | 395 |

**TABLE A.42**
**Selected Occupations of Adult Male Paupers, Prisoners, and Insane, 1880 (Percentage)**

| Occupation | Pauper | Prisoner | Insane |
|---|---|---|---|
| Skilled trade | 8.90 | 25.40 | 14.00 |
| Maritime | .00 | 1.70 | .50 |
| Labor | 59.80 | 24.70 | 19.60 |
| Agriculture | 19.00 | 14.60 | 26.70 |
| White collar | 1.40 | 4.20 | 15.00 |
| Other | 10.90 | 29.50 | 24.10 |
| N | 358 | 1436 | 569 |

**TABLE A.43**
**Occupations of Inmates and Household Heads Compared, 1880 (Percentage)**

| Status | Skilled trades | Labor | Agriculture |
|--------|---------------|-------|-------------|
| Paupers | | | |
|    Household heads | 19.5 | 24.2 | 33.8 |
|    Inmates | 7.4 | 4.2 | 1.0 |
| Blind | | | |
|    Household heads | 18.9 | 1.7 | 32.1 |
|    Inmates | 6.4 | 13.8 | 35.8 |
| Deaf-mute | | | |
|    Household heads | 12.5 | 8.9 | 37.5 |
|    Inmates | 10.3 | 30.8 | 25.6 |
| Insane | | | |
|    Household head | 19.6 | 15.2 | 41.3 |
|    Inmate | 13.6 | 16.3 | 20.3 |

**TABLE A.44**
**Marital Status of Household Heads and Inmates, 1880 (Percentage)**

| Status | Single | Married | Widowed |
|--------|--------|---------|---------|
| Paupers | | | |
|    Household heads | 7.9 | 77.2 | 15.0 |
|    Inmates | 50.2 | 9.2 | 40.6 |
| Deaf-mutes | | | |
|    Household heads | 12.1 | 65.2 | 22.7 |
|    Inmates | 82.6 | 9.1 | 8.3 |
| Blind | | | |
|    Household heads | 5.4 | 78.3 | 16.3 |
|    Inmates | 30.5 | 41.8 | 27.7 |
| Insane | | | |
|    Household heads | 5.3 | 81.3 | 13.3 |
|    Inmates | 57.1 | 31.4 | 11.5 |

**TABLE A.45**
**Residential Status of Paupers, Deaf-mutes, Blind, Insane, and Idiots, 1880 (Percentage)**

| Status | Paupers | Deaf-mute | Blind | Insane | Idiots |
|---|---|---|---|---|---|
| Household head | 7.3 | 8.6 | 21.9 | 3.9 | 1.4 |
| Spouse | 3.7 | 6.3 | 11.1 | 6.4 | 1.2 |
| Child | 13.4 | 38.0 | 21.2 | 8.2 | 61.6 |
| Inmate | 69.4 | 36.9 | 21.9 | 75.5 | 22.5 |
| Other | 6.2 | 10.2 | 23.9 | 6.0 | 13.3 |
| N | 1747 | 776 | 764 | 1968 | 768 |

**TABLE A.46**
**Tramps: Birthplaces, Age, Sex, Race, and Marital Status**

| Birthplace | Percentage |
|---|---|
| New England | 5.0 |
| New York | 28.4 |
| Other U.S. | 11.4 |
| Canada | 2.6 |
| Ireland | 26.3 |
| Great Britain | 10.1 |
| Germany | 5.5 |
| Poland | .2 |
| Other foreign | 2.6 |
| Unknown | 8.0 |
| N | 4310 |

| Age | Total percentage | Percentage male | Percentage female | Percentage single | Percentage widowed or divorced |
|---|---|---|---|---|---|
| Under 2 | .3 | .2 | 2.1 | | |
| 5–9 | .5 | .5 | 2.5 | | |
| 10–14 | 1.0 | .8 | 3.2 | | |
| 15–19 | 7.6 | 7.9 | 4.6 | 97.3 | .3 |
| 20–29 | 37.5 | 38.6 | 24.1 | 90.1 | 1.6 |
| 30–39 | 24.3 | 24.3 | 23.8 | 91.8 | 8.2 |
| 40–49 | 14.3 | 14.0 | 20.9 | 55.4 | 22.9 |
| Over 50 | 11.4 | 11.3 | 15.3 | 44.6 | 31.3 |
| Unknown | 3.0 | 2.4 | 3.6 | | |

*(continued)*

**TABLE A.46** *(continued)*

| Marital status | Total percentage | Percentage male | Percentage female |
|---|---|---|---|
| Single | 75.6 | 79.2 | 19.9 |
| Married | 14.7 | 12.3 | 51.9 |
| Divorced | 1.8 | .6 | 21.1 |
| Widowed | 7.9 | 8.0 | 7.1 |

| Sex and race | Percentage |
|---|---|
| White male | 91.4 |
| White female | 6.3 |
| Black male | 2.2 |
| Black female | .2 |

| | **Index of age by selected birthplaces** | | | |
|---|---|---|---|---|
| Birthplace | 0–9 | 10–19 | 20–40 | 40+ |
| New England | 50 | 101 | 113 | 80 |
| New York | 223 | 183 | 108 | 57 |
| Ireland | 17 | 163 | 91 | 147 |
| Great Britain | 0 | 57 | 108 | 109 |

**TABLE A.47**
**Tramps: Social Characteristics**

| Habits | Percentage |
|---|---|
| Temperate | 58.9. |
| Intemperate | 41.2 |

| Education | Percentage |
|---|---|
| None | 17.1 |
| Rudimentary | 30.8 |
| Some school | 29.2 |
| Write but cannot read | .2 |
| Read but cannot write | 4.5 |
| Read and write | 18.3 |

| Health | Percentage |
|---|---|
| Healthy | 79.9 |
| Sickly | 20.1 |

*(continued)*

**TABLE A.47** *(continued)*

| Times aided in sample | Percentage | |
|---|---|---|
| 1 | 90.9 | |
| 2 | 6.4 | |
| 3 or more | 2.7 | |

| Habits and education | Male | Female |
|---|---|---|
| Temperate | 57.2 | 79.1 |
| No education | 16.1 | 34.3 |
| Healthy | 80.5 | 70.4 |

**Temperance and education by selected birthplace**

| Birthplace | Temperate (%) | No education (%) |
|---|---|---|
| New England | 63.0 | 9.1 |
| New York | 62.9 | 15.4 |
| Ireland | 47.2 | 26.5 |
| Great Britain | 64.8 | 9.7 |
| Germany | 67.2 | 5.7 |

**TABLE A.48**
**Tramps: Years in United States and Naturalization: Selected Immigrant Groups: Known Cases Only (Percentage)**

| Birthplace | 5 or more years | 10 or more years | Naturalized |
|---|---|---|---|
| Ireland | 81.4 | 60.4 | 40.2 |
| Great Britain | 64.1 | 43.2 | 60.3 |
| Germany | 69.3 | 32.1 | 68.1 |

**TABLE A.49**
**Tramps: Occupations**

| Occupation | Percentage |
|---|---|
| Building | 4.8 |
| Metal | 8.5 |
| Food | 1.2 |
| Maritime | 4.7 |
| Domestic | 3.0 |
| Textile and apparel | 3.7 |
| Laborer | 45.1 |
| Printing | 1.1 |
| Transportation | 1.3 |
| Cabinetry and furniture | .8 |
| Agriculture | 2.9 |
| White collar | .9 |
| Other | 7.1 |
| Unknown | 15.0 |

**Proportion of females in selected occupations**

| | |
|---|---|
| Domestic | 41.8 |
| Laborer | 11.0 |
| Textile and apparel | 2.8 |
| Unknown | 39.4 |

**Major occupations by selected birthplace (percentage)**

| Birthplace | Building | Metal | Laborer | Agriculture |
|---|---|---|---|---|
| New England | 8.2 | 9.1 | 36.1 | 2.7 |
| New York | 6.4 | 9.9 | 41.7 | 4.1 |
| Ireland | 2.0 | 5.0 | 63.7 | 1.2 |
| Great Britain | 6.7 | 15.1 | 36.2 | 2.5 |
| German | 3.3 | 4.1 | 42.3 | 2.5 |

**TABLE A.50**
**Tramps: Time Tramping (Percentage)**

| Time tramping | All | Known only |
|---|---|---|
| 1–7 days | 39.4 | 49.9 |
| 8–30 days | 28.8 | 36.1 |
| 1–6 months | 8.8 | 11.0 |
| 7–12 months | .8 | 1.2 |
| 1–2 years | .7 | .9 |
| 3–5 years | .3 | .4 |
| 6–10 years | .1 | .4 |
| 11–20 years | .1 | .1 |
| Over 20 years | 2.7 | .1 |
| Unknown | 20.1 | |

**TABLE A.51**
**Tramps: Places Began Tramping, Last Aided, and Destination (New York Origin Only)**

| Location | Began tramping | Last aided | Destination | Last aided (percentage) Place began | Elsewhere in same region |
|---|---|---|---|---|---|
| Western New York city | 495 | 357 | 294 | 22.0 | 7.9 |
| Western New York noncity | 82 | 172 | 84 | 20.7 | 12.2 |
| Finger Lakes city | 176 | 68 | 189 | 5.7 | 25.6 |
| Finger Lakes noncity | 79 | 372 | 66 | 27.9 | 2.5 |
| Southern Tier city | 50 | 21 | 153 | 4.0 | 10.0 |
| Southern Tier non city | 38 | 70 | 28 | 10.5 | .0 |
| Mohawk Valley city | 148 | 120 | 90 | 12.2 | 6.8 |
| Mohawk Valley noncity | 162 | 116 | 46 | 9.3 | 3.7 |
| Catskills city | 13 | 48 | 17 | 7.7 | 46.2 |
| Catskills noncity | 131 | 430 | 91 | 52.7 | 3.8 |
| Hudson Valley city | 485 | 202 | 467 | 7.4 | 8.9 |
| Hudson Valley noncity | 145 | 287 | 105 | 22.8 | 3.5 |
| Downstate city | 650 | 188 | 667 | 20.7 | 6.8 |
| Downstate noncity | 74 | 141 | 41 | 29.7 | 14.9 |
| Adirondacks city | 6 | 0 | 0 | .0 | .0 |
| Adirondacks noncity | 91 | 42 | 39 | 9.9 | .0 |
| Other New York State | 240 | 327 | 172 | | |

**Proportion outside of New York state**

| | | | |
|---|---|---|---|
| New England | 3.7 | .2 | 2.2 |
| Mid-Atlantic states | 5.7 | 1.6 | 5.3 |
| Other | 10.9 | 2.5 | 5.2 |
| Unknown | 10.6 | 30.1 | 29.9 |

**TABLE A.52**

**Tramps: Reasons for Tramping by Age, Sex, and Color, and by Selected Occupations (Known Cases Only)**

| Factor | Reasons | | | N |
| --- | --- | --- | --- | --- |
| | Destitute | Unemployed | Sick | |
| Sex and color | | | | |
| White male | 37.7 | 57.2 | 5.2 | |
| White female | 54.6 | 37.2 | 8.2 | |
| Black male | 20.9 | 73.1 | 6.0 | |
| Black female | .0 | 83.3 | 16.7 | |
| Age and sex and color (known only) | | | | |
| White male | | | | |
| 20–29 | 38.8 | 57.8 | 3.4 | 1316 |
| 30–39 | 36.3 | 58.7 | 5.1 | 852 |
| 40–49 | 34.9 | 59.6 | 5.5 | 473 |
| 50+ | 35.6 | 52.9 | 11.5 | 365 |
| White female | | | | |
| 20–29 | 60.0 | 29.1 | 10.9 | 55 |
| 30–39 | 53.1 | 42.9 | 4.1 | 49 |
| 40–49 | 47.6 | 42.9 | 9.5 | 28 |
| 50+ | 57.1 | 32.1 | 10.7 | 28 |
| Occupations | | | | |
| Domestic | 66.3 | 26.1 | 7.6 | 92 |
| Laborer | 19.2 | 69.2 | 11.5 | 26 |

# INDEX

## A

Abbott, Edith, 219
Addams, Jane, 201n
Adolescents
  crises of, 13
  industrial work and crises of, 13
  in poorhouses
    length of stay, 84–85
    proportion entering poorhouse with
      kin, 82
    rates of entry, gender differences in,
      76
  schools and crises of, 13
Agencies
  cooperation and conflicts among, 41,
    194, 225–226
  membership overlap among, 203
  private, 226
  public, 225
  voluntary, support by public funds, 228
Aid to Families with Dependent Children,
  236
Alcohol, 54, *see also* Temperance
  as cause of dependence, 126–129, 130,
    132, 178
  as cause of pauperism, 103–105
Alexander, John F., 184n
Almshouses, 57–89, 95, 100, 188, 190, *see
  also* Poorhouses

Erie County New York Almshouse, *see*
  Erie County, N. Y., Poorhouse
Almy, Frederick, 191n
American Association for Labor
  Legislation, 221
American Social Science Association, 90,
  138n, 178
Anderson, Michael, 48
Andrews, John B., 221
Apprenticeships, 13
Association for Improving the Condition
  of the Poor, 186
Association of Public Welfare Officials,
  226
Asylums, 210, *see also* Insane, Mental
  Illness
  county, 219
  private, 216
Axinn, June, 220

## B

Benson, J. Kenneth, 235n
Berkowitz, Edward, 4
Birth control, and conflict among social
  classes, 197
Blacks
  in poorhouses and asylums, 101
  unemployment among, and tramping,
    173

Bland, Charles L., 57
Blind, 7, 70, 134, 136, 137, 140–142, 144,
    148–150
Board of Children's Guardians
    (Indianapolis), 194
Boards of State Charities, 7, 59n, 62, 91,
    92, see also New York State,
    Massachusetts
Bourne, William O., 188n
Boyer, Paul, 5, 90n, 163n, 184–201, 205,
    211n
Brace, Charles Loring, 177, 186, 193, 197,
    203, 210
Branscombe, Martha, 60n
Braverman, Harry, 154–155, 205n, 216n
Breckenridge, Sophonsiba, 219
Brenzel, Barbara M., 199n
British immigrants, see Immigrants, British
Brockway, Zebulon, 211
Brooklyn, New York, outdoor relief in,
    69, 228, 232–235, 236
Buffalo, New York, 64, 100
    aid, gender differences in, 123
    availability of work for women, and
        relief policy, 236
    Catholic aid to children's institutions, 194
    Charity Organization Society, 69, 91
    employment ratio for women, 85n
    outdoor relief, 228
    seasonality of casual labor in, 64
Bureacracy, 210, 230
Business
    coalitions with reformers, 224, 230
    size of, and relief policy, 236
    and social insurance, 222, 224
Business cycle
    and unskilled workers, 11
    and welfare, 233


C

Calhoun, Daniel, 197n
Canadian immigrants, see Immigrants,
    Canadian
Capitalism, 9n, 10, 130, 231
    dependence on mobile wage laborer
        class, 10–11
    and development of institutions, 205
    as independent influence, 200, 205
    and social insurance, 227
    as style of social relations, 200

Casework, 225
Catholic Church
    aid to dependents, 5–6, 42–43, 194–195
    aid to poor, 20, 22, 41, 47
Causal attribution, 4, 15, 175–177, 179, 180
    interdependence, 175, 179, 180
    obscures deep roots of poverty, 4
    proximate, 175–176, 178, 180
Census, U.S., 1880, special schedules,
    "Defective, Dependent, and
    Delinquent," 15
Charities Aid Association of New York,
    188
Charity, 42, 192, 239
    charity reform, 90, 93, 225, 227
    charity workers, 8, 189, 235
    and degradation, 192
    private, 107, 190–192, 219, 221
    scientific, 91–92, 185, 186, 224, 226, 228
Charity Hospital, New Orleans, 65
Charity Organization Movement
    approach to poverty, 191
    opposition to mothers' pensions, 192
    purposes of, 52
Charity Organization Society, 91–93, 179,
    184, 186, 188, 191, 192, 203
    Buffalo, 69, 91
    Indiana, 188
    Philadelphia, see Society for Organizing
        Charity (Philadelphia)
Child care, 41
Child Labor reform, 220
Child Saving Movement, 192–195, 211, 220
    attack on institutions, 211
    definition of, 192
Children
    abandoned, 102
    homeless, 134, 138, 144, 152–153
    of imprisoned parents, 102
    orphaned and abandoned, 82, 85–86, 88
    of paupers, 102
    poorhouse entry rates, gender
        differences in, 76, 86
    with kin, 82, 88
    proportion entering poorhouse
    removal from poorhouses, 100–101, 133,
        193
"Children's Act" (1875), 61, 70, 81, 85–86,
    119, 193, 217
Children's Aid Society, 186, 195
    Catholic fear of, 195

New York, 193
Philadelphia, 39, 41
Children's Bureau, 8
Philadelphia, 28, 34, 35, 41
Children's Homeopathic Hospital
(Philadelphia), 28, 41
City Beautiful movement, 187
City governments, role in providing aid, 8
City planning, 187
Civil War
effect on poorhouse entry rates, 62–63,
70, 76, 83
of men, 70, 76
of women, 76, 83, 86
effect on women's lives, 76, 86
increase in tramping, 158–159
Class relations, 200
bonds between classes, 192
conflict between models of, 200
deferential and dependent, 52
fear of class estrangement, 202
Class structure, and paupers, 218
Clement, Priscilla, 57
Cloward, Richard, 3, 5n, 58n, 113n, 132,
230–234
Coll, Blanche, 220n
Collectivism, conflict with voluntarism,
226–227
Commons, John L., 221
Community Chests, 6
Conant, James Bryant, 237n
County Superintendents of the Poor (New
York State), 191, 213–215, 235
Convention of, 8, 226
Craig, Oscar, 69–70
Crime, 202, 205, 226
rate of, 197, 200
Criminals, 206, 209
Criminal justice, innovations in, 216

Deference, 90, 186, 196, 200, 201, 236
Degler, Carl, 197n
Delinquency, 216, 226
Department of Public Health and Charity,
32
Dependence, 3, 226, 235, see also Blind,
Deaf-mutes, Death, among the
poor, Elderly, Illness, Mental
Illness, Pauperism, Unemployment
and alcohol, 126–129, 130, 132, 178
discrepancy between perceptions of and
actual patterns of, 4, 15, 132,
183–184, 198–199, 217–218, 240
explanations of, 134–135, 140–141,
175–180
gender differences in, due to availability
of work, 108, 132
historiography of, themes in, 132,
183–237
structural roots of, 132, 183
Depressions (economic), 158
effect on outdoor relief, 65, 124–125, 191
effect on poorhouse entrance rates, 61,
63
effect on poorhouses, 65, 83–88
effect on tramping, 158, 173–174, 191
Great Depression, 234
Destler, Chester McArthur, 179n
Deutsch, Albert, 61n, 91n, 193n, 203n,
213n, 219n
Deviance, definition, social construction
of, 136
Disorder, social
definitions of, 205
reactions to, 196, 197, 204
Dolan, Jay P., 194n
Domestic service, 12–13, 50–51, 123–124
domestics, 83, 173
Doucet, Michael J., 9n, 10n, 59n, 123n,
155n, 199n

**D**

Dartmouth College, 228
Davis, Susan G., 189n, 225n, 226n, 227n,
232n, 233n, 235n
Deaf, 70, 137, 150
Deaf-mutes, 7, 134, 140, 148–150, 153
Death, among the poor, 19, 20, 21
Defective populations, 134, 138, see
Dependence

**E**

Economic cycles, and pauperism, 9–11,
131, 198, 218, 240, see also
Depressions (economic),
Unemployment
Education, public, 196, 202, 210, 235
Eighteenth Amendment, 187
Eisenhauer, Paul, 211n

Elderly, 10, 70, 98, 99, 100, 102, 106, 107, 110, 111, 117, 119, 122, 123, 126–127, 130–132, 150, 174, 183, 229
gender differences among and opportunities for aid, 76, 86, 122–124, 130
poorhouse inmates, 77–78, 84–89, 119, 120, 122–123, 126, 127, 130–132, 217
proportion of, in different types of institutions, 100
Elmira Reformatory (New York), 211–213
Ely, Richard, 179
Episcopal Hospital (Philadelphia), 41
Erie County, N.Y.
Erie County Poorhouse, 57–89, 98, 142, 152, 217, see also Poorhouses
statistics of relief and institutions, 190

**F**

Families, see also Children, Elderly, Illegitimacy, Mothers' Pensions, Widows
decline in, as poorhouse inmates, 78–83, 85–88, 100–101
destitute with female household heads, sources of help, 53, 76, 86–87, 218
policy of separating poor families, 42, 52, 88, 181, 191, 192, 193–194, 206, 235
as support for elderly, 120–125, 130–132, 149–150
as support of working class during crises, 45–46, 47–49, 53, 112, 129–131, 149–151, 183, 198
working-class, kin relations among, 45–46, 47–49, 53
Family Service Association of Philadelphia, 18n
Feder, Leah H., 72n
Federal government, role in relief, 2, 8, 227–228
Fertility, marital, decline in, 13, 197
Flynt, Josiah see Willard, Josiah Flynt
Folks, Homer, 193n
Foucault, Michel, 204
Freedman, Estelle B., 202n
Friendly visiting, 6, 8, 17, 186, 196
Fuller, A. A., 193n
Furner, Mary, 90n, 92n, 176n, 178n, 224

**G**

Gender differences
in availability of aid, 76, 86, 108, 218, see also Families, Outdoor relief, Widows
in availability of work, 11–13, 76, 85
in cause of destitution, 83
in effect of the Civil War, 70, 76, 83, 86
in insane asylum composition, 100
in poorhouse demography, and length of tenure, 70, 76, 80–82, 85, 86–88, 108–110
General hospitals, see Hospitals, general
Geographical mobility, in search of work, 88
George, Henry, 178
German immigrants, see Immigrants, German
Glasco, Laurence, 172n
Gray, Robert Q., 59n
Green, Howard, 158n
Gompers, Samuel, 224
Great Awakening, Second, 204
Grob, Gerald, 178n, 202n, 204n
Gutman, Herbert G., 9n

**H**

Halbert, L. A., 189n, 226n
Hale, Edward E., 157n, 158n, 159n
Hale, Nathan J., 151n
Handlin, Mary Flug, 188n
Handlin, Oscar, 188n, 197
Haskell, Thomas L., 90, 165, 175–180, 209
Health insurance, 220
opposition to, 222
Hereditarian, explanations of dependence, 105, 130, 177–178
Hershberg, Theodore, 9n
Hoag, Julia S., 94n
Horwitz, Morton J., 188n
Hospitals, 6, 7, 233, see also Mental hospitals
general, 6, 7, 58, 184, 233
creation of, 201–202
length of treatment in, 58–59
psychopathic, 208
Housing reform, 187
Houston, Susan E., 202n
Howe, Samuel Gridley, 210

Howe, Stanley H., 189n, 226n
Hoyt, Charles, 92–133, 152, 164–165
  research biases of, 98

**I**

Idiots, 7, 134, 136, 137, 140, 144, 149, 153
Illegitimacy, 70–71, 76, 80–81, 82, 87–88, 102, 217
Illness, as cause of destitution, 46–47, 54, 83, 87–88, 108, 126
Immigrants
  British, 78, 166, 169, 170
  Canadian, 78
  German, 77–78, 105, 119, 126, 153
    tramping and, 166, 168, 170
  Irish, 12, 76, 77, 81–82, 119, 129, 153, 166, 169, 170
    constituted majority of unskilled laborers and domestic servants, 12
    disproportionately represented among dependents, 12
    lack of industrial skills and resources, 12
    as poorhouse inmates, 87, 217
    among tramps, 166, 18, 170
Immigration, 200
  fear of, 195, 202
  increase in amount of dependence, 12
  increase in pace of industrialization and urbanization, 12
  increase in rate of entrance to poorhouses, 62
  in poorhouses, 102
  and tramping, 162, 166, 169–170, 174
Indiana
  public welfare in, history of, 219
  State Board of Charity, 188
Industrial psychology, 235
Insane, 7, 70, 93, 98, 100, 101, 102, 103, 105, 108–111, 113, 126, 131, 134, 136, 149–151, see also Mental hospitals, Mental illness
  age and gender, 100, 102
  birthplace, 104, 216
  as inmates of asylums, 108–110, 213–215
Institutions, history of, 201–216, see also Almshouses, Asylums, Hospitals, Jails, Orphanages, Penitentiaries, Poorhouses, Reformatories,

Settlement houses
  for children, 193–194
Intemperance, 103–105, 126–127, 128–129, 152
Interdependence, see Causal attribution

**J**

Jacksonian period, 6, 184–185, 190, 202
Jails, 58–59, 199
Jones, Gareth Stedman, 45n, 52n, 72n, 90n, 196n, 236n
Juvenile court, 202, 208, 219

**K**

Kaestle, Carl F., 10n
Kansas City, municipal department of public welfare, 8
Katz, Michael B., 9n, 190n, 59n, 103n, 111, 123n, 127n, 155, 178n, 190n, 199n, 204n, 210n
Kett, Joseph K., 9n
Kolko, Gabriel, 211
Kuhn, Thomas, 176

**L**

Labor
  discipline and role of public welfare, 230, 233
  militancy of, 157
  organized, opposition to workmen's compensation, 224
  turnover rate, 11
  wage labor, 45–46
Laborers, 10
  as poorhouse inmates, 83
  as tramps, 170, 172–173, 174
Labor Market, changes in, 231
  effect on destitution, 88
  effect on relief policy, 236
  effect on transiency, 10, 46
  and youth, 13
Ladies benevolent societies, 108n
Lasch, Christopher, 155, 216
Lathrop, Julia, 8
Leiby, James, 4n, 91n, 184n, 220
Levin, Herman, 220
Lewis, W. David, 202n
Litchfield, Edward H., 212n

Louisiana, public welfare history of, 219
Low, Seth, 232–234
Lowell, Josephine Shaw, 91n, 178, 188, 192n
Lubove, Roy, 5n, 192n, 201, 218–237

**M**

Mann, Horace, 177
Mann Act, 187
Manufacture, domestic, decline in, effect on women, 11–12
Marcus, Steven, 197
Marx, Karl, 178
Massachusetts
    Board of State Charities, 91, 210
    public welfare in, history of, 219
McQuaid, Kim, 4
Medical care, available to the poor, quality of, 52
Medico Chi Hospital (Philadelphia), 32, 41
Mennel, Robert M., 202n
Mental hospitals, 1, 7–8, 58–59, 90, 184, 202, 204, 206, 208, see also Hospitals, psychopathic
Mental illness
    historiography, 205
    rates of, variation between natives and foreign-born, 216
    treatment, 203, 206
Mobility (geographic), 157, 171–173, 174
Mohl, Raymond, 184n
Mohr, James, 141n
Monkkonen, Eric H., 57n, 148
Moral—social control tradition, 185–187, 199–201, see also Social control
Morphology of Evil, definition, 135–136
Mothers' Pensions, 8, 192, 194, 220, 235
Municipal Departments of Public Welfare, 8, 227
Municipal Hospital (Philadelphia), 19

**N**

National Conference of Charities and Corrections, and American Social Science Association, 138n
National Welfare Rights Organization, 231
New Deal, 2
New Jersey, public welfare in, history of, 220

New York State, see also Brooklyn, Buffalo, Erie County
New York Association of Public Welfare Officials, 8
New York Board of State Charities, 7, 59n, 62, 92, 188, 203, 212, 219, 228
New York Catholic Protectory, 194
New York City Lunatic Asylum, 100, 101
New York County Superintendents of the Poor, 230
New York House of Refuge for Men, 58
New York House of Refuge for Women, 58
New York State Archives, 165
New York State Charities Aid Association, 203
New York State Commission in Lunacy, 59n
New York State Commission of Prisons, 59n
New York State Supreme Court, 228
public welfare in, history of, 219
Quarantine Hospital, 62
Randall's Island Infant Asylum, 98, 99, 100, 102
statistics of relief and institutions, 190
Norfolk Prison (Massachusetts), 208

**O**

Orphanages, 43, 53, 61, 85–86, 100, 102, 193, 233, see also Randall's Island
    effect of changes in poorhouse demography on, 85–86
    effect of changes in relief policy on, 193
    effect of Children's Act of 1875 on, 61
    effect of 1870s Depression on, 193
Osterman, Paul, 9n
Outdoor relief, 5, 6, 14, 57, 60, 63–65, 107–108, 117, 127, 130–132, 139, 144, 152, 159, 190, 193, 217–218, 230, 232–235
    attempts to abolish, 5, 6, 57–58, 69, 91, 124, 132–133, 180, 190–191, 198–199, 203, 225, 226, 228
    relation to poorhouses, 124–125, 127–129
Outpatient clinics, for treatment of mental illness, 202, 208

P

Page, Charles Hunt, 180n
Page, J. A., 192n
Parole, 207, 208
Patterson, James T., 5n, 229n, 231n
Pauperism, 134, 139, 191, 193, 198,
    218–219, 225
    interpretations of, 92–93, 103, 106, 113,
    130, 132
Paupers, 117, 134, 148, 183, 197–198, *see
    also* Poorhouses, inmates
    age and, 152
    gender, 143–144
    images of, 43–45, 217–218
        disparity between images of and
        demography, 43–45
    state paupers, 1873 legislation
        concerning, 60–61
Penitentiaries, 1, 58, 190, 204
Pennsylvania, public welfare in, history
    of, 219, *see also* Philadelphia
Pennsylvania Hospital (Philadelphia), 64
Pensions, 9, 11, 13, 132, 183, 222
Philadelphia
    business interests and Municipal
        Department of Public Welfare, 227
    Children's Aid Society, 39, 41
    Children's Bureau, 28, 34, 35, 41
    Children's Homeopathic Hospital, 28,
        41
    Department of Public Health and
        Charity, 32
    Episcopal Hospital, 41
    Family Service Association, 18n
    Medico Chi Hospital, 32, 41
    Municipal Hospital, 19
    Outdoor relief debate, 57
    Pennsylvania Hospital, 64
    Philadelphia Hospital, 21, 31, 32, 41
    Roosevelt Hospital, 26
    Saint Vincent's Society, 31, 41, 43
    Society for Organizing Charity, *see*
        Society for Organizing Charity
        (Philadelphia)
    Society for the Prevention of Cruelty to
        Children, *see* Society for the
        Prevention of Cruelty to Children
    Welfare in, 55, 189, 227
    Women's Homeopathic Hospital, 31,
Philadelphia Hospital, 21, 31, 32, 41
Philanthropy, 201, 222, 225, 228

evangelical, **184, 185, 186, 190–191**
    middle class, 54
Piore, Michael J., 236
Piven, Frances Fox, 3, 5n, 58n, 113n, 132,
    230–234
Playgrounds, 13, 196
Policy, public, 90–91, 132–133, 239–240
Poorhouses, *see also* Erie County, N.Y.,
    Poorhouse
    funds, 151–152
    history and demography in Erie County
        New York Poorhouse, 57–89
    inmates, 57–89
    removal of children from, 70, 193
    role and characteristics of, 108, 113,
        151–152
Poor laws, 5, 7, 219
Poverty, historiography of, 1–16, 175–176,
    184, 205, *see also* Pauperism
    interpretations of, 1, 3, 92, 132, 229, 240
Prisoners, 134, 142, 148, 203
    gender differences in distribution of, 142
    gender differences in reasons for
        arrests, 150
    recidivism rates among, 204
Prisons, 184, 201, 208, 211, 216
Probation, 202, 207–208, 216
Professionalization
    of welfare activity, 7
    of social science, 90–92, 175–181
Progressive Era, 177, 184, 185, 186, 201,
    202, 206, 208, 210, 211, 216
Prostitution, 197–198, 202
Protestants, and reform, 185–188, 194–195,
    202
Pruyn, John V. L., 163–165
Public
    and private, distinctions between, 7, 42,
        188, 190–192, 240–241
    cooperation between, 222, 224
Public relief, *see* Outdoor relief
Public welfare
    curtailment of, 229
    municipal departments of, 226
    professionalization of, 226
Public Welfare Department (Philadelphia),
    225
Pullman, Illinois, 9

Q

Quarantine Hospital, New York, 62

**R**

Randall's Island Infant Asylum (New
      York City), 98, 99, 100, 102
Rauch, Julia B., 18n
Reformatories and reform schools, 1, 7–8,
      57–59, 184, 190, 198, 202, 203, 204,
      206, 208, 210, 211–213, 216, *see also*
      Elmira Reformatory (New York)
Relief, *see* Outdoor relief
Ringenbach, Paul T., 157n, 158n, 162n
Rodgers, Daniel T., 9n
Roosevelt Hospital (Philadelphia), 29
Rosenberg, Charles E., 57n, 197n
Rothman, David J., 57n, 201–218, 223,
      224, 226
Rubinow, I. M., 221
Ryan, Mary P., 204n


**S**

Saint Vincent de Paul Society, 194
Saint Vincent's Society (Philadelphia), 31,
      41, 43
Samuel, Raphael, 9n, 200n
Sanborn, Frank, 176, 178, 179
Schlossman, Steven L., 59n
Scientific charity, 6, 90–92, 132–133
Settlement houses, 13, 184, 185, 186, 188
      workers in, 187, 201
Sexuality and sex roles, 196–197
Schneider, David M., 60n, 61n, 91n, 193n,
      203n, 213n, 219n
Shelton, Brenda K., 72n
Sheppherd-Towner Act, 8
Smith, Mary Roberts, 76n, 124n
Smith-Rosenberg, 185n, 197n
Social control, 90, 192, 195, 196
Social science
      early, goals of, 90–91, 132–133, 135
      professionalization of, *see*
            Professionalization, of social science
Society for Organizing Charity
      (Philadelphia), 18–54, 55–56
Society for the Prevention of Cruelty to
      Children, 21, 24–25, 30, 41, 43, 52,
      193–194
      Philadelphia (SPCC), 194
State, *see* Public
State boards of charities, *see* Boards of
      state charities

State Charities Aid Association (New
      York), 213–215
State departments of public welfare, 7–8
State governments
      mothers' pensions, 8
      role in welfare, 6–7
      workmen's compensation, 8
State prisons, 58
Steiner, Gilbert Y., 140n, 230n
Stern, Mark J., 9n, 10n, 59n, 72n, 111n,
      123n, 155n, 199n
Strikes, 90, 222
Sunday schools, 185–186, 190
Sutherland, Neil, 193n, 220n


**T**

Taxes, 1, 6, 196, 230, 241
      local, as source of most relief, 6
Temperance, 196, 197, 202, 218
Tenements, model, 202
Tract societies, 185, 190–191, 202
Trade unions, 90
Thernstrom, Stephan, 9n
Tishler, Hace Sorel, 192n, 220n, 225, 227
Tramps, 151–184
      characteristics, 165–166, 168–169, 170,
            173–174
      interpretations, 158, 162, 173, 183
      patterns of movement, 171–172, 175
Trattner, Walter I., 220
Truancy, 194


**U**

Uhlenberg, Peter, 9n
Unemployment, 8, 11, 42, 44–45, 53, 71,
      112, 183, 189, 198, 217–218


**V**

Vogel, Morris, 202n
Voluntarism, 2, 7, 222–230, 240


**W**

Wage labor
      as defining feature of capitalism, 200
      increase in proportion of, 10
Wallace, Anthony F. C., 9n

Warner, Amos G., 92–93
Watson, Frank Dekker, 18n, 43, 91n, 192n
Wayland, Francis, 93, 157, 159, 161n, 162n
Welfare, 107, 130–131, 151–152, *see also*
    Indiana, Louisiana, Massachusetts,
    New Jersey
  expansion, 228–229, 231
  historiography, 184, 218–237, 239, 241
  history to 1930, 5
  in Philadelphia, 55, 189, 227
  reform, 130–133, 241
Welfare capitalism, 9, 222, 235, 240
White, Morton, 175n, 179n
Whitehead, John S., 188n
White House Conference on Children
    (1909), 8
Wiberley, Stephen E. (Jr), 57n
Widows, 11, 12, 82, 88, 100, 108, 111,
    120–124, 129–131, 148, 168, 191–192,
    223

Wiebe, Robert, 211
Willard, Josiah Flynt (Josiah Flynt), 163
Willard Asylum, (New York), 61, 213–214
Wines, Frederic H., 134–142, 151
Wishy, Bernard, 177n
Women's Homeopathic Hospital
    (Philadelphia), 31, 41
Work, characteristics of, 10–11, 93, 107,
    183
Working class, 9, 10, 11, 47–54, 107, 126,
    130, 157, 170, 175, 180, 196, 198,
    200, 218, 239–240
  life among, 54–55, 183
  youth, 13
Workmen's compensation, 8, 220–222,
    228, 235
  opposition to, 222
World War I, 226
World War II, 230
Wright, Carroll, 178

## STUDIES IN SOCIAL DISCONTINUITY
*(Continued from page ii)*

*Elizabeth Hafkin Pleck.* Black Migration and Poverty: Boston 1865-1900

*Harvey J. Graff.* The Literacy Myth: Literacy and Social Structure in the Nineteenth-Century City

*Michael Haines.* Fertility and Occupation: Population Patterns in Industrialization

*Keith Wrightson and David Levine.* Poverty and Piety in an English Village: Terling, 1525-1700

*Henry A. Gemery and Jan S. Hogendorn* (Eds.). The Uncommon Market: Essays in the Economic History of the Atlantic Slave Trade

*Tamara K. Hareven* (Ed.). Transitions: The Family and the Life Course in Historical Perspective

*Randolph Trumbach.* The Rise of the Egalitarian Family: Aristocratic Kinship and Domestic Relations in Eighteenth-Century England

*Arthur L. Stinchcombe.* Theoretical Methods in Social History

*Juan G. Espinosa and Andrew S. Zimbalist.* Economic Democracy: Workers' Participation in Chilean Industry 1970-1973

*Richard Maxwell Brown and Don E. Fehrenbacher* (Eds.). Tradition, Conflict, and Modernization: Perspectives on the American Revolution

*Harry W. Pearson.* The Livelihood of Man by Karl Polanyi

*Frederic L. Pryor.* The Origins of the Economy: A Comparative Study of Distribution in Primitive and Peasant Economies

*Charles P. Cell.* Revolution at Work: Mobilization Campaigns in China

*Dirk Hoerder.* Crowd Action in Revolutionary Massachusetts, 1765-1780

*David Levine.* Family Formations in an Age of Nascent Capitalism

*Ronald Demos Lee* (Ed.). Population Patterns in the Past

*Michael Schwartz.* Radical Protest and Social Structure: The Southern Farmers' Alliance and Cotton Tenancy, 1880-1890

*Jane Schneider and Peter Schneider.* Culture and Political Economy in Western Sicily

*Daniel Chirot.* Social Change in a Peripheral Society: The Creation of a Balkan Colony

*Stanley H. Brandes.* Migration, Kinship, and Community: Tradition and Transition in a Spanish Village

*James Lang.* Conquest and Commerce: Spain and England in the Americas

*Kristian Hvidt.* Flight to America: The Social Background of 300,000 Danish Emigrants

*D. E. H. Russell.* Rebellion, Revolution, and Armed Force: A Comparative Study of Fifteen Countries with Special Emphasis on Cuba and South Africa

*John R. Gillis.* Youth and History: Tradition and Change in European Age Relations 1770-Present

# STUDIES IN SOCIAL DISCONTINUITY

*Immanuel Wallerstein.* The Modern World-System I: Capitalist Agriculture and the Origins of the European World-Economy in the Sixteenth Century; II: Mercantilism and the Consolidation of the European World-Economy, 1600-1750

*John W. Cole and Eric R. Wolf.* The Hidden Frontier: Ecology and Ethnicity in an Alpine Valley

*Joel Samaha.* Law and Order in Historical Perspective: The Case of Elizabethan Essex

*William A. Christian, Jr.* Person and God in a Spanish Valley